Preface

THE FREE PRESS SOURCES IN AMERICAN HISTORY series reviews the history of the United States from its beginnings in the seventeenth century to the present. Each of the nine volumes consists of from 15 to 35 carefully chosen contemporary documents illustrating the major themes—political, economic, social, and cultural—of American history and civilization. The volume editors, selected for their specialized knowledge of the periods into which the series is divided, have drawn upon the rich resources of the American past for the materials to be included in their respective books. They have ranged over the principal geographical areas of the United States and have exploited a wide variety of genres—governmental and political party documents, descriptive and analytical accounts, theoretical writings, and literary products. History is a seamless web and one learns about himself and his past by exploring the multivarious experiences of his forbears and their reflections upon those experiences.

The editors have kept the student in mind while selecting the items to be reprinted in each volume. They have not only chosen significant documents, but have respected the intentions of the original writers to the extent that the materials are offered substantially as the authors produced them with a minimum of cutting and editing. We have, therefore, put together a set of volumes containing a limited number of major documents reproduced *in extenso* rather than a series containing hundreds of snippets which can suggest, at best, only an impressionistic view of history. To promote thoughtful reading and discussion of these materials we have introduced each selection with headnotes containing biographical and bibliographical data. Moreover, we have included in each headnote four or five suggestions indicating what students should look for in reading the documents; these do not tell the reader what is in the material, but they are very useful in directing his attention to the salient points covered. Finally, the editors have added to each note two or three titles of books that might be consulted for further study of the author of the document or of the problem or episode dealt with in the selection.

Each volume contains an extended introductory essay, an interpretive narrative written by the volume editor, which treats the period as a whole and relates the documents to the history under consideration. These essays incorporate both factual and conceptual information obtained from recent historical research; they reflect the new findings of contemporary scholarship.

The American people in the quarter-century prior to 1789 had lived through exciting days. The crisis that developed after 1763 involving the mother country and her American colonies achieved a climax in 1775 when fighting broke out between the king's troops and the colonials. A little over a year later representatives from the colonies declared their independence from Great Britain, giving the war a quasi-legal status in international law. By 1781 a government had come to power in England willing to negotiate a peace with the Americans; plenipotentiaries signed the Treaty of Paris in 1785 which among other things recognized the sovereignty of what was called the United States of America.

Working at differing rates of speed, leaders in America transformed colonial governments into state governments and organized a central government under a constitution, the Articles of Confederation. Independence, far from ushering in an era of domestic peace and tranquillity, brought the American people a number of thorny problems which seemed to defy solution. By 1787 dissatisfaction with the loose structure of the central government had grown to such an extent that leadership sought to strengthen the bonds of union. Representatives assembled at Philadelphia in the summer of 1787 and wrote a new constitution for the United States which, after ratification, supplanted the Articles of Confederation as the basic framework of government.

Professor Miller's volume deals with another quarter-century of American history, perhaps not quite as full of drama as the previous twenty-five years, but in its way every bit as fateful for the future. The success of the experiment was not guaranteed in advance. When the newly chosen electoral college named George Washington President of the United States in 1789, it was by no means clear that

The Young Republic,

1789-1815

SOURCES IN AMERICAN HISTORY

GENERAL EDITOR: *George H. Knoles*

Professor of History and Director of
the Institute of American History,
Stanford University

The Young Republic, 1789-1815

John C. Miller

Stanford University

The Free Press, New York
Collier-Macmillan Limited, London

Collier-Macmillan Canada Ltd., Toronto, Ontario

Library of Congress Catalog Card Number: 74–80472

printing number

1   2   3   4   5   6   7   8   9   10

Contents

the converging forces within the nation would overcome the diverging forces operating within it. Innumerable decisions faced the young republic. The constitution was a document; how should its words be fleshed out into living institutions? How could the government develop confidence and strength needed to establish its character as a new nation at home and abroad? In an age of international anarchy and almost universal warfare involving all the major nations of Europe, how could the independence and integrity of the United States be maintained? How could a people who understood what it meant to be a Virginian, or a Pennsylvanian, or a Massachusetts man but who little sensed what it meant to be an American develop a strong and unifying sense of national self-consciousness?

Professor Miller has gathered a significant collection of documents to aid the student in understanding some of the major domestic and international issues and problems confronting the young republic. One group of documents (1–6) treats aspects of the launching of the new government and efforts to establish its financial stability at home and abroad. Another group (7–12) deals primarily with political problems arising from differing views as to the nature and proper functioning of the government. A third group (13–15) relates to foreign affairs and domestic complications arising out of the war of 1812. The last documents have to do with features of social and intellectual life during the first quarter-century of the republic. The student will find this volume a valuable aid in understanding these years of beginnings so fraught with meaning for the future of the United States.

Stanford University   George Harmon Knoles

Introduction

In 1789, the paramount task of American statesmen was to create a nation, based upon the principle of ordered liberty, out of the sectional diversity and variant economic interests and social institutions of which the republic was composed. In this endeavor, they were aided by the recent experience of the American people under the Articles of Confederation—an experience that had convinced most influential citizens of the necessity of a stronger national government—and by the adoption of the Federal constitution in 1787–1788.

Yet, although the constitution provided the framework of a government in which order might coexist with liberty, it did not automatically create a nation. The constitution, a relatively short document (reading time: 23 minutes), merely outlined in broad strokes a general government of three branches and, again broadly, established a division of powers between it and the State governments. Whether this complex system by which every citizen was brought under the jurisdiction of two governments, each empowered to tax, could be made to function as the Framers hoped, depended upon whether the American people would consent to live under the restraints imposed by the constitution upon their freedom of action and whether the States would submit to the authority of the general government.

In short, as the Framers themselves admitted, the constitution was an experiment. What was wanting to ensure the success of this venture was an overriding sense of loyalty to the nation. Most Americans of this generation tended to center their affections upon their States: the union was a decidedly lesser love. Moreover, the constitution lacked the sanction of consensus. It had been ratified

1]

by hardly more than 5 per cent of the adult males in the United States, and two States, North Carolina and Rhode Island, remained loyal to the government of the Articles of Confederation. Finally, the new government could not ignore the Antifederalists who, although they professed willingness to abide by the decision registered in 1787–1788, made clear that they intended to shift the focus of power from the Federal government to the States.

It devolved upon the First Congress (1789–1791) and the Executive Department to construct and administer the Federal government along the lines laid down by the Framers. In this work, the House of Representatives took the lead. As the most influential member of the House, James Madison continued to play in Congress the same dominant role he had taken in the Constitutional Convention. Under his direction, Congress gave the new government a solid financial base by enacting a tariff law; fostered American shipping by the imposition of discriminatory duties upon foreign ships entering American ports; adopted and proposed to the States the Bill of Rights—the first ten amendments to the constitution; organized the Departments of State, Treasury, and War; and established the Federal Judiciary, including the Supreme Court. For these achievements, the first Congress earned acclaim as the most productive of the ninety sessions of the National legislature.

MADISON

Early in 1790, the direction of affairs passed from Congress and James Madison to Alexander Hamilton, the Secretary of the Treasury and co-author, with Madison, of the *Federalist*. Hamilton, a West Indian by birth, was a thoroughgoing nationalist who wished to see established in the United States a powerful, highly centralized government. He was captivated by a vision of the future wealth and grandeur of the American republic. Unlike Madison and Jefferson, who made liberty their lodestar, Hamilton feared that the American people were too fond of liberty for the good of order, liberty, and the rights of property.

HAMILTON

To make sure that power gravitated to the general government—where, in his opinion, it belonged—Hamilton undertook to attach the most affluent citizens to the Federal government by bonds of self-interest. The Report on National Credit which he submitted to Congress in January, 1790, proposed that the purchasers of government securities should receive full facevalue from the Federal government regardless of the fact that in many instances they had bought these certificates of indebtedness for a fraction of their nominal price. At the same time, to depreciate the influence of the States, he recommended that the Federal government assume the unpaid debts contracted by the States during the War of Independence. *HAMILTON/*

Although Madison did not oppose funding (i.e., converting the government's obligations into a long-term debt at fixed interest) the national debt, he objected strenuously to rewarding speculators in the public funds and to assuming State debts to the amount advocated by Hamilton. The first part of Hamilton's plan, Madison said, would injure the civilians and soldiers who had found it necessary to sell their certificates at a small part of their face value. As for the assumption of State debts, Madison complained that Virginia and other States that had liquidated a large part of their war debts would be penalized for the benefit of less provident states. *MADISON STRUGGLE*

Because neither Hamilton nor Madison would yield, Congress remained for six months in a state of deadlock. Finally, in the summer of 1790, Hamilton struck a bargain with James Madison and Thomas Jefferson, the Secretary of State, whereby in exchange for the transfer of the national government from New York to Philadelphia and, after ten years, from the City of Brotherly Love to the Potomac, the two Virginians agreed to induce four Congressmen to switch their votes, enough to secure the adoption of Hamilton's plan. The assumption of State debts was made more palatable for Virginia and several other States by rewarding them for having paid a portion of their debt. *HAMILTONS VICTORY*

Thus Hamilton, at comparatively small price, carried his main points: the purchasers of government securities were not obliged to share their profits with the original holders and the State debts were assumed by the Federal government. Public creditors all over the union were made to look upon the United States government as a source whence all financial blessings flowed. Equally important, for the first time in its history, the credit of the United States was firmly established abroad. In 1792, the Federal government borrowed money in Holland, then the financial capital of the world, upon terms more advantageous than those granted any other country.

Hamilton's next step toward centralizing power and integrating the American economy was to propose in his *Report on the Bank of the United States* (1791) a quasi-public bank designed to facilitate the *National BANK* banking operations of the government, provide a circulating medium, and advance loans to the government and private borrowers. When Madison and Jefferson questioned the constitutionality of the proposed Bank, President Washington asked written opinions from all the members of his cabinet. Hamilton defended the constitutionality of the Bank of the United States in a forceful exposition of the loose or permissive method of interpreting the constitution. Although Hamilton's opinion did not wholly dispel President Washington's doubts, he signed the bill incorporating the Bank of the United States.

By virtue of the services it rendered both the government and the private sector of the economy, the Bank of the United States fully vindicated Hamilton's confidence in its utility but it did not persuade Jefferson and Madison of its constitutionality. Although he remained in the cabinet, Jefferson did not cease to oppose the acts of the Washington administration which he considered to be beyond the scope of the powers assigned the Federal government. Southerners' dislike of the Bank of the United States was aggravated by the fact that most of its stockholders were Northerners and Britons: the South enjoyed little representation upon its Board of Directors. Moreover, although the banknotes it issued helped meet the need of a stable circulating medium, they circulated mainly in the Northern, commercial section of the country. For the most part, farmers and planters remained outside the orbit of the Bank of the United States's paper currency and credit facilities.

Hamilton submitted to Congress in December, 1791, the *Report on Manufactures*, intended to provide the capstone of his effort to give the union solid economic and financial base. By means of bounties, subsidies, and tariffs, he proposed to make the United States less dependent upon foreign sources of supply and, by creating domestic markets for the products of American plantations and farms, to relieve the republic of its dependence upon fluctuating and precarious foreign demand. Again Jefferson and Madison raised constitutional objections, but Hamilton asserted that the general welfare clause provided ample sanction for government aid to manufactures.

In response to Hamilton's Report, Congress granted some aid to distressed industries, particularly the fisheries. But the results fell far short of his expectations. Hamilton's discomfiture was owing, however, less to the indifference of Congress than to the unexpectedly brisk demand for American products that resulted from bad harvests in Europe and, in 1792, from the outbreak of the Wars of the French Revolution. For the next two decades, Americans enjoyed unprecedented prosperity while Europeans, in John Adams's words, went about their business of cutting each other's throats.

In order to carry his measures through Congress, Hamilton was obliged to act very much like the leader of a political party, organizing and exhorting his followers, furnishing them with arguments and, in some cases, even speeches in support of his policies. But the opposition, too, organized and disciplined itself to thwart the Secretary of the Treasury and his "phalanx." As a result, an embryonic two-party system came about in 1790–1792. Since James Madison led the opposition forces, it was originally called the *Madisonian* party whereas the Hamiltonians retained the name of *Federalist*. These two parties did not originate in the struggle between Federalists and Antifederalists. Rather, they were created by the schism within the Federalist party itself produced by Hamilton's efforts to centralize power in the Federal government and to concentrate wealth in the hands of those who, by his reckoning, could best devote it to the advancement of manufacturing and commerce.

During the struggle in Congress between the Hamiltonian Federalists and the Madisonian Republicans, Secretary of State Jefferson, except for his state papers on constitutional questions, remained in the background. The differences between the two cabinet officers were brought to the fore by Hamilton's efforts to bend American foreign policy in a more pro-British direction than Jefferson or, indeed, President Washington himself, favored. Jefferson assumed that Hamilton's ulterior objective was the establishment of a monarchy in the United States and an alliance with Great Britain. Firmly persuaded that the fate of republicanism was at stake, Jefferson and Madison induced Philip Freneau, the "poet of the Revolution," to establish a newspaper in Philadelphia. The two Virginians made no offer to Freneau of financial support but Jefferson intimated through Madison that a post in the State Department as a translating clerk was open.

Freneau came to Philadelphia, took a position in the State Department and established a newspaper, the *National Gazette*, which pilloried Hamilton as the Colossus of Federalism and Monarchism. When Hamilton learned of Jefferson's and Madison's part in this affair, he rushed into print in the newspapers where, under a nom de plume, he demanded that Jefferson resign as Secretary of State. Although Jefferson did not respond to this attack, his friends engaged the Secretary of the Treasury in a full-scale newspaper war. Both Hamilton and Jefferson informed President Washington that they would not remain in the cabinet if the other stayed on. Washington himself was eager to lay down the cares of office and retire to Mount Vernon but he could not bring himself to abandon the presidency while his cabinet was torn with dissension. It ended with Washington agreeing to stand for a second term and with Jefferson and Hamilton remaining at their posts. But before his retirement in December, 1793, Jefferson aided his friends in Congress in their effort to compel the President to dismiss Hamilton. The effort failed and Hamilton did not relinquish the Treasury until 1795.

CABINET
DISSENSION

By attacking Jefferson in the newspapers, Hamilton succeeded in making the Virginian appear to be the head and front of the opposition to the Treasury—a role Jefferson would not have claimed of his own accord. As a result, when in February, 1793, the outbreak of war between France and Great Britain intensified the political conflict in the United States, Jefferson had begun to eclipse Madison as the leader of the Republican party.

For the next twenty years, with only brief periods of remission, foreign affairs continued to agitate and divide the American people. Yet in 1793 and for most of the subsequent period, Americans were united in wishing to stay out of the European war. Division occurred over the questions whether a British or French victory would best serve the national interests of the United States and whether, in consequence, American neutrality ought to incline to the advantage of one or the other of the belligerents.

FRENCH -
ENGLISH
WAR

In April, 1793, without claiming the right to bind Congress in any way, President Washington issued an Executive Proclamation that set forth the conditions of American neutrality. But Citizen Edmond Genêt, the first Minister of the French Republic to the United States, acted in such complete disregard of the President's orders that Jefferson began to fear that the impetuous young Frenchman would "sink the Republican interest." Late in 1793, the strain

Genêt imposed upon Franco-American relations was eased by his recall. Thereupon the focal point of crisis shifted to Great Britain which in 1793–1794 began the systematic seizure of American ships carrying supplies to France from the French West Indies. When, in May, 1794, the Washington administration decided to send John Jay, Chief Justice of the United States Supreme Court, as envoy extraordinary to Great Britain, the two countries were on the verge of war. Hostilities also seemed imminent between the United States and the Barbary pirates who, in default of tribute from the United States, preyed upon American shipping in the Mediterranean and enslaved captured American seamen. To meet this threat Congress ordered the construction of six frigates but before they could be completed, the United States government purchased peace with Algiers by agreeing to pay tribute and to ransom captive American officers and sailors.

While John Jay was in London, an armed uprising against the excise tax occurred in western Pennsylvania. An overwhelming military force led by President Washington himself quickly suppressed the so-called Whiskey Rebellion. Had the government failed to put down the uprising, Jay's position in London would have been seriously undermined. Even so, the treaty signed by Jay in November, 1794, was not an unqualified success: although the United States gained possession of the Northwest posts which the British had promised in 1783 to surrender with all convenient speed, Jay made concessions to British seapower at the expense of American neutral rights.

Jay's Treaty precipitated a bitter conflict between the Federalists and Jeffersonian Republicans that was not resolved until April, 1796, when the House of Representatives finally agreed to appropriate the funds necessary to carry the treaty into effect. The Jeffersonians regarded the Treaty as tantamount to an Anglo-American alliance, a point of view in which the French concurred. The French minister to the United States did everything in his power to prevent the ratification of Jay's Treaty. This interference in the domestic affairs of the United States called forth President Washington's strictures in his Farewell Address of September, 1796, upon the baneful effect of foreign influence and political parties. Yet even after the publication of the Farewell Address, the French minister threatened the United States with the condign displeasure of France if John Adams won the presidential election of 1796.

XYZ
dispatches

Jay's Treaty, together with the election of John Adams as President (Thomas Jefferson, who received the second highest number of votes in the electoral college became Vice President), led to the seizure of American ships on the high seas by French cruisers and privateers. President Adams's efforts to settle the dispute by diplomacy failed: the American envoys were approached by French agents who were referred to in the American version of the negotiations as *X*, *Y* and *Z*, with demands for a bribe, a loan, and an apology for President Adams's unflattering remarks upon the conduct of the French government. The publication of the *XYZ* dispatches produced an outburst of patriotism in the United States that reminded President Adams of the days of 1776. It also produced the Alien and Sedition Act of July, 1798, by which the Federalists hoped to rid the country of "foreign incendiaries" and stifle criticism of the government's policies. Under the Sedition Act, some leading Republican newspaper editors and one Republican member of Congress, Matthew Lyon of Vermont, were fined and imprisoned. But for every newspaper suppressed, two papers sprang up in its place.

Alien and
Sedition Acts

States Rights
Acts

Of even greater significance were the Virginia and Kentucky Resolutions adopted in 1798–1799 by the legislatures of these two States. Drafted by Jefferson and Madison, these resolutions enunciated the compact theory of the origin of the Federal union. The sovereign States, they held, had created the general government and had granted it only certain enumerated powers. If the general government transgressed its constitutional authority, Jefferson and Madison recommended that the states interpose their authority. In the second Kentucky Resolution of 1799, Jefferson declared that the legal remedy was State nullification of the offensive act of Congress.

Contrary to all expectations, neither France nor the United States declared war. From 1798–1801, the two countries engaged in an undeclared naval war as a result of which the seas were made safe for American shipping from French maritime power. But early in 1799, President Adams initiated peace negotiations with the French Directory. The President's action split the Federalist party—the Hamiltonians wished to escalate the war into an Anglo-

American attack upon Spanish America—but it did eventuate in the Convention of 1800, which terminated the Franco-American alliance of 1778. As a result, after 1801, the United States was free of "entangling alliances."

Saddled with the responsibility of a war that became progressively more unpopular after it had achieved its objective of stopping French depredations upon American commerce, with direct Federal taxes upon houses, land, and slaves, and with the Alien and Sedition Acts, the Federalists went into the election divided by a struggle for power between Hamilton and Adams. The Jeffersonian Republicans, on the other hand, stood for peace, economy in government, and the maintenance of civil liberties.

In the election of 1800 President John Adams proved to be more popular than his party. Although he received only seven fewer electoral votes than in 1796, the Federalists lost heavily in Congress. Because Jefferson and Burr were tied in the electoral college with 73 votes apiece, the election of the president was thrown into the House of Representatives. The Federalists made a determined effort to make Burr president but on February 16, 1801, after thirty-six ballots, enough Federalists abstained from voting to enable the Republicans to elect Jefferson. *Republican*

JEFFERSON
ELECTED

In his inaugural address, President Jefferson laid down the principles by which, he believed, a republican government ought to be guided: economy, neutrality, financial integrity, and respect for the rights of minorities. The principal minority in the country was now the Federalist party and to it the President held out the olive branch. Like President Washington, he called for an end of partisan politics in the interests of national union: "We are all Federalists, we are all Republicans," he told his countrymen.

President Jefferson believed that the election of 1800 ought to be regarded as a revolution as important, in its way, as the events of 1776. As he saw it, the election that had brought him to the presidency and had given the Republican party control of Congress saved the country from monarchism, centralization of power, and involvement in the European war on the side of Great Britain. His task as president, in his opinion, was to put the country back on the republican tack—which meant, to him, sharply reversing direction and signing aboard a new crew.

The President set out to restore the republic to the pristine

Republican
Repeal of
Laws.

purity it had possessed before the Federalists had laid impious hands upon the Constitution. Essentially, his work, as he conceived it, was to be an undoing, not a launching out upon new, positive governmental programs. To achieve this goal, the President acted as the leader of his party in Congress. Under his auspices, Congress repealed such Federalist-inspired legislation as the Judiciary Act of 1801, the excise (the principal cause of the Whiskey Rebellion), and the Naturalization Act. The Alien and Sedition Acts expired despite Federalist efforts to keep them on the statute books. But the President made no move against the Bank of the United States. Albert Gallatin, the Secretary of the Treasury, told Jefferson that the Bank could not be dispensed with.

MARBURY vs.
MADISON

The repeal of the Judiciary Act of 1801 and the adoption of a new Judiciary Act in 1802 was designed by Jefferson to clip the wings of the Federal judiciary. Few Republicans—certainly not the President—doubted that Chief Justice John Marshall and the Federalist Associate Justices would declare the Judiciary Act unconstitutional. Yet Marshall wisely avoided a confrontation with the President and his party upon this issue: instead, in 1803, in the case of *Marbury v. Madison*, the Supreme Court declared unconstitutional a minor section of the Judiciary Act of 1789. Marshall thereby established the principle of judicial review without clashing head-on with the Republicans. Jefferson and his party thereupon brought impeachments against two Federal judges. Although Judge John Pickering was found guilty and removed from office, the biggest fish—Supreme Court Justice Samuel Chase—got away. Had the proceedings against Chase succeeded, the Republicans planned to move against Chief Justice Marshall himself.

BARBARY
PIRATES

President Jefferson said that "peace is my passion" but during his first administration he had little opportunity to indulge it. From 1801 to 1805 the United States was engaged in war with Tripoli. The Barbary pirates brought on the conflict by seizing unarmed American merchant ships in the Mediterranean. Although Jefferson always regarded the Navy as a prime object for economizing, he was forced to employ it against Tripoli. The war ended with the Navy blockading the port of Tripoli. But it did not put an end to the payment of tribute by the United States to the Barbary states. Until 1815, the United States continued to procure protection for its shipping in the Mediterranean by annual outlays of cash.

In 1801–1803, the peace of Amiens between France and Great Britain gave the United States a brief respite from depredations upon its ships and impressment of its seamen. But peace in Europe permitted Napoleon to turn his undivided attention to the western hemisphere where he planned to erect a new French empire. In 1800, he secured from Spain the retrocession of Louisiana. When President Jefferson learned of this transaction, he ordered Lewis and Clark to undertake a military reconnaisance of Louisiana and he directed the army to hold itself in readiness for all emergencies. He went further: if France took possession of Louisiana, he said that the United States would be obliged to marry itself to the British fleet and nation. But before taking a step that ran counter to his passion for peace and neutrality and for keeping Great Britain at arm's length, President Jefferson was determined to exhaust all the *MONROE* resources of diplomacy. In 1802, James Monroe was sent to France *LIVINGSTON* as special envoy to back up Edward Livingston, the resident United States Minister in Paris. The American diplomats were instructed to buy New Orleans and its environs. To their astonishment, Napoleon offered to sell all of Louisiana to the United States for $15 million. Because of the resistance of the blacks under Touissant *LOUISIANA* L'Ouverture on Santo Domingo and Napoleon's decision to renew *PURCHASE* the war with Great Britain, Louisiana had ceased to have much value to the First Consul. Monroe and Livingston eagerly accepted the opportunity to buy all of Louisiana and, despite the opposition of the Federalists, the United States Senate ratified the treaty. It proved to be the greatest real estate bargain in American history.

Jefferson's reelection in 1804 demonstrated that the Federalist party had been reduced to the position of an impotent minority. Indeed, some of the New England Federalists, turning their backs upon their earlier nationalism, began to work secretly for the creation of a Northern Confederacy but Burr's failure to win the governorship of New York foiled the plan. Burr thereupon tried to use the Western states as a base for a filibustering expedition against Mexico. President Jefferson believed that Burr's real objective was to sever the West from the rest of the union. Burr's expedition was broken up by Federal authority and Burr himself was put on trial for treason in Richmond, Virginia. Chief Justice John Marshall's strict interpretation of the law governing the legal proof of treason saved Burr.

But President Jefferson's real problem came not from disaffection at home but from the European belligerents. Caught between the upper and nether millstones of French and British maritime power, neutral rights were ground exceedingly small. The British compounded the seizure of American vessels by impressing American seamen as well as British deserters from American merchant vessels. In 1807, H.M.S. *Leopard* fired upon U.S.S. *Chesapeake*, inflicted casualties upon the crew, and forcibly removed four seamen from the American ship. For a brief time, the two countries were poised on the brink of war but President Jefferson kept the dispute within diplomatic channels. Well aware that the British government had never claimed the right to board and remove men from an American warship, Jefferson expected that an apology and an offer of reparation would be forthcoming from the British government. Under these circumstances, while preparing for the worst, President Jefferson gave the Ministry an opportunity to retreat from the dangerous position in which it had been placed by the unauthorized acts of British naval officers.

As Jefferson expected, the British government apologized for the "Chesapeake outrage," promised compensation to the families of the dead seamen, and otherwise satisfied the demands of the United States. But because Jefferson and Secretary of State Madison insisted upon coupling the impressment of seamen from the *Chesapeake* with the impressment question in general, the matter was not closed until 1810 when the surviving seamen were returned with full honors to the deck of the *Chesapeake*.

France showed no more respect for American neutral rights than did the British. In 1806–1807, Napoleon issued the Milan and Berlin Decrees, which declared the British Isles to be in a state of blockade. Any neutral ship touching at a British port or carrying British merchandise was declared to be lawful prize. The British retaliated by issuing Orders in Council, which required every neutral ship to enter a British port and there secure a license authorizing it to proceed to a Continental port.

In December, 1807, rather than permit the British government to dictate the terms upon which American ships could trade with France and its satellites, President Jefferson recommended that Congress impose an embargo upon all American shipping. Congress acted with the promptitude the President had some to expect of that body, and the United States, in effect, adopted the posture of a self-blockade. By thus confining American ships to port, President Jefferson and his party expected that the belligerents would soon be compelled by sheer economic necessity to admit American neutral rights to the fullest degree.

The enforcement of the embargo required an exertion of power by the Federal government far beyond anything dreamed of by the Federalists. Even the last resort of power was used: in 1808 the United States Army and Navy were called upon to prevent citizens from smuggling. Opposition to the embargo centered in New England where the Federalist party embraced the doctrines promulgated by the Virginia and Kentucky Resolutions. The party of Washington and Hamilton became the party of State rights. In this new guise, it returned to power in several New England States and made an impressive showing in the Congressional elections of 1808.

The embargo inflicted greater economic hardship upon the United States than upon the belligerents at which it was aimed. Although President Jefferson did not lose faith in the efficacy of economic coercion as a means of securing American neutral rights, early in 1809, faced with mounting disaffection in New England, he was compelled to consent to the repeal of the embargo. The problem of establishing the freedom of the seas was left to Jefferson's successor, James Madison.

Madison, a scholar in politics, did not possess Jefferson's quality MADISON of firm leadership. Madison's cabinet became the scene of a struggle PRESIDENT for power between Albert Gallatin and the Smith faction of Maryland. Congress filled the vacuum created by the absence of a clear sense of direction on the part of the Executive by taking the initiative in formulating foreign policy. The Nonintercourse Act, passed by Congress in March, 1809, to replace the embargo, failed, like its predecessor, to bring Great Britain and France to terms. In 1810, accordingly, Congress enacted Macon's Act #2, which offered to each of the belligerents the repeal of the penalties imposed by the Nonintercourse Act if it withdrew its controls upon American commerce. If one belligerent accepted this offer and the other belligerent refused, the Nonintercourse Act would remain in force against the noncomplying power.

Perceiving in Macon's Act #2 an opportunity to sow dissension between the United States and Great Britain and to use American shipping for his own purposes, Napoleon ostensibly repealed the Berlin and Milan Decrees. Despite continued French seizures of American ships and merchandise, President Madison professed to be satisfied that the Emperor had acted in good faith. By playing Napoleon's game, the American President hoped to compel the British to abandon Orders in Council. But the British Ministry refused to accept Napoleon's assurances that the Berlin and Milan Decrees had been repealed. As a result, in March, 1811, the United States government declared that trade with France was open to American ships while trade with Great Britain and its possessions remained closed.

Apart from this official certification that the government of Great Britain was the archenemy of American rights at sea, many Americans had already awarded the British government that distinction on the strength of its performance on land. In the West, British traders, agents, and even high government officials were accused of supplying the Indians with arms and inciting them to take the warpath against the American settlements. In actuality, the influence of the British government, but not that of some British traders, was exerted on the side of avoiding committing the Indian allies of George III to a premature and, therefore, necessarily unsupported, war. But Tecumseh and his brother, The Prophet, two of the most remarkable Indians to appear in recorded history, could not easily be dissuaded from their resolution to protect the tribal lands from the advance of the whites. In November, 1811, William Henry Harrison, governor of Indiana Territory, led an army against Tecumseh and his braves. Although Harrison succeeded in destroying the Indian village at Tippecanoe Creek, Tecumseh escaped to fight another day—this time with British support—against the Americans.

Neither economic pressure by the United States nor the repeated assurances of President Madison that the Berlin and Milan Decrees had indeed been rescinded, failed to persuade the British government of the necessity of repealing the Orders in Council. Americans' rising anger against Great Britain was manifested in the elections of 1810–1811 when a large number, but by no means a majority, of War Hawks were elected to Congress. By the end of 1811, President Madison himself was becoming convinced that his policy had failed: British obduracy offered no scope to diplomatic finesse. It was under this persuasion that in June, 1812, the United States substituted war for the seemingly discredited policy of peaceful economic coercion.

WHR OF 1812

In actuality, the President and Congress abandoned Nonintercourse at almost the very moment it was achieving a striking success. On June 16, 1812, the British government announced that as regards the United States, the Orders in Council would be suspended. But nothing was said about impressment—the issue upon which President Madison and the War Hawks had grounded their case for war with Great Britain. Until November, 1812, hopeful that the United States government would reconsider its action of June, the British government refrained from embarking upon hostilities at sea.

Although the acquisition of Canada did not figure as an official objective of the war—the slogan of 1812 was "free ships and sailors' rights"—its supposed vulnerability determined the course of military strategy. But, much to Americans' chagrin, their efforts to conquer Canada in 1812 ended in a rout. By the end of the first year of war, the only Americans in Canada were prisoners of war, and the British regulars, aided by Canadians and Indians, were in possession of key posts in the Northwest including Fort Dearborn, the site of Chicago. Oliver Perry's victory on Lake Erie in 1813, while it saved the American West, did not open the way to Canada. At the end of 1813, the United States Army was no closer to Montreal and Quebec than at the beginning of the war.

Inability to capture CANADA

During these months of defeat and frustration, Americans' morale was sustained by the victories won by the frigates and sloops of the United States Navy over their British counterparts in single-ship duels. But in 1814, strengthened by the downfall of Napoleon and his temporary exile in Elba, the British Navy ceased to engage in single-ship actions, using instead their overwhelming naval superiority to blockade the American coast—a blockade that in April, 1814, was extended to New England. In August, 1814, the British Navy landed a large force of marines and infantry near Washington, D.C. After putting to rout the American militiamen assembled at Bladensburg, the British marched to Washington where they burned the public buildings, including the President's house. But when they attempted to capture Baltimore they were repulsed with heavy loss, an event that inspired Francis Scott Key to write the verse of *The Star Spangled Banner*.

Attack on Washington

But the withdrawal of the British fleet and army from the Chesapeake did not dispel the republic's peril. Reinforced by 10,000 veterans of the Napoleonic Wars, the British Army in Canada mounted an invasion of the United States. In September, 1814, the British force was checked at Plattsburg on Lake Champlain by a small flotilla under the command of Thomas Macdonough. Chastened by this reverse, the British expeditionary force returned to Canada.

In the meantime, disaffection upon the home front was beginning to take the ominous form of secessionism. Although the War of 1812 was known to the Federalists as "Mr. Madison's War," it was primarily the work of Western and Southern Republican Congressmen. The New England businessmen, bankers, and professional men, most of whom had remained loyal to the Federalist party, deplored a war certain to weaken Great Britain, "the world's best hope" in its struggle against Napoleonic France. As the commercial section of the union, New England bore the brunt of the losses in trade incurred in fighting the mistress of the seas. Several New England governors tried to take their States out of the war by refusing to cooperate with the United States government. Even so, New England furnished more recruits for the United States Army than did any other section of the union.

Despite the lamentations of the Federalists, New England was the only part of the country that prospered from the war. Specie flowed from the Southern, Western, and Middle states to New England banks, and manufacturing was stimulated by the virtual stoppage of British imports. Nevertheless, Timothy Pickering and a few other bitter-enders, argued that New England was doomed to suffer economic ruin and political "slavery." But the majority of the Federalist leaders opposed separation. If New England seceded, they pointed out, it would in effect be cutting itself off from its customers and debtors. Late in 1814, the Massachusetts legislature, responding to the wishes of the moderate, not the radical, Federalists, summoned a convention of delegates from the New England States to meet at Hartford, Connecticut. Instead of sounding the tocsin for secession, the delegates asked only for amendments to the Federal constitution. Secession was pronounced to be strictly a last resort.

Few assemblages have been more inopportune than was the Hartford Convention. While the delegates were ventilating the grievances of New England, peace was being made at Ghent in the Netherlands and at New Orleans Andrew Jackson was winning a decisive victory over the British expeditionary force assigned to conquer Louisiana. In the light of these developments, the New England Federalists were made by the Jeffersonian Republicans to appear as defeatists and even as traitors.

The treaty signed at Ghent on December 24, 1814—"the peace of Christmas Eve"—made no mention of any of the objectives for which the United States had gone to war: impressment, freedom of the seas, blockades, or compensation for seizures under the Orders in Council. The United States gained no territory—a circumstance that at least precluded sectional quarrels over the spoils of victory. On the other hand, the peace was not wholly without advantage to the United States: the British government abandoned its plan of creating an Indian buffer state in the Upper Mississippi Valley and the boundary dispute between Canada and United States was referred to mixed commissions for settlement.

With the advent of peace in Europe in 1815, Americans were free to turn their undivided attention to the internal development of the country. For almost the first time since independence, they were liberated not only from foreign entanglements but from the foreign sympathies and involvements that had divided them and weakened the nation. At last the attitude toward Europe that Washington had urged his countrymen to adopt appeared realizable. In a war distinguished by frustration and defeat quite as much as by victory, national feeling won an ascendancy that was not seriously impaired until the great conflict over the sectional balance of power and slavery.

During the period 1789–1815, the foundations were laid for Jacksonian Democracy. In many states, the franchise was broadened and the westward movement created new states based upon the principle of universal suffrage. Even before 1815, Federalists were complaining that the United States was rushing into democracy before the people had been sufficiently prepared for the responsibilities thrust upon them.

The inescapable paradox of the American republic was that the freest white society in the world lived in juxtaposition to a large and ever-increasing population of black slaves. In a nation dedicated to the realization of the ideals of the Declaration of Independence, the

PARADOX
OF THE
AMERICAN
REPUBLIC

color of one's skin was a sovereign determinant. The census of 1810 revealed that every sixth American was in bondage. And, despite the Act of Congress of 1808 which prohibited the importation of slaves from Africa, they continued to be smuggled into the country. The institution of slavery was entrenched in the constitution and the Fugitive Slave Act of 1793 put the Federal government into the business of returning fugitive slaves to their masters.

In the early republic, art and literature were directed toward inculcating patriotism, morality, and "republican virtue." In 1810, the Society of Artists of the United States was organized for the purpose of promoting the "prosperity, glory and independence of the United States" by establishing art schools, holding public exhibitions of the work of American artists, and commemorating upon canvas the events of the American Revolution. John Turnbull's "The Declaration of Independence" was perhaps the finest exemplification of the aspiration, general among American artists, "to preserve and diffuse the memory of the noblest series of actions which have ever presented themselves in the history of man."

The national character that emerged from the War of 1812 represented the consummation of a long effort on the part of American patriots to propagate "Americanism" by means of literature. By separating themselves from the "decadence" of Great Britain and Europe, some Americans expected that an American Renaissance would follow almost automatically. Poets, orators, and historians, it was predicted, would emerge after the "long night" of British rule and American ideals would become a guiding light to humanity.

Animated by this sense of high destiny, American men of letters addressed themselves to the task of crowning the Revolution with a truly republican literature. A coterie of Yale graduates, the so-called Hartford Wits, produced epics which, they flattered themselves, would rank beside the *Iliad* and *Aeneid*. Joel Barlow spent eight years writing *The Vision of Columbus* (1787), which he later rewrote and published under the title of *The Columbiad*. But instead of receiving the critical acclaim he confidently expected, his work was pronounced to be a libel upon the memory of Columbus.

With the exception of Joel Barlow, all the Wits became pillars of the Federalist Establishment and inveterate enemies of the French Revolution. Timothy Dwight, later President of Yale

University, was a staunch champion of orthodoxy against the "heresies" of Deism and Unitarianiam. In *The Triumph of Infidelity* (1788), he recounted in verse Satan's efforts to subvert Christ's Kingdom by means of his favorite instrument for effecting this purpose, the Roman Catholic Church.

Noah Webster, whose *American Spelling Book* (1783) and *American Dictionary of the English Language* (1828) entitled him to be called "Schoolmaster to America," sought to create a national character by fostering the "cultural independence" of the United States in manners, education, spelling, and pronunciation. He believed that a sense of common purpose and national identity could most easily be instilled into the minds of the younger generation. His *Readers* and other classroom books drew examples not from the Bible but from American history, especially the American Revolution. "Every child in America," he said, "should be acquainted with his own country. . . . As soon as he opens his lips, he should lisp the praises of liberty and of those illustrious heroes and statesmen who have wrought a revolution in his favor."

Yet this tone of self-congratulation was considerably muted in Hugh Henry Brekinridge's *Modern Chivalry* (1792–1815). In form a picaresque novel dealing with the adventures of Teague O'Regan and Captain Farrago, it was actually a satire upon many facets of American life. In describing the antics of Teague and the even more reprehensible follies of the American people, Breckinridge meant to reveal what he believed to be fundamental defects of democracy. His message was that the United States could not afford incompetence and ignorance either in its electorate or in its elected officials and that levellism, if given free rein, would destroy excellence.

Washington Irving became the first American professional writer to win a reputation abroad. Irving, a native New Yorker, began his career as an essayist. In 1807, he and a number of friends began the publication of the *Salmagundi*, a magazine devoted to satirizing the foibles of the bon ton of Gotham (*Salmagundi* was the first to apply this name to New York City), reviewing plays, and purveying gossip. Later, Irving turned the legends dating from the days of Dutch rule into such enduring works of literature as *The Legend of Sleepy Hollow*.

The cultural life of the nation was enriched by the growth of public libraries, state and local historical societies, musical and artistic groups, magazines devoted to literary criticism, and theaters. American playwrights drew their plots and characters from the American Revolution. Royall Tyler's *The Contrast*, a play designed to exhibit the superiority of plain, down-to-earth American manners over those of Europe was first presented in 1787. William Dunlap, "the father of the American Drama," produced a repertoire of box-office successes, including *The Glory of Columbia—Her Yeomanry*. Among American poets, Philip Freneau and William Cullen Bryant drew inspiration from distinctively American scenes and experiences. In 1817, Bryant published *Thanatopsis*, a poem celebrating the "noble" rivers, lakes, and mountains of the United States. It was said that "whoever saw Bryant, saw America."

Except for the ubiquitous newspaper, the novel became the most popular literary art-form in the early republic. But it was in the field of architecture rather than of literature that Americans succeeded in emancipating themselves most decisively from contemporary English and European influences. Thomas Jefferson, almost the last of a long line of amateur architects who dominated the colonial period, found inspiration in the architecture of the Roman Empire. His design for the Virginia State Capitol was an enlarged version of the *Maison Carrée* at Nîmes, France, which Jefferson had observed while serving as Minister to France in 1785–1789. Jefferson established the national style in public buildings. Based upon the temple form, these structures were intended to give stability, dignity, and permanence to the public edifices of the republic. To achieve this effect, Americans looked back not only to the grandeur that was Rome but also to the glory that was Greece: the Roman Revival in the United States was followed by the Greek Revival.

During the period 1789–1815 Americans made important contributions to technology. The labor shortage and the immense distances to be overcome put a high premium upon inventions. Heralding the epochal advances that lay ahead, the steamboat, an American invention, began to ply the rivers of the United States, opening up large areas of the West. Canals, turnpikes, and new bridges brought hitherto isolated communities into contact with the cities. The cotton gin, invented by Eli Whitney in 1793, made possible the Cotton Kingdom and thereby gave slavery a fresh lease on life. In his factory in Connecticut, Whitney introduced the prototype of a highly sophisticated technique: he used machines to make parts of muskets so exactly alike that they were interchangeable. Even the assembly-line method of production existed as early as 1818. Thus the American was beginning to appear upon the stage of history as The Man with the Machine. "The time is approaching," a Swedish traveler remarked in 1820, "when people will come here from the old continent to learn about invention and perfected methods of production made by this Nation."

Initiating the New Government

George Washington's
First Inaugural Address, 1789

The inauguration of President George Washington (1732–1799) in New York City on April 30, 1789 was marked by the "monarchical" etiquette of which Thomas Jefferson and his followers so strongly disapproved. President Washington delivered his inaugural address in person to the two Houses of Congress, whereupon each house delivered an address to the President and the President in turn delivered replies to the House and Senate. To some apprehensive republicans, all this formality was reminiscent of the British monarch's Speech from the Throne.

In his Inaugural Address, Washington disclaimed any intention of assuming leadership of Congress. The doctrine of the separation of powers seemed to him to preclude interference by the executive in legislative affairs. Finally, because the new government found itself in serious financial straits less than because of his own wealth (Washington was so land and slave poor that he had to borrow money to make the journey from Mount Vernon to New York) he renounced the salary set aside for the President. During his two terms, Washington merely asked that his expenses as President be paid, but, in actuality, his expenses proved to be only slightly less than his salary. Douglas S. Freeman's Pulitzer-prize-winning, multi-volume biography, *George Washington*, 7 volumes, (New York: Charles Scribner's Sons, 1948–1957), provides a life-sized, sympathetic portrait of the father of his country. The English scholar, Marcus Cunliffe, affords a balanced estimate in his *George Washington: Man and Monument* (Boston: Little, Brown and Company, 1958). For an authoritative biography of one of the framers of the constitution see Irving Brant's nine-volume study of *James Madison* (Indianapolis: The Bobbs-Merrill Company, 1941-1961).

James D. Richardson, ed., *A Compilation of the Messages and Papers of the Presidents, 1789–1897* (Washington, D.C.: Government Printing Office, 1898), I, pp. 51–57.

The volume subtitled *Father of the Constitution, 1787–1800* (1950) is particularly valuable for the 1790s. An interesting mid-nineteenth-century account of the beginnings of the republic can be found in R. W. Griswold's *The Republican Court or American Society in the Days of Washington* (New York: Appleton, 1855). In reading this selection note (1) with what sentiments Washington approached his presidency; (2) to what agency Washington attributed the rise of the United States; (3) upon what principles he thought the success of the new government would depend; (4) Washington's estimate of the relationships of the new constitution to the fate of republican government in the world; (5) his position in the then current debate over the advisability of adding a group of amendments to the constitution; (6) the nature of Washington's style and rhetoric; (7) what substitutes for the word *God* he employed; and (8) the form and style of the addresses of the Senate and the House of Representatives.

April 30th, 1789

Fellow-citizens of the Senate and of the House of Representatives:

Among the vicissitudes incident to life no event could have filled me with greater anxieties than that of which the notification was transmitted by your order, and received on the 14th day of the present month. On the one hand, I was summoned by my country, whose voice I can never hear but with veneration and love, from a retreat which I had chosen with the fondest predilection, and, in my flattering hopes, with an immutable decision, as the asylum of my declining years—a retreat which was rendered every day more necessary as well as more dear to me by the addition of habit to inclination, and of frequent interruptions in my health to the gradual waste committed on it by time. On the other hand, the magnitude and difficulty of the trust to which the voice of my country called me, being sufficient to awaken in the wisest and most experienced of her citizens a distrustful scrutiny into his qualifications, could not but overwhelm with despondence one who (inheriting inferior endowments from nature and unpracticed in the duties of civil administration) ought to be peculiarly conscious of his own deficiencies. In this conflict of emotions all I dare aver is that it has been my faithful study to collect my duty from a just appreciation of every circumstance by which it might be affected. All I dare hope is that if, in executing this task, I have been too much swayed by a grateful remembrance of former instances, or by an affectionate sensibility to this transcendent proof of the confidence of my fellow-citizens, and have thence too little consulted my incapacity as well as disinclination for the weighty and untried cares before me, my error will be palliated by the motives which mislead me, and its consequences be judged by my country with some share of the partiality in which they originated.

Such being the impressions under which I have, in obedience to the public summons, repaired to the present station, it would be peculiarly improper to omit in this first official act my fervent supplications to that Almighty Being who rules over the universe, who presides in the councils of nations, and whose providential aids can supply every human defect, that His benediction may consecrate to the liberties and happiness of the people of the United States a Government instituted by themselves for these essential purposes, and may enable every instrument employed in its administration to execute with success the functions allotted to his charge. In tendering this homage to the Great Author of every public and private good, I assure myself that it expresses your sentiments not less than my own, nor those of my fellow-citizens at large less than either. No people can be bound to acknowledge and adore the Invisible Hand which conducts the affairs of men more than those of the United States. Every step by which they have advanced to the character of an independent nation seems to have been distinguished by some token of providential agency; and in the important revolution just accomplished in the system of their united government the tranquil deliberations and voluntary consent of so many distinct communities from which the event has resulted can not be compared with the means by which most governments have been established without some return of pious gratitude, along with an humble anticipation of the future blessings which the past seem to presage. These reflections, arising out of the present crisis, have forced themselves too strongly on my mind to be suppressed. You will join with me, I trust, in thinking that there are none under the influence of which the proceedings of a new and free government can more auspiciously commence.

By the article establishing the executive department it is made the duty of the President "to recommend to your consideration such

Role of President

Work for good of all - not self-interests

measures as he shall judge necessary and expedient." The circumstances under which I now meet you will acquit me from entering into that subject further than to refer to the great constitutional charter under which you are assembled, and which, in defining your powers, designates the objects to which your attention is to be given. It will be more consistent with those circumstances, and far more congenial with the feelings which actuate me, to substitute, in place of a recommendation of particular measures, the tribute that is due to the talents, the rectitude, and the patriotism which adorn the characters selected to devise and adopt them. In these honorable qualifications I behold the surest pledges that as on one side no local prejudices or attachments, no separate views nor party animosities, will misdirect the comprehensive and equal eye which ought to watch over this great assemblage of communities and interests, so, on another, that the foundation of our national policy will be laid in the pure and immutable principles of private morality, and the preeminence of free government be exemplified by all the attributes which can win the affections of its citizens and command the respect of the world. I dwell on this prospect with every satisfaction which an ardent love for my country can inspire, since there is no truth more thoroughly established than that there exists in the economy and course of nature an indissoluble union between virtue and happiness; between duty and advantage; between the genuine maxims of an honest and magnanimous policy and the solid rewards of public prosperity and felicity; since we ought to be no less persuaded that the propitious smiles of Heaven can never be expected on a nation that disregards the eternal rules of order and right which Heaven itself has ordained; and since the preservation of the sacred fire of liberty and the destiny of the republican model of government are justly considered, perhaps, as *deeply*, as *finally*, staked on the experiment intrusted to the hands of the American people.

Besides the ordinary objects submitted to your care, it will remain with your judgment to decide how far an exercise of the occasional power delegated by the fifth article of the Constitution is rendered expedient at the present juncture by the nature of objections which have been urged against the system, or by the degree of inquietude which has given birth to them. Instead of undertaking particular recommendations on this subject, in which I could be guided by no lights derived from official opportunities, I shall again give way to my entire confidence in your discernment and pursuit of the public good; for I assure myself that whilst you carefully avoid every alteration which might endanger the benefits of an united and effective government, or which ought to await the future lessons of experience, a reverence for the characteristic rights of freemen and a regard for the public harmony will sufficiently influence your deliberations on the question how far the former can be impregnably fortified or the latter be safely and advantageously promoted.

emphasize fact that he is not tyrant.

To the foregoing observations I have one to add, which will be most properly addressed to the House of Representatives. It concerns myself, and will therefore be as brief as possible. When I was first honored with a call into the service of my country, then on the eve of an arduous struggle for its liberties, the light in which I contemplated my duty required that I should renounce every pecuniary compensation. From this resolution I have in no instance departed; and being still under the impressions which produced it, I must decline as inapplicable to myself any share in the personal emoluments which may be indispensably included in a permanent provision for the executive department, and must accordingly pray that the pecuniary estimates for the station in which I am placed may during my continuance in it be limited to such actual expenditures as the public good may be thought to require.

Having thus imparted to you my sentiments as they have been awakened by the occasion which brings us together, I shall take my present leave; but not without resorting once more to the benign Parent of the Human Race in humble supplication that, since He has been pleased to favor the American people with opportunities for deliberating in perfect tranquillity, and dispositions for deciding with unparalleled unanimity on a form of government for the security of their union and the advancement of their happiness, so His divine blessing may be equally *conspicuous* in the enlarged views, the temperate consultations, and the wise measures on which the success of this Government must depend.

Address of the Senate to George Washington, President of the United States

Sir: We, the Senate of the United States, return you our sincere thanks for your excellent speech delivered to both Houses of Congress, congratulate you on the complete organization of the Federal Government, and felicitate ourselves and our fellow-citizens on your elevation to the office of President, an office highly important by the powers constitutionally annexed to it and extremely honorable from the manner in which the appointment is made. The unanimous suffrage of the elective body in your favor is peculiarly expressive of the gratitude, confidence, and affection of the citizens of America, and is the highest testimonial at once of your merit and their esteem. We are sensible, sir, that nothing but the voice of your fellow-citizens could have called you from a retreat chosen with the fondest predilection, endeared by habit, and consecrated to the repose of declining years. We rejoice, and with us all America, that in obedience to the call of our common country you have returned once more to public life. In you all parties confide; in you all interests unite; and we have no doubt that your past services, great as they have been, will be equaled by your future exertions, and that your prudence and sagacity as a statesman will tend to avert the dangers to which we were exposed, to give stability to the present Government and dignity and splendor to that country which your skill and valor as a soldier so eminently contributed to raise to independence and empire.

When we contemplate the coincidence of circumstances and wonderful combination of causes which gradually prepared the people of this country for independence; when we contemplate the rise, progress, and termination of the late war, which gave them a name among the nations of the earth, we are with you unavoidably led to acknowledge and adore the Great Arbiter of the Universe, by whom empires rise and fall. A review of the many signal instances of divine interposition in favor of this country claims our most pious gratitude; and permit us, sir, to observe that among the great events which have led to the formation and establishment of a Federal Government we esteem your acceptance of the office of President as one of the most propitious and important.

In the execution of the trust reposed in us we shall endeavor to pursue that enlarged and liberal policy to which your speech so happily directs. We are conscious that the prosperity of each State is inseparably connected with the welfare of all, and that in promoting the latter we shall effectually advance the former. In full persuasion of this truth, it shall be our invariable aim to divest ourselves of local prejudices and attachments, and to view the great assemblage of communities and interests committed to our charge with an equal eye. We feel, sir, the force and acknowledge the justness of the observation that the foundation of our national policy should be laid in private morality. If individuals be not influenced by moral principles, it is in vain to look for public virtue. It is therefore the duty of legislators to enforce, both by precept and example, the utility as well as the necessity of a strict adherence to the rules of distributive justice. We beg you to be assured that the Senate will at all times cheerfully cooperate in every measure which may strengthen the Union, conduce to the happiness or secure and perpetuate the liberties of this great confederated Republic.

We commend you, sir, to the protection of Almighty God, earnestly beseeching Him long to preserve a life so valuable and dear to the people of the United States, and that your Administration may be prosperous to the nation and glorious to yourself.

May 7, 1789

Reply of the President

Gentlemen: I thank you for your address, in which the most affectionate sentiments are expressed in the most obliging terms. The coincidence of circumstances which led to this auspicious crisis, the confidence reposed in me by my fellow-citizens, and the assistance I may expect from counsels which will be dictated by an enlarged and liberal policy seem to presage a more prosperous issue to my Administration than a diffidence of my abilities had taught me to anticipate. I now feel myself inexpressibly happy in a belief that Heaven, which has done so much for our infant nation, will not withdraw its providential influence before our political felicity shall have been completed, and in a conviction that the Senate will at all times cooperate in every measure which may tend to promote the welfare of this conferated Republic. Thus supported by a firm trust in the Great Arbiter of the Universe, aided by the collected wisdom of the Union, and imploring the divine benediction on our joint exertions in the service of our country, I readily engage with you in the arduous but pleasing task of attempting to make a nation happy.

GO. WASHINGTON

May 18, 1789

Address of the House of Representatives to George Washington, President of the United States

Sir: The Representatives of the people of the United States present their congratulations on the event by which your fellow-citizens have attested the preeminence of your merit. You have long held the first place in their esteem. You have often received tokens of their affection. You now possess the only proof that remained of their gratitude for your services, of their reverence for your wisdom, and of their confidence in your virtues. You enjoy the highest, because the truest, honor of being the first Magistrate by the unanimous choice of the freest people on the face of the earth.

We well know the anxieties with which you must have obeyed a summons from the repose reserved for your declining years into public scenes, of which you had taken your leave forever. But the obedience was due to the occasion. It is already applauded by the universal joy which welcomes you to your station. And we can not doubt that it will be rewarded with all the satisfaction with which an ardent love for your fellow-citizens must review successful efforts to promote their happiness.

This anticipation is not justified merely by the past experience of your signal services. It is particularly suggested by the pious impressions under which you commence your Administration and the enlightened maxims by which you mean to conduct it. We feel with you the strongest obligations to adore the Invisible Hand which has led the American people through so many difficulties, to cherish a conscious responsibility for the destiny of republican liberty, and to seek the only sure means of preserving and recommending the precious deposit in a system of legislation founded on the principles of an honest policy and directed by the spirit of a diffusive patriotism.

The question arising out of the fifth article of the Constitution will receive all the attention demanded by its importance, and will, we trust, be decided under the influence of all the considerations to which you allude.

In forming the pecuniary provisions for the executive department we shall not lose sight of a wish resulting from motives which give it a peculiar claim to our regard. Your resolution, in a moment critical to the liberties of your country, to renounce all personal emolument, was among the many presages of your patriotic services which have been amply fulfilled; and your scrupulous adherence now to the law then imposed on yourself can not fail to demonstrate the purity, whilst it increases the luster, of a character which has so many titles to admiration.

Such are the sentiments which we have thought fit to address to you. They flow from our own hearts, and we verily believe that among the millions we represent there is not a virtuous citizen whose heart will disown them.

All that remains is that we join in our fervent supplications for the blessings of Heaven on our country, and that we add our own for the choicest of these blessings on the most beloved of her citizens.

May 5, 1789

Reply of the President

Gentlemen: Your very affectionate address produces emotions which I know not how to express. I feel that my past endeavors in the service of my country are far overpaid by its goodness, and I fear much that my future ones may not fulfill your kind anticipation. All that I can promise is that they will be invariably directed by an honest and an ardent zeal. Of this resource my heart assures me. For all beyond I rely on the wisdom and patriotism of those with whom I am to cooperate and a continuance of the blessings of Heaven on our beloved country.

GO. WASHINGTON

May 8, 1789

2

Washington and the Senate

Entries from the Journal of Senator William Maclay

As President (1789–1797), Washington scrupulously avoided exceeding his constitutional mandate, and at the beginning of his administration he was willing to concede the Senate a larger measure of co-ordinate authority than that body was prepared to exercise. With regard to the making of treaties the constitution directs the President to act with "the advice and consent" of the Senate. Washington interpreted that directive in its most literal sense. In August, 1789, while negotiations with the southern Indians were still pending, the President, accompanied by Secretary of War Henry Knox (1750–1806), went to the Senate Chamber, took the Vice-President's chair, and informed the senators that he had come to ask their advice and consent regarding the instructions to be given the American commissioners who were to treat with the Creek Indians. Thereupon he submitted seven questions to the Senate. Vice-President John Adams (1735–1826) read the questions to the senators, asking at the end of each question, "Do you advise and consent?" An unwonted silence fell upon the Senate until, finally, Senator Robert Morris (1734–1806), remarking that the President's questions required study, moved that they be referred to a committee of five. According to Senator William Maclay (1734–1804) of Pennsylvania, who seconded Morris's motion, President Washington "started up in a violent fret. 'This defeats every purpose of my coming here,'" he exclaimed angrily. In order to conciliate the outraged Chief Executive, the Senate had to agree to give its answer within three days. Having scored this small victory, Washington left the Senate Chamber with "sullen dignity."

Edgar S. Maclay, ed., *Journal of William Maclay* (New York: D. Appleton and Company, 1890), pp. 128–32.

Contrary to Senator Maclay—a waspish-tempered and cross-grained man who, when Washington invited him to dinner, suspected that the President was trying to corrupt him—that last thing the President had in mind was to overawe the Senate by making a display of his authority. Nevertheless, in expecting the Senate to give an immediate answer to the questions he propounded, the President obviously demanded too much of the members. He realized his mistake and when he met the Senate for the second time his demeanor was "placid and serene." After the Senate had expressed its opinion, the President withdrew, well satisfied with the result. And yet he never repeated the experiment of conducting personal consultations with the Senate; during the remainder of his term of office he communicated with that body exclusively by means of written messages. On occasion, most notably in the case of Jay's Treaty (1794–1795), he neglected to ask its advice prior to entering upon negotiations. It is improbable, however, that Washington was so deeply offended by the reception he met with at the hands of the Senate in August, 1789, that he swore "he would be damned if he ever went there again." The formality and precision of written communications were much more to Washington's taste than were the jars and irritations of personal interviews.

John C. Miller has written a very useful survey of the period for the new American Nation Series, *The Federalist Era, 1789–1801* (New York: Harper and Row, 1960). An older, although still a highly reputable study, is W. Stull Holt's *Treaties Defeated by the Senate; a Study of the Struggle Between the President and Senate Over the Conduct of Foreign Relations* (Baltimore: The Johns Hopkins Press, 1933). Leonard D. White began in 1948 a series of books dealing with the administrative history of the Federal government. The first of these, * *The Federalists: A Study in Administrative History, 1789–1801* (New York: The Macmillan Company, 1948), tells the fascinating story of how the leaders of the new nation organized the republic and what they thought about the problems of managing the public business. In reading the following selection note (1) the temper and tone of Senator Maclay's attitude toward the President; (2) Maclay's descriptions of the interplay between the President of the Senate, John Adams (under the constitution the Vice-President of the United States is the President of the Senate), and Washington's Secretary of War, General Henry Know; (3) the ostensible and probable genuine purport of Senator Robert Morris's interposition in the proceedings; (4) the purpose of Senator Maclay's request for delay; (5) Maclay's estimate of Washington's various responses to his reception by the Senate; (6) Senator Maclay's judgment concerning the methods of procedure proper to the business at hand; and (7) Maclay's estimate of the Senate's response to the presence of the President of the United States in the Senate chamber.

August 21, 1789

NOTICE WAS GIVEN JUST BEFORE WE BROKE UP THAT
the President would be in the Senate chamber at
half after eleven tomorrow to take the advice and consent of the
Senate on some matters of consequence; but nothing communicated.

August 22d, Saturday

Senate met, and went on the Coasting bill. The doorkeeper
soon told us of the arrival of the President. The President was
introduced, and took our Vice-President's chair. He rose and told
us bluntly that he had called on us for our advice and consent to
some propositions respecting the treaty to be held with the Southern
Indians. Said he had brought General Knox with him, who was
well acquainted with the business. He then turned to General
Knox, who was seated on the left of the chair. General Knox
handed him a paper, which he handed to the President of the
Senate, who was seated on a chair on the floor to his right. Our
Vice-President hurried over the paper. Carriages were driving
past, and such a noise, I could tell it was something about "Indians,"
but was not master of one sentence of it. Signs were made to the
doorkeeper to shut down the sashes. Seven heads, as we have since
learned, were stated at the end of the paper which the Senate were
to give their advice and consent to. They were so framed that this
could not be done by aye or no.

The President told us that a paper from an agent of the Cherokees
was given to him just as he was coming to the Hall. He motioned
to General Knox for it, and handed it to the President of the Senate.
It was read. It complained hard of the unjust treatment of the people
of North Carolina, etc., their violation of treaties, etc. Our Vice-
President now read off the first article, to which our advice and
consent were requested. It referred back principally to some
statements in the body of the writing which had been read.

Mr. Morris rose. Said the noise of carriages had been so great that
he really could not say that he had heard the body of the paper
which had been read, and prayed that it might be read again. It
was so [read]. It was no sooner read than our Vice-President
immediately read the first head over again, and put the question:

Do you advise and consent, etc.? There was a dead pause. Mr.
Morris whispered me, "We will see who will venture to break
silence first." Our Vice-President was proceeding, "As many
as—"

I rose reluctantly, indeed, and, from the length of the pause, the
hint given by Mr. Morris, and the proceeding of our Vice-President,
it appeared to me that if I did not no other one would, and we
should have these advices and consents ravished, in a degree, from
us.

Mr. President: The paper which you have now read to us
appears to have for its basis sundry treaties and public transactions
between the Southern Indians and the United States and the
States of Georgia, North Carolina, and South Carolina. The
business is new to the Senate. It is of importance. It is our duty to
inform ourselves as well as possible on the subject. I therefore call
for the reading of the treaties and other documents alluded to in the
paper before us.

I cast an eye at the President of the United States. I saw he
wore an aspect of stern displeasure. General Knox turned up some
of the acts of Congress and the protest of one Blount, agent for
North Carolina. Mr. Lee rose and named a particular treaty which
he wished read. The business labored with the Senate. There
appeared an evident reluctance to proceed. The first article was
about the Cherokees. It was hinted that the person just come from
there might have more information. The President of the United
States rose; said he had no objection to that article being postponed,
and in the mean time he would see the messenger.

The second article, which was about the Chickasaws and
Choctaws, was likewise postponed. The third article more immediately concerned Georgia and the Creeks. Mr. Gunn, from
Georgia, moved that this be postponed till Monday. He was
seconded by Mr. Few. General Knox was asked when General
Lincoln would be here on his way to Georgia. He answered *not till
Saturday next*. The whole House seemed against Gunn and Few. I
rose and said, when I considered the newness and importance of
the subject, that one article had already been postponed; that
General Lincoln, the first named of the commissioners, would not
be here for a week; the deep interest Georgia had in this affair—I
could not think it improper that the Senators from the State should

be indulged in a postponement until Monday; and more especially as I had not heard any inconvenience pointed out that could possibly flow from it.

The question was put and actually carried; but Elsworth immediately began a long discourse on the merits of the business. He was answered by Lee, who appealed to the Constitution with regard to the power of making war. Butler and Izard answered, and Mr. Morris at last informed the disputants that they were debating on a subject that was actually postponed. Mr. Adams denied, in the face of the House, that it had been postponed. This very trick had been played by him and his New England men more than once. The question was, however, put a second time and carried.

I had at an early stage of the business whispered Mr. Morris that I thought the best way to conduct the business was to have all the papers committed. My reasons were, that I saw no chance of a fair investigation of subjects while the President of the United States sat there, with his Secretary of War, to support his opinions and overawe the timid and neutral part of the Senate. Mr. Morris hastily rose and moved that the papers communicated to the Senate by the President of the United States should be referred to a committee of five, to report as soon as might be on them. He was seconded by Mr. Gunn. Several members grumbled some objections. Mr. Butler rose; made a lengthy speech against commitment; said we were acting as a council. No council ever committed anything. Committees were an improper mode of doing business; it threw business out of the hands of the many into the hands of the few, etc.

I rose and supported the mode of doing business by committees; that committees were used in all public deliberative bodies, etc. I thought I did the subject justice, but concluded the commitment can not be attended with any possible inconvenience. Some articles are already postponed until Monday. Whoever the committee are, if committed, they must make their report on Monday morning. I spoke through the whole in a low tone of voice. Peevishness itself, I think, could not have taken offense at anything I said.

As I sat down, the President of the United States started up in a violent fret. "*This defeats every purpose of my coming here,*" were the first words that he said. He then went on that he had brought his Secretary of War with him to give every necessary information; that the Secretary knew all about the business, and yet he was delayed and could not go on with the matter. He cooled, however, by degrees. Said he had no objection to putting off this matter until Monday, but declared he did not understand the matter of commitment. He might be delayed; he could not tell how long. He rose a second time, and said he had no objection to postponement until Monday at ten o'clock. By the looks of the Senate this seemed agreed to. A pause for some time ensued. We waited for him to withdraw. He did so with a discontented air. Had it been any other man than the man whom I wish to regard as the first character in the world, I would have said, with sullen dignity.

I can not now be mistaken. The President wishes to tread on the necks of the Senate. Commitment will bring the matter to discussion, at least in the committee, where he is not present. He wishes us to see with the eyes and hear with the ears of his Secretary only. The Secretary to advance the premises, the President to draw the conclusions, and to bear down our deliberations with his personal authority and presence. Form only will be left to us. This will not do with Americans. But let the matter work; it will soon cure itself.

August 24th, Monday

The Senate met. The President of the United States soon took his seat, and the business began. The President wore a different aspect from what he did Saturday. He was placid and serene, and manifested a spirit of accommodation; declared his consent that his questions should be amended. A tedious debate took place on the third article. I was called on by Mr. Lee, of Virginia, to state something respecting the treaty held by Pennsylvania. This brought me up. I did not speak long, but endeavored to be as pointed as possible. The third article consisted of two questions. The first I was for. I disliked the second, but both were carried. The fourth article consisted of sundry questions. I moved pointedly for a division. Got it. Voted for the first and opposed the second part. A long debate ensued, which was likely to end only in words. I moved to have the words "in failure thereof by the United States" struck out, and, although Elsworth, Wyngate, and Dalton had spoken on the same side with me, yet I was not seconded. My colleague had in private declared himself of my opinion also. It was an engagement that the United States would pay the stipulated purchase money for Georgia in case Georgia did not. The arguments

I used on this subject were so plain I need not set them down. Yet a shamefacedness, or I know not what, flowing from the presence of the President, kept everybody silent.

The next clause was for a free port on the Altamaha or Saint Mary's River. This produced some debate, and the President proposed "secure" port in place of "free" port. Agreed to. Now followed something of giving the Indians commissions on their taking the oaths to Government. It was a silly affair, but it was carried without any debate. Now followed a clause whether the cession of lands should be made an ultimatum with the Creeks. There was an alternative in case this should be negatived; but, strange to tell, the Senate negatived both, when it was plain one only should have been so. A boundary was named by a following clause which the commissioners were to adhere to. Money and honorary commissions were to be given to the Indians. The old treaties with the Creeks, Choctaws, and Chickasaws were made the basis of future treaty, though none of them were read to us nor a single principle of them explained (but it was late). The twenty thousand dollars applied to this treaty, if necessary. This closed the business. The President of the United States withdrew, and the Senate adjourned. . . .

3

Hamilton's Report on National Credit

A Communication to the House of Representatives, January 14, 1790

On January 14, 1790, Alexander Hamilton (1755–1804), the 33-year-old Secretary of the Treasury, delivered to Congress one of the truly epoch-making state papers submitted to that body. Its credit strained by years of fiscal irresponsibility, the government of the United States by 1790 reached the point at which its financial house had to be set in order if the vision of "a more perfect union" were to be realized. In order to establish the credit of the Federal government, Hamilton saw that its existing obligations, foreign and domestic, would have to be honored. Hamilton therefore proposed that the foreign debt, including accrued interest, be paid in full and that the domestic creditors be given almost equally favorable treatment.

Hamilton's most audacious proposal was that the Federal government assume that part of the debts incurred by the States in the prosecution of the War of Independence that had not yet been paid. Here his motives were a mixture of political, economic, and fiscal considerations. By this measure he hoped to concentrate the financial power of the country in the Federal government—for the responsibility of paying the debt required the exercise of the authority to tax—and to compel the State creditors to look to the Federal government for the redemption of their certificates. In short, Hamilton hoped that the States, stripped of their functions by an all-powerful central government, would simply wither away into mere administrative districts of the Federal government. The irresistible force of self-interest, by enlisting public creditors and men of property in general

John C. Hamilton, ed., *The Works of Alexander Hamilton* (New York: Charles S. Francis and Co., 1850), III, pp. 1–15, 20, 41.

on the side of the central government, would, he hoped, remake the political face of the nation. And, finally, by giving the public creditors more than the most sanguine had expected, Hamilton intended to concentrate large quantities of negotiable securities (which served the function of capital) in the hands of those best able to employ that capital for the economic advancement of the country. For a study of late eighteenth- and early nineteenth-century economic policy in America by means of a detailed study of one State, see Louis Hartz, *Economic Policy and Democratic Thought: Pennsylvania, 1776–1860* (Cambridge: Harvard University Press, 1948). Nathan Schachner has written one of the better biographies of the colorful and controversial first Secretary of the Treasury in his *Alexander Hamilton* (New York: Appleton-Century, 1946). In reading Hamilton's report note (1) what, in his judgment, were the basic principles upon which the public credit of a nation rested; (2) what he thought had happened to those principles during the Confederation period; (3) how he related the public debt to liberty; (4) the effect the initiation of the new government had had upon the public credit; (5) what general results could be expected to occur from a proper management of the public credit; (6) the arguments that led him to claim that the public debt, properly managed, could become a public blessing; (7) why he rejected the argument that the government should discriminate between the original holders of its securities and the subsequent purchasers; (8) why he thought the United States ought to assume the obligation of paying, not only its own debt, but those of the States as well; and (9) his opinion as to the "true secret for rendering public credit immortal."

THE SECRETARY OF THE TREASURY, IN OBEDIENCE TO the resolution of the House of Representatives of the twenty-first day of September last, has, during the recess of Congress, applied himself to the consideration of a proper plan for the support of the public credit, with all the attention which was due to the authority of the House, and to the magnitude of the object. . . .

With an ardent desire that his well meant endeavors may be conducive to the real advantage of the nation, and with the utmost deference to the superior judgment of the House, he now respectfully submits the result of his inquiries and reflections to their indulgent construction.

In the opinion of the Secretary, the wisdom of the House, in giving their explicit sanction to the proposition which has been stated, cannot but be applauded by all who will seriously consider and trace, through their obvious consequences, these plain and undeniable truths:

That exigencies are to be expected to occur, in the affairs of nations, in which there will be a necessity for borrowing.

That loans in times of public danger, especially from foreign war, are found an indispensable resource, even to the wealthiest of them.

And that, in a country which, like this, is possessed of little active wealth, or, in other words, little moneyed capital, the necessity for that resource must, in such emergencies, be proportionably urgent.

And as, on the one hand, the necessity for borrowing, in particular emergencies, cannot be doubted, so, on the other, it is equally evident, that, to be able to borrow upon good terms, it is essential that the credit of a nation should be well established.

For, when the credit of a country is in any degree questionable, it never fails to give an extravagant premium, in one shape or another, upon all the loans it has occasion to make. Nor does the evil end here; the same disadvantage must be sustained upon whatever is to be bought on terms of future payment.

From this constant necessity of borrowing and buying dear, it is easy to conceive how immensely the expenses of a nation, in a course of time, will be augmented by an unsound state of the public credit.

To attempt to enumerate the complicated variety of mischiefs in the whole system of the social economy, which proceed from a neglect of the maxims that uphold public credit, and justify the solicitude manifested by the House on this point, would be an improper intrusion on their time and patience.

In so strong a light, nevertheless, do they appear to the Secretary, that, on their due observance, at the present critical juncture, materially depends, in his judgment, the individual and aggregate prosperity of the citizens of the United States; their relief from the embarrassments they now experience; their character as a people; the cause of good government.

If the maintenance of public credit, then, be truly so important, the next inquiry which suggests itself is, By what means is it to be effected? The ready answer to which question is, by good faith; by a punctual perforamce of contracts. States, like individuals, who observe their engagements, are respected and trusted, while the reverse is the fate of those who pursue an opposite conduct.

Every breach of the public engagements, whether from choice or necessity, is, in different degrees, hurtful to public credit. When such a necessity does truly exist, the evils of it are only to be palliated by a scrupulous attention, on the part of the Government to carry the violation no further than the necessity absolutely requires, and to manifest, if the nature of the case admit of it, a sincere disposition to make reparation whenever circumstances shall permit. But, with every possible mitigation, credit must suffer, and numerous mischiefs ensue. It is, therefore, highly important, when an appearance of necessity seems to press upon the public councils, that they should examine well its reality, and be perfectly assured that there is no method of escaping from it, before they yield to its suggestions. . . .

While the observance of that good faith, which is the basis of public credit, is recommended by the strongest inducements of political expediency, it is enforced by considerations of still greater authority. There are arguments for it which rest on the immutable principles of moral obligation. And in proportion as the mind is disposed to contemplate, in the order of Providence, an intimate connection between public virtue and public happiness, will be its repugnancy to a violation of those principles.

This reflection derives additional strength from the nature of the debt of the United States. It was the price of liberty. The faith of America has been repeatedly pledged for it, and with solemnities that give peculiar force to the obligation. There is, indeed, reason to regret that it has not hitherto been kept; that the necessities of the war, conspiring with inexperience in the subjects of finance, produced direct infractions; and that the subsequent period has been a continued scene of negative violation or non-compliance. But a diminution of this regret arises from the reflection, that the last seven years have exhibited an earnest and uniform effort, on the part of the Government of the Union, to retrieve the national credit, by doing justice to the creditors of the nation; and that the embarrassments of a defective constitution, which defeated this laudable effort, have ceased.

From this evidence of a favorable disposition given by the former Government, the institution of a new one, clothed with powers competent to calling forth the resources of the community, has excited correspondent expectations. A general belief accordingly prevails, that the credit of the United States will quickly be established on the firm foundation of an effectual provision for the existing debt. The influence which this has had at home, is witnessed by the rapid increase that has taken place in the market value of the public securities. From January to November, they rose thirty-three and a third per cent.; and, from that period to this time, they have risen fifty per cent. more; and the intelligence from abroad announces effects proportionably favorable to our national credit and consequence.

It cannot but merit particular attention, that, among ourselves, the most enlightened friends of good government are those whose expectations are the highest.

To justify and preserve their confidence; to promote the increasing respectability of the American name; to answer the calls of justice; to restore landed property to its due value; to furnish new resources, both to agriculture and commerce; to cement more closely the union of the States; to add to their security against foreign attack; to establish public order on the basis of an upright and liberal policy;—these are the great and invaluable ends to be secured by a proper and adequate provision, at the present period, for the support of public credit.

To this provision we are invited, not only by the general considerations which have been noticed, but by others of a more particular nature. It will procure, to every class of the community, some important advantages, and remove some no less important disadvantages.

The advantage to the public creditors, from the increased value of that part of their property which constitutes the public debt, needs no explanation.

But there is a consequence of this, less obvious, though not less true, in which every other citizen is interested. It is a well known fact, that, in countries in which the national debt is properly funded, and an object of established confidence, it answers most of the purposes of money. Transfers of stock or public debt, are there equivalent to payments in specie; or, in other words, stock, in the principal transactions of business, passes current as specie. The same thing would, in all probability, happen here under the like circumstances.

The benefits of this are various and obvious:

First. Trade is extended by it, because there is a larger capital to carry it on, and the merchant can, at the same time, afford to trade for smaller profits; as his stock, which, when unemployed, brings him in an interest from the Government, serves him also as money when he has a call for it in his commercial operations.

Secondly. Agriculture and manufactures are also promoted by it, for the like reason, that more capital can be commanded to be employed in both; and because the merchant, whose enterprise in foreign trade gives to them activity and extension, has greater means for enterprise.

Thirdly. The interest of money will be lowered by it, for this is always in a ratio to the quantity of money, and to the quickness of circulation. This circumstance will enable both the public and individuals to borrow on easier and cheaper terms.

And from the combination of these effects, additional aids will be furnished to labor, to industry, and to arts of every kind. But these good effects of a public debt are only to be looked for, when, by being well funded, it has acquired an adequate and stable value; till then, it has rather a contrary tendency. The fluctuation and insecurity incident to it, in an unfunded state, render it a mere commodity, and a precarious one. As such, being only an object of occasional and particular speculation, all the money applied to it is so much diverted from the more useful channels of circulation, for which the thing itself affords no substitute; so that, in fact, one serious inconvenience of an unfunded debt is, that it contributes to the scarcity of money.

This distinction, which has been little if at all attended to, is of the greatest moment; it involves a question immediately interesting to every part of the community, which is no other than this: Whether the public debt, by a provision for it on true principles, shall be rendered a substitute for money; or whether, by being left as it is, or by being provided for in such a manner as will wound those principles, and destroy confidence, it shall be suffered to continue as it is, a pernicious drain of our cash from the channels of productive industry? . . .

Having now taken a concise view of the inducements to a proper provision for the public debt, the next inquiry which presents itself is, What ought to be the nature of such a provision? This requires some preliminary discussions.

It is agreed, on all hands, that that part of the debt which has been contracted abroad, and is denominated the foreign debt, ought to be provided for according to the precise terms of the contracts relating to it. The discussions which can arise, therefore, will have reference essentially to the domestic part of it, or to that which has been contracted at home. It is to be regretted that there is not the same unanimity of sentiment on this part as on the other.

The Secretary has too much deference for the opinions of every part of the community, not to have observed one, which has more than once made its appearance in the public prints, and which is occasionally to be met with in conversation. It involves this question: Whether a discrimination ought not to be made between original holders of the public securities, and present possessors, by purchase? Those who advocate a discrimination, are for making a full provision for the securities of the former at their nominal value; but contend that the latter ought to receive no more than the cost to them, and the interest. And the idea is sometimes suggested, of making good the difference to the primitive possessor. . . .

The Secretary, after the most mature reflection on the force of this argument, is induced to reject the doctrine it contains, as equally unjust and impolitic; as highly injurious, even to the original holders of public securities; as ruinous to public credit.

It is inconsistent with justice, because, in the first place, it is a breach of contract—a violation of the rights of a fair purchaser. . . .

That he is to be considered as a fair purchaser, results from this: whatever necessity the seller may have been under, was occasioned by the Government, in not making a proper provision for its debts. The buyer had no agency in it, and therefore ought not to suffer. He is not even chargeable with having taken an undue advantage. He paid what the commodity was worth in the market, and took the risks of reimbursement upon himself. He, of course, gave a fair equivalent, and ought to reap the benefit of his hazard—a hazard which was far from inconsiderable, and which, perhaps, turned on little less than a revolution in government. . . .

But, though many of the original holders sold from necessity, it does not follow that this was the case with all of them. It may well be supposed that some of them did it either through want of confidence in an eventual provision, or from the allurements of some profitable speculation. How shall these different classes be discriminated from each other? How shall it be ascertained, in any case, that the money which the original holder obtained for his security, was not more beneficial to him, than if he had held it to the present time, to avail himself of the provision which shall be made? How shall it be known whether, if the purchaser had employed his money in some other way, he would not be in a better situation than by having applied it in the purchase of securities, though he should now receive their full amount? And, if neither of these things can be known, how shall it be determined, whether a discrimination, independent of the breach of contract, would not do a real injury to purchasers; and, if it included a compensation to the primitive proprietors, would not give them an advantage to which they had no equitable pretension? . . .

Questions of this sort, on a close inspection, multiply themselves without end, and demonstrate the injustice of a discrimination, even on the most subtile calculations of equity, abstracted from the obligation of contract. . . .

The impolicy of a discrimination results from two considerations: one, that it proceeds upon a principle destructive of that quality of the public debt, or the stock of the nation, which is essential to its capacity for answering the purposes of money, that is, the security of transfer; the other, that, as well on this account as because it includes a breach of faith, it renders property, in the funds, less valuable, consequently, induces lenders to demand a higher premium for what they lend, and produces ever other inconvenience of a bad state of public credit. . . .

But there is still a point of view, in which it will appear perhaps even more exceptionable than in either of the former. It would be repugnant to an express provision of the Constitution of the United States. This provision is, that "all debts contracted, and engagements entered into, before the adoption of that Constitution, shall be as valid against the United States under it, as under the Confederation;" which amounts to a constitutional ratification of the contracts respecting the debt, in the state in which they existed under the Confederation. And, resorting to that standard, there can be no doubt that the rights of assignees and original holders must be considered as equal. . . .

The Secretary, concluding that a discrimination between the different classes of creditors of the United States cannot, with propriety, be made, proceeds to examine whether a difference ought to be permitted to remain between them and another description of public creditors—those of the States, individually. The Secretary, after mature reflection on this point, entertains a full conviction, that an assumption of the debts of the particular States by the Union, and a like provision for them, as for those of the Union, will be a measure of sound policy and substantial justice.

It would, in the opinion of the Secretary, contribute, in an eminent degree, to an orderly, stable, and satisfactory arrangement of the national finances. Admitting, as ought to be the case, that a provision must be made, in some way or other, for the entire debt, it will follow that no greater revenues will be required, whether that provision be made wholly by the United States, or partly by them, and partly by the States separately.

The principal question, then, must be, whether such a provision cannot be more conveniently and effectually made, by one general plan, issuing from one authority, than by different plans, originating in different authorities? In the first case, there can be no competition for resources; in the last, there must be such a competition. The consequences of this, without the greatest caution on both sides, might be interfering regulations, and thence, collision and confusion. Particular branches of industry might also be oppressed by it. The most productive objects of revenue are not numerous. Either these must be wholly engrossed by one side, which might lessen the efficacy of the provisions by the other, or both must have recourse to the same objects, in different modes, which might occasion an accumulation upon them, beyond what they could properly bear. . . .

If all the public creditors receive their dues from one source, distributed with an equal hand, their interest will be the same. And, having the same interests, they will unite in the support of the fiscal arrangements of the Government—as these, too, can be made with more convenience where there is no competition. These circumstances combined, will insure to the revenue laws a more ready and more satisfactory execution.

If, on the contrary, there are distinct provisions, there will be distinct interests, drawing different ways. That union and concert of views, among the creditors, which in every Government is of great importance to their security, and to that of public credit, will not only not exist, but will be likely to give place to mutual jealousy and opposition. And from this cause, the operation of the systems which may be adopted, both by the particular States and by the Union, with relation to their respective debts, will be in danger of being counteracted. . . .

The result of the foregoing discussions is this: That there ought to be no discrimination between the original holders of the debt, and present possessors by purchase; that it is expedient there should be an assumption of the State debts by the Union; and that the arrears of interest should be provided for on an equal footing with the principal. . . .

Persuaded, as the Secretary is, that the proper funding of the present debt will render it a national blessing, yet he is so far from acceding to the position, in the latitude in which it is sometimes laid down, that "public debts are public benefits"—a position inviting to prodigality, and liable to dangerous abuse—that he ardently wishes to see it incorporated, as a fundamental maxim, in the system of public credit of the United States, that the creation of debt should always be accompanied with the means of extinguishment. This he regards as the true secret for rendering public credit immortal. And he presumes that it is difficult to conceive a situation in which there may not be an adherence to the maxim. At least, he feels an unfeigned solicitude that this may be attempted by the United States, and that they may commence their measures for the establishment of credit with the observance of it.

Thomas Jefferson's Account of the Adoption of Hamilton's Report on National Credit

Thomas Jefferson's *The Anas*

Alexander Hamilton's Report on National Credit, submitted to Congress in January, 1790, produced a crisis that threatened to disrupt the newly formed union. Hamilton proposed the funding of the national debt virtually at par and the assumption by the Federal government of State debts. James Madison (1751–1836), Hamilton's collaborator in the writing of the *Federalist*, took the lead in Congress in opposing the adoption of Hamilton's Report, and thereby signalized the dissolution of the sectional alliance that had made possible the ratification of the Federal Constitution. Rather than enrich speculators who had bought public securities at depreciated prices, Madison demanded an equitable division between the original holders and later purchasers of the profit that was certain to accrue from the funding of the debt. Thus Madison injected a humanitarian note into American politics, for most of those who had sold their certificates to speculators and investors were soldiers and farmers who had fought or labored for American independence. Madison also pleaded for "justice" to the States, Virginia among them, that had paid off a large part of their debts. If these two points were agreed to, Madison was willing to accept Hamilton's principle that the national debt ought to be paid in full and that the State debts ought to be assumed by the Federal government. Because Hamilton refused to yield upon either point, a deadlock was produced in Congress between the Madisonians (as the opposition group was called) and the partisans of the Secretary of the Treasury. For six months, virtually all business in Congress was halted.

Uncertainty and delay tended to increase the incidence of speculation

Thomas Jefferson, *The Anas*, 1791–1806, in Paul Leicester Ford, ed., *The Writings of Thomas Jefferson* (New York: G. P. Putnam's Sons, 1894), I, pp. 159–64.

in the public debt—the evil Madison sought to curb. But by the summer of 1790, some speculators had become thoroughly alarmed by the prospect of the defeat of Hamilton's plan. Many of those who had acclaimed the courage and wisdom of the Secretary of the Treasury now blamed him for rashness and overconfidence.

Yet a basis for compromise existed and there were men ready to act upon it. Throughout the debate over Hamilton's Report, the question of the permanent site of the Federal government had never been lost sight of. Hamilton himself tried to strike a bargain with the Pennsylvania Representatives and Senators whereby in exchange for enough votes to ensure the adoption of his Report the national capital would be located in Philadelphia or on the Susquehanna River. When the Pennsylvanians failed to produce the necessary votes, Hamilton turned perforce to the Virginians, who, despite the vehemence of their opposition to the funding-assumption plan, were eager to move the capital to the Potomac River where, far removed from "the marts of trade" and in rural surroundings calculated to remind the legislators that the United States was a farmers' republic, the interests of agriculture would be given the primacy they deserved.

No one felt more strongly the importance of transferring the capital to the Potomac than did Thomas Jefferson (1743–1826). Hitherto, the Secretary of State had taken no direct part in the controversy, but he was known to be a moderate and to fear for the continuance of the union. When Hamilton accosted Jefferson, the Virginian agreed to arrange a meeting of the leaders of the contending factions. Over a bottle of wine—the Secretary of State served only the finest French vintages—the two cabinet officers agreed to a compromise, by which the debt was to be funded much as Hamilton had proposed, the present holders of government certificates were to be paid in full, the assumption of State debts was to be "sweetened" for Virginia and other States that had paid a considerable part of their war debts, and the national capital, after a ten years' temporary relocation at Philadelphia, was to be established permanently on the Potomac.

Although it ran against the grain of Virginia Congressmen to vote for the settlement worked out by Jefferson, Madison, and Hamilton, the Virginians mustered enough votes to carry it through Congress. Still, it was a sectional victory; for more Northerners than Southerners voted to adopt Hamilton's Report. Nor was there any question as to who reaped the financial windfall: in 1795, citizens of Massachusetts were paid over $300,000 in interest on United States government securities whereas Virginians received only $62,000. The speculators, upon whom descended a golden harvest in the form of unearned increment, sang hosannas to the sagacious Secretary of the Treasury.

And with good reason. The funding of the debt incurred by the Continental Congress and the assumption of State debts gave security holders about $70 million for their depreciated paper. Backed by the financial resources of the Federal government, these securities had a cash surrender value that permitted them to be used as money in business transactions, including the payment of private debts to foreign creditors. Moreover, the credit of the United States was so firmly established that by 1792 the Federal government enjoyed a better credit rating than any continental European country.

Hamilton was well satisfied with the bargain he had struck with Jefferson: to secure the passage of the funding-assumption bills, he would gladly have moved the national capital to an even hotter spot than the Potomac in August. At first, too, Jefferson was content. Among other advantages he foresaw from this arrangement was an opportunity to participate personally in the planning of the Federal city and in designing its public buildings. Captivated by this prospect, Jefferson momentarily forgot his aversion to cities; he expressed the hope that the Federal capital would attract "foreigners, manufacturers and settlers" to the Potomac, thereby shifting southward the balance of population, political power, and wealth. But after 1791 when the Virginia legislature condemned the assumption of State debts, Jefferson changed his mind about the transaction. Jefferson kept notes relating to the public events of the day while he was Secretary of State (1789–1793). Several years later he reworked these notes giving the results the title of *The Anas*. The validity of *The Anas* as an exact historical record is compromised by Jefferson's later revisions at a time when party lines had become more clearly marked than during Washington's first administration. Yet, the account provides us with an intimate judgment and estimate of events by a participant in one of the more significant episodes in the life of the young republic.

An account written in the Progressive tradition of historiography popular in the 1920s and 1930s by Claude G. Bowers, **Jefferson and Hamilton: The Struggle for Democracy in America* (Boston: Houghton Mifflin Company, 1926), stresses the dramatic elements in the confrontation between Washington's two principal associates and advisers. John C. Miller's later study, **Alexander Hamilton: Portrait in Paradox* (New York: Harper and Row, 1959), emphasizes the long-range implications of some of Hamilton's achievements while at the same time giving weight to his libertarian and humanitarian sentiments—sentiments frequently overlooked by authors searching for ways to add spice to their histories of the Federalist period. In reading this selection note (1) Jefferson's estimate of the political confrontation emerging in the early 1790s; (2) the evidence he found to support the contention that a monarchical conspiracy existed in the United States; (3) what side Jefferson took in the controversy over payment to holders of public securities; (4) the evidence he cited in justification of his taking

sides; (5) what position Jefferson took, and why, respecting the assumption
of State debts; (6) considerations that led him to support Hamilton's
proposals; and (7) what seemed to Jefferson to be the political results of the
adoption of Hamilton's Report.

I RETURNED FROM THAT MISSION [TO FRANCE] IN THE
1st. year of the new government, having landed in
Virginia in Dec. [17]89. & proceeded to N. York in March [17]90.
to enter on the office of Secretary of State. Here certainly I found
a state of things which, of all I had ever contemplated, I the least
expected. I had left France in the first year of its revolution, in the
fervor of natural rights, and zeal for reformation. My conscientious
devotion to these rights could not be heightened, but it had been
aroused and excited by daily exercise. The President received me
cordially, and my Colleagues & the circle of principal citizens,
apparently, with welcome. The courtesies of dinner parties given me
as a stranger newly arrived among them, placed me at once in
their familiar society. But I cannot describe the wonder and mortification with which the table conversations filled me. Politics were
the chief topic, and a preference of kingly, over republican, government, was evidently the favorite sentiment. An apostate I could
not be; nor yet a hypocrite: and I found myself, for the most part,
the only advocate on the republican side of the question, unless,
among the guests, there chanced to be some member of that party
from the legislative Houses. Hamilton's financial system had then
past. It had two objects: 1st as a puzzle, to exclude popular understanding & inquiry. 2dly, as a machine for the corruption of the
legislature; for he avowed the opinion that man could be governed
by one of two motives only, force or interest: force he observed, in
this country, was out of the question; and the interests therefore of
the members must be laid hold of, to keep the legislature in unison
with the Executive. And with grief and shame it must be acknowledged that his machine was not without effect. That even in this, the
birth of our government, some members were found sordid enough
to bend their duty to their interests, and to look after personal,
rather than public good. It is well-known that, during the war, the
greatest difficulty we encountered was the want of money or means,

to pay our souldiers who fought, or our farmers, manufacturers & merchants who furnished the necessary supplies of food & clothing for them. After the expedient of paper money had exhausted itself, certificates of debt were given to the individual creditors, with assurance of payment, so soon as the U.S. should be able. But the distresses of these people often obliged them to part with these for the half, the fifth, and even a tenth of their value; and Speculators had made a trade of cozening them from the holders, by the most fraudulent practices and persuasions that they would never be paid. In the bill for funding & paying these, Hamilton made no difference between the original holders, & the fraudulent purchasers of this paper. Great & just repugnance arose at putting these two classes of creditors on the same footing, and great exertions were used to pay to the former the full value, and to the latter the price only which he had paid, with interest. But this would have prevented the game which was to be played, & for which the minds of greedy members were already tutored and prepared. When the trial of strength on these several efforts had indicated the form in which the bill would finally pass, this being known within doors sooner than without, and especially than to those who were in distant parts of the Union, the base scramble began. Courtiers & relay horses by land, and swift sailing pilot boats by sea, were flying in all directions. Active part[n]ers & agents were associated & employed in every state, town and country neighborhood, and this paper was bought up at 5/ and even as low as 2/ in the pound, before the holder knew that Congress had already provided for it's redemption at par. Immense sums were thus filched from the poor & ignorant, and fortunes accumulated by those who had themselves been poor enough before. Men thus enriched by the dexterity of a leader, would follow of course the chief who was leading them to fortune, and become the zealous instruments of all his enterprises. This game was over, and another was on the carpet at the moment of my arrival; and to this I was most ignorantly & innocently made to hold the candle. This fiscal maneuvre is well known by the name of the Assumption. Independantly of the debts of Congress, the states had, during the war, contracted separate and heavy debts; and Massachusetts particularly in an absurd attempt, absurdly conducted, on the British post of Penobscot: and the more debt Hamilton could rake up, the more plunder for his mercenaries.

This money, whether wisely or foolishly spent, was pretended to have been spent for general purposes, and ought therefore to be paid from the general purse. But it was objected that nobody knew what these debts were, what their amount, or what their proofs. No matter; we will guess them to be 20. millions. But of these 20. millions we do not know how much should be reimbursed to one state, nor how much to another. No matter; we will guess. And so another scramble was set on foot among the several states, and some got much, some little, some nothing. But the main object was obtained, the phalanx of the treasury was reinforced by additional recruits. This measure produced the most bitter & angry contests every known in Congress, before or since the union of the states. I arrived in the midst of it. But a stranger to the ground, a stranger to the actors on it, so long absent as to have lost all familiarity with the subject, and as yet unaware of it's object, I took no concern in it. The great and trying question however was lost in the H. of Representatives. So high were the feuds excited by this subject, that on it's rejection, business was suspended. Congress met and adjourned from day to day without doing any thing, the parties being too much out of temper to do business together. The Eastern members particularly, who, with Smith from South Carolina, were the principal gamblers in these scenes, threatened a secession and dissolution. Hamilton was in despair. As I was going to the President's one day, I met him in the street. He walked me backwards & forwards before the President's door for half an hour. He painted pathetically the temper into which the legislature had been wrought, the disgust of those who were called the Creditor states, the danger of the secession of their members, and the separation of the states. He observed that the members of the administration ought to act in concert, that tho' this question was not of my department, yet a common duty should make it a common concern that the President was the center on which all administrative questions ultimately rested, and that all of us should rally around him, and support with joint efforts measures approved by him; and that the question having been lost by a small majority only, it was probable that an appeal from me to the judgment and discretion of some of my friends might effect a change in the vote, and the machine of government, now suspended, might be again set into motion. I told him that I was really a stranger to the whole subject; not having yet informed myself of the system of finances adopted, I knew not how far this was a necessary sequence; that undoubtedly if it's rejection endangered a dissolution of our union at this incipient stage, I should deem that the most unfortunate of all consequences, to avert which all partial and temporary evils should be yielded. I proposed to him however to dine with me the next day, and I would invite another friend or two, bring them into conference together, and I thought it impossible that reasonable men, consulting together coolly, could fail, by some mutual sacrifices of opinion, to form a compromise which was to save the union. The discussion took place. I could take no part in it, but an exhortatory one, because I was a stranger to the circumstances which should govern it. But it was finally agreed that, whatever importance had been attached to the rejection of this proposition, the preservation of the union, & and of concord among the states was more important, and that therefore it would be better that the vote of rejection should be rescinded, to effect which some members should change their votes. But it was observed that this pill would be peculiarly bitter to the Southern States, and that some concomitant measure should be adopted to sweeten it a little to them. There had before been propositions to fix the seat of government either at Philadelphia, or at Georgetown on the Potomac; and it was thought that by giving it to Philadelphia for ten years, and to Georgetown permanently afterwards, this might, as an anodyne, calm in some degree the ferment which might be excited by the other measure alone. So two of the Potomac members ([Alexander] White & [Richard Henry] Lee, but White with a revulsion of stomach almost convulsive) agreed to change their votes, & Hamilton undertook to carry the other point. In doing this the influence he had established over the Eastern members, with the agency of Robert Morris with those of the middle states, effected his side of the engagement, and so the assumption was passed, and 20. millions of stock divided among favored states, and thrown in as pabulum to the stock-jobbing herd. This added to the number of votaries to the treasury and made its Chief the master of every vote in the legislature which might give to the government the direction suited to his political views. I know well, and so must be understood, that nothing like a majority in Congress had yielded to this corruption. Far from it. But a division, not very unequal, had already taken place in the honest part of that body, between the parties styled republican and federal. The latter being monarchists in principle, adhered to Hamilton of course, as their leader in that principle, and this mercenary phalanx added to them ensured him always a majority in both houses: so that the whole action of the legislature was now under the direction of the treasury. . . .

5

The Federalists' Defense of the Bank of the United States

Hamilton's Opinion on the Constitutionality of the Bank of the United States, February 23, 1791

In December, 1790, Hamilton submitted to Congress a Report in which he urged that a quasi-public bank called the Bank of the United States be chartered for twenty years by the Federal government. Ownership and control of the Bank were to be shared by the government and the private stockholders: the government would contribute part of the Bank's capital of $10 million and appoint five members of a Board consisting of 25 Directors, but the larger share of the capital and the actual management of the Bank would be vested in Directors appointed by the private stockholders. A measure of public control was provided by the privilege accorded the Secretary of the Treasury of examining the Bank's books periodically. The Bank was to be authorized to use bank notes that enjoyed the status of legal tender, to receive deposits, and to make loans to private borrowers as well as to the government.

Hamilton believed that a central bank was necessary to the proper functioning of the government and to the commercial and industrial development of the nation. In the United States, the lack of a national circulating medium made such an institution especially imperative. The three banks operating in 1790 in New York, Philadelphia, and Boston issued paper banknotes that circulated as money but not even the mercantile needs of those cities were fully met by these notes. In the interior of the country, money, whether bank notes or specie, was rarely seen. A British traveler reported that the words *buy* and *sell* were almost unknown; in business transactions, everything was conducted as *trade*.

The bill chartering the Bank of the United States passed Congress but

John C. Hamilton, ed., *The Works of Alexander Hamilton* (New York: Charles S. Francis and Co., 1850), IV, pp. 104–38.

not before the constitutionality of the measure had been called in question by James Madison. President Washington, who attached great weight to Madison's view of the constitution, was deeply troubled. Before signing the bill, therefore, he asked each member of his cabinet to submit in writing an opinion regarding the constitutionality of the proposed Bank. Secretary of State Jefferson made clear in his opinion that he regarded the Bank of the United States as another milestone on the road to monarchism, centralization, and the Leviathan state. From his reading of the constitution it appeared that the Federal government had no power to create corporations of any kind. Yet Jefferson gladly conceded this power to the States. The Secretary of State insisted that he was seeking to preserve the "beautiful balance" established by the constitution between the States and the Federal government but his constitutional theory would have given the States exclusive control of a vital segment of the national economy.

The brief presented by Hamilton to President Washington justifying the constitutionality of the Bank of the United States took a more permissive view of the powers of the Federal government under the constitution. Applying what came to be called the broad interpretation of that document, the Secretary of the Treasury argued that the necessary and proper and general welfare clauses contained in the preamble to the constitution gave Congress the power to charter corporations when they were necessary to the execution of an enumerated power. In short, the Federal government, like all other viable governments, was authorized by the constitution to fulfill the ends for which it had been instituted.

Although his doubts and misgivings were not wholly removed by Hamilton's arguments, President Washington signed the bill incorporating the Bank of the United States. The Bank opened its doors in April, 1791. But the question of its constitutionality would not die down; when President Jackson moved against the Second Bank of the United States it was on the ground that it was unconstitutional.

The economist and economic historian, Broadus Mitchell, has written a study of Hamilton, *Alexander Hamilton*, 2 vols. (New York: The Macmillan Company, 1957–1962), which might be consulted with profit. An older account still useful is Davis R. Dewey's *Financial History of the United States* (New York: Longmans, Green and Company, 1903). Bray Hammond's Pulitzer prize-winning *Banks and Politics in America, From the Revolution to the Civil War* (Princeton: Princeton University Press, 1957) is indispensable for one interested in the relationships between government and finance. In reading this selection note (1) Hamilton's argument supporting his contention that the Federal government possessed the power to create corporations; (2) his view of the significance of the doctrine of implied powers to the success of government under the constitution; (3) how he would distinguish between the constitutional and unconstitutional use of the Federal power to create corporations; (4) how he explained the difference between his own and Jefferson's definition of the word *necessary*; (5) what he believed were the criteria for what was constitutional and what was unconstitutional; (6) his reasons for believing the Bank to be constitutional; and (7) his characterization of the objections raised against the Bank.

 IF IT WOULD BE NECESSARY TO BRING PROOF TO A proposition so clear, as that which affirms that the powers of the federal government, as to *its objects*, were sovereign, there is a clause of its Constitution which would be decisive. It is that which declares that the Constitution, and the laws of the United States made in pursuance of it, and all treaties made, or which shall be made, under their authority, shall be the *supreme law of the land*. The power which can create the *supreme law of the land* in *any case* is doubtless *sovereign* as to such case.

This general and indisputable principle puts at once an end to the *abstract* question whether the United States have power to erect a *corporation*; that is to say, to give a *legal* or *artificial capacity* to one or more persons, distinct from the *natural*. For it is unquestionably incident to *sovereign power* to erect corporations, and consequently to *that* of the United States, in *relation* to the *objects* intrusted to the management of the government. The difference is this: where the authority of the government is general, it can create corporations in *all cases*; where it is confined to certain branches of legislation, it can create corporations *only* in those cases. . . .

It is not denied that there are *implied* as well as *express powers* and that the *former* are as effectually delegated as the *latter*. And for the sake of accuracy it shall be mentioned that there is another class of powers which may be properly denominated *resulting powers*. It will not be doubted that, if the United States should make a conquest of any of the territories of its neighbors, they would possess sovereign jurisdiction over the conquered territory. This would be rather a result, from the whole mass of the powers of the government, and from the nature of political society, than a consequence of either of the powers specially enumerated. . . .

It is conceded that *implied powers* are to be considered as delegated equally with *express ones*. Then it follows that, as a power of erecting a corporation may as well be *implied* as any other thing, it may as well be employed as an *instrument* or *mean* of carrying into execution any of the specified powers, as any other *instrument* or *mean* whatever. The only question must be, in this, as in every other case, whether the mean to be employed or, in this instance, the corporation to be erected, has a natural relation to any of the acknowledged objects or lawful ends of the government. Thus a corporation may not be erected by Congress for superintending the police of the city of Philadelphia, because they are not authorized to *regulate* the *police* of that city. But one may be erected in relation to the collection of taxes, or to the trade with foreign countries, or to the trade between the states, or with the Indian tribes; because it is the province of the federal government to *regulate* those objects, and because it is incident to a general *sovereign* or *legislative* power to *regulate* a thing, to employ all the means which relate to its regulation to the best and greatest advantage. . . .

Through this mode of reasoning respecting the right of employing all the means requisite to the execution of the specified powers of the government, it is objected that none but necessary and proper means are to be employed; and the Secretary of State maintains that no means are to be considered as *necessary* but those without which the grant of the power would be *nugatory*. Nay, so far does he go in his restrictive interpretation of the *word*, as even to make the case of the *necessity* which shall warrant the constitutional exercise of the power to depend on *casual* and *temporary* circumstances; an idea which alone refutes the construction. The *expediency* of exercising a particular power, at a particular time, must, indeed, depend on circumstances; but the constitutional right of exercising it must be uniform and invariable, the same today as tomorrow. . . .

It is essential to the being of the national government that so erroneous a conception of the meaning of the word *necessary* should be exploded.

It is certain that neither the grammatical nor popular sense of the term requires that construction. According to both, *necessary* often means no more than *needful, requisite, incidental, useful,* or *conducive to*. It is a common mode of expression to say that it is *necessary* for a government or a person to do this or that thing, when nothing more is intended or understood than that the interests of the government or person require, or will be promoted by, the doing of this or that thing. The imagination can be at no loss for exemplifications of the use of the word in this sense. And it is the true one in which it is to be understood as used in the Constitution. . . .

To understand the word as the Secretary of State does would be to depart from its obvious and popular sense and to give it a restrictive operation, an idea never before entertained. It would be to give it the same force as if the word *absolutely* or *indispensably* had been prefixed to it.

Such a construction would beget endless uncertainty and embarrassment. The cases must be palpable and extreme, in which it could be pronounced, with certainty, that a measure was absolutely necessary, or one, without which, the exercise of a given power would be nugatory. There are few measures of any government which would stand so severe a test. To insist upon it would be to make the criterion of the exercise of any implied power a *case of extreme necessity*; which is rather a rule to justify the overleaping of the bounds of constitutional authority than to govern the ordinary exercise of it. . . .

This restrictive interpretation of the word *necessary* is also contrary to this sound maxim of construction, namely, that the powers contained in a constitution of government, especially those which concern the general administration of the affairs of a country, its finances, trade, defense, etc., ought to be construed liberally in advancement of the public good. This rule does not depend on the particular form of a government, or on the particular demarcation of the boundaries of its powers, but on the nature and objects of government itself. The means by which national exigencies are to be provided for, national inconveniences obviated, national prosperity promoted, are of such infinite variety, extent, and complexity, that there must of necessity be great latitude of discretion in the selection and application of those means. Hence, consequently, the necessity and propriety of exercising the authorities intrusted to a government on principles of liberal construction. . . .

The doctrine which is contended for is not chargeable with the consequences imputed to it. It does not affirm that the national government is sovereign in all respects but that it is sovereign to a certain extent; that is, to the extent of the objects of its specified powers.

It leaves, therefore, a criterion of what is constitutional and of what is not so. This criterion is the *end*, to which the measure relates as a *mean*. If the *end* be clearly comprehended within any of the specified powers, and if the measures have an obvious relation to that *end*, and is not forbidden by a particular provision of the Constitution, it may safely be deemed to come within the compass of the national authority. There is also this further criterion, which may materially assist the decision: Does the proposed measure abridge a pre-existing right of any state or of any individual? If it does not, there is a strong presumption in favor of its constitutionality, and slighter relations to any declared object of the Constitution may be permitted to turn the scale. . . .

A bank has a natural relation to the power of collecting taxes—to that of regulating trade—to that of providing for the common defense—and . . . as the bill under consideration contemplates the government in the light of a joint proprietor of the stock of the bank, it brings the case within the provision of the clause of the Constitution which immediately respects the property of the United States.

Under a conviction that such a relation subsists, the Secretary of the Treasury, with all deference, conceives, that it will result as a necessary consequence from the position, that all the specified powers of government are sovereign, as to the proper objects; that the incorporation of a bank is a constitutional measure; and that the objections taken to the bill, in this respect, are ill founded. . . .

6

Jefferson and Hamilton Explain Their Rift

Letters Written in May, 1792

To Jefferson, the struggle for control of the Federal government that began in 1789 was nothing less than a confrontation between monarchism and republicanism. On every hand, especially within the Federal government itself, he saw evidences of the rising power of monarchism: in the effort in the Senate to give the President a title such as "His Highness the President of the United States and Protector of their Liberties"; in John Adams's alleged defection from republicanism to the monarchical camp; in the levees and other evidences of "monarchical pomp" affected by President Washington; and in the dinner-table conversation in New York and Philadelphia where the British system of government was openly praised. At the head of this "monarchical conspiracy" Jefferson placed Alexander Hamilton: in Jefferson's book (he set down his opinions, together with the rumors and gossip he picked up from his friends, in a book he called *The Anas*), Hamilton figured not merely as the advocate of consolidated government but as a monarchist bent upon subverting the constitution and establishing in the United States a government of king, lords, and commons.

In consequence, the controversy between Hamilton and Jefferson could not be conducted wholly under the decorous guise of constitutional interpretation. Jefferson and Madison were well aware that as long as the dispute was kept upon this lofty intellectual plane, the American people were not likely to realize the full danger in which they and their free institutions stood from Hamilton and his partisans. Persuaded that nothing

Thomas Jefferson to George Washington, Philadelphia, May 23, 1792 in Paul Leicester Ford, ed., *The Writings of Thomas Jefferson*, VI, pp. 1–5. Alexander Hamilton to Edward Carrington, Philadelphia, May 26, 1792 in John C. Hamilton, *History of the Republic of the United States . . .* (New York: Charles S. Francis and Co., 1859), IV, pp. 524–26; 530; 532–37.

less than the fate of republicanism was at issue, Jefferson and Madison keenly felt the need of a national newspaper capable of alerting the people to Hamilton's real designs. Such a newspaper seemed all the more essential in view of the fact that since 1789 the *Gazette of the United States*, edited by John Fenno and subsidized by Hamilton and his friends, had been engaged in fabricating an image of Secretary of the Treasury as a patriot and statesman beyond reproach.

To counteract the adulation dispensed by Fenno's *Gazette of the United States*, Jefferson and Madison persuaded Philip Freneau, the "Poet of the Revolution" turned newspaper editor, to establish in Philadelphia a newspaper called the *National Gazette*. The main financial inducement held out by Jefferson to bring Freneau to Philadelphia was the offer of a clerkship in the State Department.

As editor of the *National Gazette*, Philip Freneau made the Federalists regret that he had not confined his talents to the writing of poetry. He specialized in heaping coals upon Hamilton: every measure conceived by the Secretary of the Treasury, Freneau declared, had as its ulterior objective the creating of a king, lords, and commons in the United States. On July Fourth, 1792, for example, the *National Gazette* printed an article entitled: "Rules for changing a limited republican government into an unlimited hereditary one." The first rule listed was to increase the national debt and to establish a central bank.

What Freneau was saying about Hamilton in the *National Gazette*, Jefferson was saying directly to President Washington. Early in 1792, the Secretary of State told the President that Hamilton was interfering in the conduct of foreign affairs, ruling Congress by means of a "corrupt squadron," and working to make the United States a monarchy. In May, 1792, he asserted that the crisis of republicanism was at hand: Congress must either be purged of all holders of government securities and bank stock or the monarchists would take over the country. Monarchists, according to Jefferson's definition, sought to aggrandize the power of the Executive; true republicans, on the other hand, exalted the legislature as the direct representative of the people. He wished to see Congress wholly free of direction from the executive branch; only then, he said, could separation of powers ordained by the constitution be preserved.

Despite the deep respect in which he held Jefferson, President Washington refused to be alarmed by the bogey of monarchism. He did not know of ten reputable men in the United States, he told Jefferson, who seriously contemplated erecting a monarchy and, he added, he would give the last drop of his blood to ensure that the republican experiment was given a fair trial. As for Hamilton's work, the President took the position that failing some infallible rule of reason, it must be judged pragmatically. When he contrasted the state of the country as he had known it under the Articles of

Confederation with its present prosperity and financial stability, he was prepared to give Hamilton the benefit of every constitutional doubt.

Hamilton, too, registered his complaints of his colleague with the President. He told Washington that Jefferson intrigued with members of Congress to defeat administration measures and discredit Hamilton himself and that Jefferson's ambition was so inordinate that he aspired to the presidency itself. But neither man succeeded in shaking the President's confidence in the other; instead of taking sides, Washington urged them to compose their differences. To which both men replied that they could never sacrifice their principles. As Jefferson said, republicanism and monarchism could never lie down together in peace.

In August, 1792, Hamilton learned that while remaining discreetly in the background, Jefferson had been instrumental in bringing Freneau to Philadelphia. He immediately assumed that Jefferson was responsible for everything that appeared in the *National Gazette* and that he supplied the libels and gossip with which Freneau regaled his readers. Writing in the newspapers under a pseudonym, Hamilton accused the Secretary of State of having hired with government money a character-assassin to destroy the people's confidence in the Secretary of the Treasury. Although Jefferson himself did not respond publicly, his friends, including James Monroe, filled the newspapers with attacks upon Hamilton. Among other things, he was called an apostate from the principles of 1776, who wished to introduce into republican America that "class of human lions, tygers and mammoths called kings."

By singling out Jefferson as his prime enemy, Hamilton succeeded in making the Secretary of State appear to be the leader of the anti-Hamiltonian opposition. Hitherto, because James Madison had been regarded as its chief spokesman, that opoosition had been known as the *Madisonian* party; but henceforth, it was called the *Jeffersonian* or Republican party. Madison continued to supply ideas and to devise political strategy but he took care to subordinate himself to his older friend. It was to the author of the Declaration of Independence to whom the adversaries of the Hamiltonian system looked for leadership.

The student might consult the biographies of Hamilton by John C. Miller and Nathan Schachner and the account of Jefferson and Hamilton by Claude G. Bowers already cited. Adrienne Koch in **Jefferson and Madison: The Great Collaboration* (New York: Alfred A. Knopf, 1950) has explored the relationships between the two famous Virginia neighbors. The major modern biography of Jefferson is Dumas Malone's thorough *Jefferson and His Time*, three volumes of which have appeared to date; volume II, *Jefferson and the Rights of Man* (Boston: Little, Brown and Company, 1951) deals primarily with the period of the 1790s. A brilliant essay suggesting that American political parties arose out of foreign rather than domestic agreements can be found in Joseph Charles, * *The Origins of the American Party System: Three Essays* (Williamsburg: Institute of Early American History and Culture, 1956). In reading Jefferson's letter to President Washington note (1) what led him to believe that Hamilton intended to saddle a permanent public debt upon the United States; (2) the consequences he envisioned resulting from this action; (3) the political purpose he thought motivated Hamilton's fiscal policies; (4) by what processes he believed Hamilton gained support for his objectives; (5) his opinion of what might eventually occur should Hamilton not be checked; and (6) how he thought Washington might assist in maintaining republicanism in the United States. In reading Hamilton's letter to Colonel Carrington note (1) the charges he lodged against Jefferson and Madison; (2) the evidence he advanced in support of his contention; (3) how, it appeared to him, that foreign policy was implicated in the dispute; (4) the influence on Jefferson's thought he ascribed to Jefferson's residence in France; (5) how he accounted for Madison's and Jefferson's charge that he (Hamilton) aimed to convert the United States into a monarchy; and (7) what warning he suggested concerning the future of the national government.

Thomas Jefferson to George Washington

Philadelphia May 23 1792

WHEN YOU FIRST MENTIONED TO ME YOUR PURPOSE of retiring from the government, tho' I felt all the magnitude of the event, I was in a considerable degree silent. . . . I knew we were some day to try to walk alone . . . The public mind . . . was calm & confident, and therefore in a favorable state for making the experiment. Had no change of circumstances intervened, I should not, with any hope of success, have now ventured to propose to you a change of purpose. But the public mind is no longer confident and serene; and that from causes in which you are in no ways personally mixed. . . .

It has been urged . . . that a public debt, greater than we can possibly pay before other causes of adding new debt to it will occur, has been artificially created, by adding together the whole amount of the debtor & creditor sides of accounts, instead of taking only their balances, which could have been paid off in a short time: That this accumulation of debt has taken for ever out of our power those easy sources of revenue, which, applied to the ordinary necessities and exigencies of government, would have answered them habitually, and covered us from habitual murmurings against taxes & tax-gatherers, reserving extraordinary calls, for those. extraordinary occasions which would animate the people to meet them: That though the calls for money have been no greater than we must generally expect, for the same or equivalent exigencies, yet we are already obliged to strain the impost till it produces clamour, and will produce evasion, & war on our own citizens to collect it: and even to resort to an *Excise* law, of odious character with the people, partial in it's operation, unproductive unless enforced by arbitrary & vexatious means, and committing the authority of the government in parts where resistance is most probable, & coercion least practicable. They cite propositions in Congress and suspect other projects on foot still to increase the mass of debt. They say that by borrowing at $\frac{2}{3}$ of the interest, we might have paid off the principal in $\frac{2}{3}$ of the time: but that from this we are precluded by it's being made irredeemable but in small portions & long terms: That this irredeemable quality was given it for the avowed purpose of inviting it's transfer to foreign countries. They predict that this transfer of the principal, when compleated, will occasion an exportation of 3. millions of dollars annually for the interest, a drain of coin, of which as there has been no example, no calculation can be made of it's consequences: That the banishment of our coin will be compleated by the creation of 10. millions of paper money, in the form of bank bills, now issuing into circulation. They think the 10. or 12. percent annual profit paid to the lenders of this paper medium taken out of the pockets of the people, who would have had without interest the coin it is banishing: That all the capital employed in paper speculation is barren & useless, producing, like that on a gaming table, no accession to itself, and is withdrawn from commerce & agriculture where it would have produced addition to the common mass: That it nourishes in our citizens habits of vice and idleness instead of industry & morality: That it has furnished effectual means of corrupting such a portion of the legislature, as turns the balance between the honest voters which ever way it is directed: That this corrupt squadron, deciding the voice of the legislature, have manifested their dispositions to get rid of the limitations imposed by the constitution on the general legislature, limitations, on the faith of which, the states acceded to that instrument: That the ultimate object of all this is to prepare

the way for a change, from the present republican form of government, to that of a monarchy, of which the English constitution is
to be the model. That this was contemplated in the Convention
is no secret, because it's partisans have made none of it. To effect it
then was impracticable, but they are still eager after their object,
and are predisposing every thing for it's ultimate attainment. So
many of them have got into the legislature, that, aided by the
corrupt squadron of paper dealers, who are at their devotion, they
make a majority in both houses. . . .

Of all the mischiefs objected to the system of measures before
mentioned, none is so afflicting, and fatal to every honest hope, as
the corruption of the legislature. As it was the earliest of these
measures, it became the instrument for producing the rest, & will be
the instrument for producing in future a king, lords & commons,
or whatever else those who direct it may chuse. Withdrawn such a
distance from the eye of their constituents, and these so dispersed
as to be inaccessible to public information, & particularly to that of
the conduct of their own representatives, they will form the most
corrupt government on earth, if the means of their corruption be
not prevented. The only hope of safety hangs now on the numerous
representation which is to come forward the ensuing year. Some of
the new members will probably be either in principle or interest,
with the present majority, but it is expected that the great mass
will form an accession to the republican party. They will not be
able to undo all which the two preceding legislatures, & especially
the first, have done. Public faith & right will oppose this. But
some parts of the system may be rightfully reformed; a liberation
from the rest unremittingly pursued as fast as right will permit, &
the door shut in future against similar commitments of the nation. . . .
But should the majority of the new members be still in the same
principles with the present, & shew that we have nothing to expect
but a continuance of the same practices, it is not easy to conjecture
what would be the result, nor what means would be resorted to
for correction of the evil. True wisdom would direct that they should
be temperate & peaceable, but the division of sentiment & interest
happens unfortunately to be so geographical, that no mortal can
say that what is most wise & temperate would prevail against what
is most easy & obvious? I can scarcely contemplate a more in-
calculable evil than the breaking of the union into two or more

parts. Yet when we review the mass which opposed the original coalescence, when we consider that it lay chiefly in the Southern quarter, that the legislature have availed themselves of no occasion of allaying it, but on the contrary whenever Northern & Southern prejudices have come into conflict, the latter have been sacrificed & the former soothed; that the owners of the debt are in the Southern & the holders of it in the Northern division; that the Anti-federal champions are now strengthened in argument by the fulfilment of their predictions; that this has been brought about by the Monarchical federalists themselves, who, having been for the new government merely as a stepping stone to monarchy, have themselves adopted the very constructions of the constitution, of which, when advocating it's acceptance before the tribunal of the people, they declared it insusceptible; that the republican federalists, who espoused the same government for it's intrinsic merits, are disarmed of their weapons, that which they denied as prophecy being now become true history: who can be sure that these things may no proselyte the small number which was wanting to place the majority on the other side? And this is the event at which I tremble, & to prevent which I consider your continuance at the head of affairs as of the last importance. . . . North & South will hang together, if they have you to hang on; and, if the first correction of a numerous representation should fail in it's effect, your presence will give time for trying others not inconsistent with the union & peace of the states.

Philadelphia May 26, 1792

IT WAS NOT, TILL THE LAST SESSION, THAT I BECAME UNEQUIVOCALLY CONVINCED OF THE FOLLOWING TRUTH, *"that Mr. Madison, co-operating with Mr. Jefferson, is at the head of a faction, decidedly hostile to me, and my administration; and actuated by views, in my judgment, subversive of the principles of good government, and dangerous to the Union, peace and happiness of the country.". . .*

This conviction in my mind, is the result of a long train of circumstances; many of them minute. To attempt to detail them all, would fill a volume. I shall therefore confine myself to the mention of a few.

First, As to the point of opposition to me, and my administration.

Mr. Jefferson, with very little reserve, manifests his dislike of the funding system, generally; calling in question, the expediency of funding a debt, at all. Some expressions, which he has dropped in my own presence, (sometimes without sufficient attention to delicacy,) will not permit me to doubt on this point, representations, which I have had from various respectable quarters. I do not mean, that he advocates directly the undoing of what has been done; but he censures the whole, on principles, which, if they should become general, could not but end in the subversion of the system.

In various conversations with *foreigners*, as well as citizens, he has thrown censure on my *principles* of government, and on my measures of administration. He had predicted, that the people would not long tolerate my proceedings; and, that I should not long maintain my ground. Some of those, whom he *immediately* and *notoriously* moves, have *even* whispered suspicions of the rectitude of my motives and conduct. In the question concerning the Bank, he not only, delivered an opinion in writing against its constitutionality and expediency; but he did it *in a stile and manner*, which I felt as partaking of asperity and ill humor towards me. As one of the trustees of the Sinking fund, I have experienced, in almost every leading question, opposition from him. When any turn of things in the community has threatened either odium or embarrassment to me, he has not been able to suppress the satisfaction, which it gave him. . . .

I find a strong confirmation in the following circumstances. *Freneau*, the present printer of the "National Gazette," who was a journeyman, with Childs & Swain, at New York, was a known Anti-federalist. It is reduced to a certainty, that he was brought to Philadelphia, by Mr. Jefferson to be the conductor of a newspaper. It is notorious, that cotemporarily with the commencement of his paper, he was a clerk in the department of State, for foreign languages. Hence a clear inference, that his paper has been set on foot, and is conducted, under the patronage, and not against the views of Mr. Jefferson. What then is the complexion of this paper? Let any impartial man peruse all the numbers down to the present day; and, I never was more mistaken, if he does not pronounce, that it is a paper, devoted to the subversion of me and the measures in which I have had an agency; and, I am little less mistaken, if he do not pronounce, that it is a paper, of a tendency *generally unfriendly* to the Government of the United States.

It may be said, that a newspaper being open to all the publications, which are offered to it, its complexion may be influenced by other views, than those of the editor. But the fact here is, that, whenever the editor appears, it is in a correspondent dress. The paragraphs which appear as his own, the publications, not original, which are selected for his press, are of the same malignant and unfriendly aspect; so, as not to leave a doubt, of the temper which directs the publication. . . .

Secondly, As to the tendency of the views of the two gentlemen, who have been named. . . .

In almost all the questions, great and small, which have arisen, since the first session of Congress, Mr. Jefferson and Mr. Madison have been found among those who are disposed to narrow the Federal authority. . . .

In respect to our foreign politics, the views of these gentlemen, are, in my judgment, equally unsound, and dangerous. THEY HAVE A WOMANISH ATTACHMENT TO FRANCE, AND A WOMANISH RESENTMENT AGAINST GREAT BRITAIN. They would draw us into the closest embrace of the former, and involve us in all the consequences of her politics; and they would risk the peace of the country, in their endeavors, to keep us at the greatest possible distance from the latter. This disposition goes to a length, particularly in Mr. Jefferson, of which, till lately, I had no adequate idea. Various circumstances prove to me, that, if these gentlemen were left to pursue their own course, there would be, in less than six months, AN OPEN WAR BETWEEN THE UNITED STATES AND GREAT BRITAIN. . . .

Having delineated to you, what I conceive, to be the true complexion of the politics of these gentlemen, I will now attempt a solution of these strange appearances.

Mr. Jefferson, it is known, did not, in the first instance, cordially acquiesce in the new Constitution for the United States; he had many doubts, and reserves. He left this country, before we had experienced the imbecilities of the former.

In France, he saw government, only on the side of its abuses. He drank deeply of the French philosophy, in religion, in science, in politics. He came from France, in the moment of a fermentation, which he had a share in exciting; and in the passions and feelings of which, he shared, both from temperament and situation. He came here, probably with a too partial idea of his own powers;

and, with the expectation of a greater share in the direction of our councils, than he has, in reality, enjoyed. I am not sure, that he had not peculiarly marked out for himself, the department of the finances.

He came, electrified *plus* with attachment to France, and with the project of knitting together, the two countries, in the closest political bands. . . .

Attempts were made by these gentlemen, in different ways, to produce a commercial warfare with Great Britain. In this, too, they were diappointed. And, as they had the liveliest wishes on the subject, their dissatisfaction has been proportionably great; and, as I had not favored the project, I was comprehended in their displeasure. . . .

Another circumstance has contributed to widening the breach. 'Tis evident, beyond a question, from every movement, that Mr. Jefferson aims, with ardent desire, at the Presidential chair. This, too, is an important object of the party—politics. It is supposed, from the nature of my former personal and political connections, that I may favor some other candidate, more than Mr. Jefferson, when the question shall occur, by the retreat of the present gentleman. My influence, therefore, with the community, becomes a thing, on ambitious and personal grounds, to be resisted and destroyed. . . .

It is possible, too, (for men easily heat their imaginations when their passions are heated,) that they have, by degrees, persuaded themselves of what they may have at first only sported, to influence others; namely, that there is some dreadful combination against State Government, and Republicanism; which, according to them, are convertible terms. But there is so much absurdity in this supposition, that the admission of it tends to apologize for their hearts, at the expense of their heads.

Under the influence of all these circumstances, the attachment to the Government of the United States, originally weak in Mr. Jefferson's mind, has given way to something very like dislike in Mr. Madison's, it is so counteracted by personal feelings, as to be more an affair of the head than of the heart . . .

In such a state of mind, both these gentlemen are prepared to hazard a great deal to effect a change. Most of the important measures of every Government are connected with the Treasury.

To subvert the present head of it, they deem it expedient to risk rendering the Government itself odious; perhaps, foolishly thinking, that they can easily recover the lost affections and confidence of the people; and not appreciating, as they ought to do, the natural resistance to Government, which, in every community, results from the human passions, the degree to which this is strengthened by the *organized rivality* of State Governments; and the infinite danger that the National Government, once rendered odious, will be kept so by these powerful and indefatigable enemies.

They forget an old, but a very just, though a coarse saying, that it is much easier to raise the devil than to lay him.

7

Washington's Advice to his Fellow Countrymen

An Address to the Nation, (Washington's Farewell Address), September 17, 1796

For about 25 years beginning early in the 1790s, Europe, led by revolutionary and postrevolutionary France on one side and England on the other, experienced almost continuous warfare. The big powers paid scant heed to the efforts of smaller nations to maintain their neutrality; as a matter of fact, each of the big powers sought to enlist on his side the aid of powerful or weak but useful neutrals. President Washington had, when war broke out in 1793 between France and England, proclaimed American neutrality. Divisions of opinion within America over domestic policies between the Jeffersonians and Hamiltonians were sharpened and deepened by the debates over foreign policy, with the Jeffersonians favoring a pro-French, anti-British posture and the Hamiltonians maintaining a pro-British, anti-French stance. The Hamiltonian administration in pursuit of its policy sought to abate some of the exacerbating issues outstanding with Great Britain by sending Chief Justice John Jay (1745–1829) to the Court of St. James to negotiate a settlement. Jay concluded and signed a treaty (which bears his name) in 1794 and the Senate ratified the document in 1795. The Jeffersonians very strongly opposed the treaty on a number of grounds, whereas the French government regarded it as an alliance in everything but name between the United States and Great Britain. For this reason, Pierre Adet, French minister at Philadelphia, had embodied himself with the Jeffersonian opposition and lobbied against the treaty in the Congress—the kind of intervention in the affairs of independent nations

Washington's Farewell Address, in James D. Richardson, ed., *A Compilation of the Messages and Papers of the Presidents* (Washington, D.C.: Government Printing Office, 1898), I, pp. 213–24.

that in Europe usually preceded "emancipation" by the French Army. Against the background of this type of interference in American affairs President Washington delivered his Farewell Address (it was not actually spoken, but printed in the newspapers) in 1796 giving advice to his fellow countrymen concerning the future conduct of their public affairs.

Of all the American statesmen of the day, President Washington was the most impartial in his attitude toward the European belligerents. Mindful of the part played by France in the winning of American independence and of the importance to the United States in having at least one friendly power upon the European continent, Washington always declared himself to be a friend of France and the French Revolution. Even so, he keenly resented French efforts to bend to its will American foreign policy as a derogation of the honor and independence of the United States.

This consideration was uppermost in his mind when, in the spring of 1796, having resolved not to stand for a third term, Washington asked Alexander Hamilton to aid in writing a valedictory to the American people. The President and the former Secretary of the Treasury agreed that political partisanship had been carried to dangerous lengths in the United States and that the division of the American people into Republicans and Federalists gave France an opportunity of undermining American independence. It was the Republican party's devotion to the cause of France that seemed to Washington and Hamilton to have made it possible for Adet to have become a power in American politics. The root of the trouble, as Washington and Hamilton saw it, was that the American people, as a result of their preoccupation with events in Europe and the inordinate attachment they felt for one or the other of the belligerents, had ceased to think and act as Americans. Instead, they thought and acted as transplanted Europeans imbued with all the nationalistic passions of the Old World. Even though the United States was officially neutral, the people had permitted themselves to be drawn emotionally into the vortex of the European war.

Therefore, in his Farewell Address, President Washington called upon the American people to turn away from Europe, to cultivate a sense of American nationalism, and to give primacy to the interests of the United States. When Americans thought and acted like true indigenous men of the western world, the President was persuaded that political parties would disappear; for how could they exist if they were deprived of foreign attachments, their principal source of sustenance?

For the guidance of his countrymen, President Washington laid down in the Farewell Address what he thought to be the basic principles of a sound foreign policy. In 1795, he had succinctly expressed the ideas which he elaborated in his valedictory: "to be upon friendly terms with, but independent of all, the nations of the earth. To share in the broils of none. To fulfill our own engagements. To supply the wants, and be the carriers for them all." By following this prescription, Washington believed that the United States could be sure of extracting the maximum profit from the distresses Europeans brought upon themselves by their rivalries and wars and enjoying the kind of internal harmony that was essential to the preservation of the union.

The Farewell Address, the so-called charter of American isolationism, was not so isolationist as it appeared to succeeding generations. Washington did not say that it was of no concern to Americans which side won in Europe or that the United States had no vital interest in the maintenance of a balance of power in Europe. Moreover, in warning his countrymen against foreign partisanship, President Washington did not suggest that the Franco-American alliance (1778) be repudiated nor did he exclude the possibility that future events might make other alliances imperative for the security of the United States. He hoped that the United States would be able to pursue a policy of neutrality and that the wars of Europe would pass the republic by, but he never made hope alone the basis of American foreign policy.

In his Bancroft prize-winning *To the Farewell Address: Ideas of Early American Foreign Policy* (Princeton: Princeton University Press, 1961), Felix Gilbert provides an interesting account of the elements of American foreign policy that preceded Washington's announcement. For a careful assessment of the address see Samuel Flagg Bemis, "Washington's Farewell Address: A Foreign Policy of Independence," in *The American Historical Review*, XXXIX (1934), pp. 250–68. E. Wilson Lyon, whose scholarly interest focused on early Franco-American relations, discusses some of the problems giving rise to Washington's address in his article "The [French] Directory and the United States," in *The American Historical Review*, XLIII (1938), pp. 514–32. In reading Washington's Farewell Address note (1) suggestions of the character of the man in the sentiments expressed and in the rhetoric used; (2) the proportions of the address devoted to domestic and foreign affairs; (3) Washington's estimate of the value of the new government; (4) what he thought the new government had, and could, accomplish for each of the nation's major sections; (5) the extent to which he was willing to rely on experience as a test of validity in political affairs; (6) his judgment of the new constitution of 1787; (7) what he thought of the spirit of party, its causes, its effects, and the means of avoiding some of its consequences; (8) his estimate of the role of religion and morality in society; (9) the extent to which he was concerned with liberty as well as with union and security; (10) his advice and the reasons therefor concerning relations with foreign powers; (11) the basic principles he laid down for the conduct of foreign policy and what exceptions he was willing to countenance; and (12) his defense of his neutralist policy during the war between England and France.

F RIENDS AND FELLOW-CITIZENS:

The period for a new election of a citizen to administer the Executive Government of the United States being not far distant, and the time actually arrived when your thoughts must be employed in designating the person who is to be clothed with that important trust, it appears to me proper, especially as it may conduce to a more distinct expression of the public voice, that I should now apprise you of the resolution I have formed to decline being considered among the number of those out of whom a choice is to be made.

I beg you at the same time to do me the justice to be assured that this resolution has not been taken without a strict regard to all the considerations appertaining to the relation which binds a dutiful citizen to his country; and that in withdrawing the tender of service, which silence in my situation might imply, I am influenced by no diminution of zeal for your future interest, no deficiency of grateful respect for your past kindness, but am supported by a full conviction that the step is compatible with both.

The acceptance of and continuance hitherto in the office to which your suffrages have twice called me have been a uniform sacrifice of inclination to the opinion of duty and to a deference for what appeared to be your desire. I constantly hoped that it would have been much earlier in my power, consistently with motives which I was not at liberty to disregard, to return to that retirement from which I had been reluctantly drawn. The strength of my inclination to do this previous to the last election had even led to the preparation of an address to declare it to you; but mature reflection on the then perplexed and critical posture of our affairs with foreign nations and the unanimous advice of persons entitled to my confidence impelled me to abandon the idea. I rejoice that the state of your concerns, external as well as internal, no longer renders the pursuit of inclination incompatible with the sentiment of duty or propriety, and am persuaded, whatever partiality may be retained for my services, that in the present circumstances of our country you will not disapprove my determination to retire.

The impressions with which I first undertook the arduous trust were explained on the proper occasion. In the discharge of this trust I will only say that I have, with good intentions, contributed toward the organization and administration of the Government the best exertions of which a very fallible judgment was capable. Not unconscious in the outset of the inferiority of my qualifications, experience in my own eyes, perhaps still more in the eyes of others, has strengthened the motives to diffidence of myself; and every day the increasing weight of years admonishes me more and more that the shade of retirement is as necessary to me as it will be welcome. Satisfied that if any circumstances have given peculiar value to my services they were temporary, I have the consolation to believe that, while choice and prudence invite me to quit the political scene, patriotism does not forbid it.

In looking forward to the moment which is intended to terminate the career of my political life my feelings do not permit me to suspend the deep acknowledgment of that debt of gratitude which I owe to my beloved country for the many honors it has conferred upon me, still more for the steadfast confidence with which it has supported me, and for the opportunities I have thence enjoyed of manifesting my inviolable attachment by services faithful and persevering, though in usefulness unequal to my zeal. If benefits have resulted to our country from these services, let it always be remembered to your praise and as an instructive example in our annals that under circumstances in which the passions, agitated in every direction, were liable to mislead; amidst appearances sometimes dubious; vicissitudes of fortune often discouraging; in situations in which not unfrequently want of success has countenanced the spirit of criticism, the constancy of your support was the essential prop of the efforts and a guaranty of the plans by which they were effected. Profoundly penetrated with this idea, I shall carry it with me to my grave as a strong incitement to unceasing vows that Heaven may continue to you the choicest tokens of its beneficence; that your union and brotherly affection may be perpetual; that the free Constitution which is the work of your hands may be sacredly maintained; that its administration in every department may be stamped with wisdom and virtue; that, in fine, the happiness of the people of these States, under the auspices of liberty, may be made complete by so careful a preservation and so prudent a use of this blessing as will acquire to them the glory of recommending it to the applause, the affection, and adoption of every nation which is yet a stranger to it.

Here, perhaps, I ought to stop. But a solicitude for your welfare which can not end but with my life, and the apprehension of danger natural to that solicitude, urge me on an occasion like the present to offer to your solemn contemplation and to recommend to your frequent review some sentiments which are the result of much reflection, of no inconsiderable observation, and which appear to me all important to the permanency of your felicity as a people. These will be offered to you with the more freedom as you can only see in them the disinterested warnings of a parting friend, who can possibly have no personal motive to bias his counsel. Nor can I forget as an encouragement to it your indulgent reception of my sentiments on a former and not dissimilar occasion.

Interwoven as is the love of liberty with every ligament of your hearts, no recommendation of mine is necessary to fortify or confirm the attachment.

The unity of government which constitutes you one people is also now dear to you. It is justly so, for it is a main pillar in the edifice of your real independence, the support of your tranquillity at home, your peace abroad, of your safety, of your prosperity, of that very liberty which you so highly prize. But as it is easy to foresee that from different causes and from different quarters much pains will be taken, many artifices employed, to weaken in your minds the conviction of this truth, as this is the point in your political fortress against which the batteries of internal and external enemies will be most constantly and actively (though often covertly and insidiously) directed, it is of infinite moment that you should properly estimate the immense value of your national union to your collective and individual happiness; that you should cherish a cordial, habitual, and immovable attachment to it; accustoming yourselves to think and speak of it as of the palladium of your political safety and prosperity; watching for its preservation with jealous anxiety; discountenancing whatever may suggest even a suspicion that it can in any event be abandoned, and indignantly frowning upon the first dawning of every attempt to alienate any portion of our country from the rest or to enfeeble the sacred ties which now link together the various parts.

For this you have every inducement of sympathy and interest. Citizens by birth or choice of a common country, that country has a right to concentrate your affections. The name of American, which belongs to you in your national capacity, must always exalt the just pride of patriotism more than any appellation derived from local discriminations. With slight shades of difference, you have the same religion, manners, habits, and political principles. You have in a common cause fought and triumphed together. The independence and liberty you possess are the work of joint councils and joint efforts, of common dangers, sufferings, and successes.

But these considerations, however, powerfully they address themselves to your sensibility, are greatly outweighed by those which apply more immediately to your interest. Here every portion of our country finds the most commanding motives for carefully guarding and preserving the union of the whole.

The *North*, in an unrestrained intercourse with the *South*, protected by the equal laws of a common government, finds in the productions of the latter great additional resources of maritime and commercial enterprise and precious materials of manufacturing industry. The *South*, in the same intercourse, benefiting by the same agency of the *North*, sees its agriculture grow and its commerce expand. Turning partly into its own channels the seamen of the *North*, it finds its particular navigation invigorated; and while it contributes in different ways to nourish and increase the general mass of the national navigation, it looks forward to the protection of a maritime strength to which itself is unequally adapted. The *East*, in a like intercourse with the *West*, already finds, and in the progressive improvement of interior communications by land and water will more and more find, a valuable vent for the commodities which it brings from abroad to manufactures at home. The *West* derives from the *East* supplies requisite to its growth and comfort, and what is perhaps of still greater consequence, it must of necessity owe the *secure* enjoyment of indispensable *outlets* for its own productions to the weight, influence, and the future maritime strength of the Atlantic side of the Union, directed by an indissoluble community of interest as *one nation*. Any other tenure by which the *West* can hold this essential advantage, whether derived from its own separate strength or from an apostate and unnatural connection with any foreign power, must be intrinsically precarious.

While, then, every part of our country thus feels an immediate and particular interest in union, all the parts combined can not fail to find in the united mass of means and efforts greater strength, greater resource, proportionably greater security from external danger, a less frequent interruption of their peace by foreign nations, and what is of inestimable value, they must derive from union an exemption from those broils and wars between themselves which so frequently afflict neighboring countries not tied together by the same governments, which their own rivalships alone would be sufficient to produce, but which opposite foreign alliances, attachments, and intrigues would stimulate and imbitter. Hence, likewise, they will avoid the necessity of those overgrown military establishments which, under any form of government, are inauspicious to liberty, and which are to be regarded as particularly hostile to republican liberty. In this sense it is that your union ought to be considered as a main prop of your liberty, and that the love of the one ought to endear to you the preservation of the other.

These considerations speak a persuasive language to every reflecting and virtuous mind, and exhibit the continuance of the union as a primary object of patriotic desire. Is there a doubt whether a common government can embrace so large a sphere? Let experience solve it. To listen to mere speculation in such a case were criminal. We are authorized to hope that a proper organization of the whole, with the auxiliary agency of governments for the respective subdivisions, will afford a happy issue to the experiment. It is well worth a fair and full experiment. With such powerful and obvious motives to union affecting all parts of our country, while experience shall not have demonstrated its impracticability, there will always be reason to distrust the patriotism of those who in any quarter may endeavor to weaken its bands.

In contemplating the causes which may disturb our union it occurs as matter of serious concern that any ground should have been furnished for characterizing parties by *geographical* discriminations—*Northern* and *Southern*, *Atlantic* and *Western*—whence designing men may endeavor to excite a belief that there is a real difference of local interests and views. One of the expedients of party to acquire influence within particular districts is to misrepresent the opinions and aims of other districts. You can not shield yourselves too much against the jealousies and heartburning which spring from these misrepresentations; they tend to render alien to each other those who ought to be bound together by fraternal affection. The inhabitants of our Western country have lately had a useful lesson on this head. They have seen in the negotiation by the Executive and in the unanimous ratification by the Senate of the treaty with Spain, and in the universal satisfaction at that event throughout the United States, a decisive proof how unfounded were the suspicions propagated among them of a policy in the General Government and in the Atlantic States unfriendly to their interests in regard to the Mississippi. They have been witnesses to the formation of two treaties—that with Great Britain and that with Spain—which secure to them everything they could desire in respect to our foreign relations toward confirming their prosperity. Will it not be their wisdom to rely for the preservation of these advantages on the union by which they were procured? Will they not henceforth be deaf to those advisers, if such there are, who would sever them from their brethren and connect them with aliens?

To the efficacy and permanency of your union a government for the whole is indispensable. No alliances, however strict, between the parts can be an adequate substitute. They must inevitably experience the infractions and interruptions which all alliances in all times have experienced. Sensible of this momentous truth, you have improved upon your first essay by the adoption of a Constitution of Government better calculated than your former for an intimate union and for the efficacious management of your common concerns. This Government, the offspring of our own choice, uninfluenced and unawed, adopted upon full investigation and mature deliberation, completely free in its principles, in the distribution of its powers, uniting security with energy, and containing within itself a provision for its own amendment, has a just claim to your confidence and your support. Respect for its authority, compliance with its laws, acquiescence in its measures, are duties enjoined by the fundamental maxims of true liberty. The basis of our political systems is the right of the people to make and to alter their constitutions of government. But the constitution which at any time exists till changed by an explicit and authentic act of the whole people is sacredly obligatory upon all. The very idea of the power and the right of the people to establish government presupposes the duty of every individual to obey the established government.

All obstructions to the execution of the laws, all combinations and associations, under whatever plausible character, with the real design to direct, control, counteract, or awe the regular deliberation and action of the constituted authorities, are destructive of this fundamental principle and of fatal tendency. They serve to organize faction; to give it an artificial and extraordinary force; to put in the place of the delegated will of the nation the will of a party, often a small but artful and enterprising minority of the community, and, according to the alternate triumphs of different parties, to make the public administration the mirror of the ill-concerted and incongruous projects of faction rather than the organ of consistent and wholesome plans, digested by common counsels and modified by mutual interests.

However combinations or associations of the above description may now and then answer popular ends, they are likely in the course of time and things to become potent engines by which cunning, ambitious, and unprincipled men will be enabled to subvert the power of the people, and to usurp for themselves the reins of government, destroying afterwards the very engines which have lifted them to unjust dominion.

Toward the preservation of your Government and the permanency of your present happy state, it is requisite not only that you steadily discountenance irregular oppositions to its acknowledged authority, but also that you resist with care the spirit of innovation upon its principles, however specious the pretexts. One method of assault may be to effect in the forms of the Constitution alterations which will impair the energy of the system, and thus to undermine what can not be directly overthrown. In all the changes to which you may be invited remember that time and habit are at least as necessary to fix the true character of governments as of other human institutions; that experience is the surest standard by which to test the real tendency of the existing constitution of a country; that facility in changes upon the credit of mere hypothesis and opinion exposes to perpetual change, from the endless variety of hypothesis and opinion; and remember especially that for the efficient management of your common interests in a country so extensive as ours a government of as much vigor as is consistent with the perfect security of liberty is indispensable. Liberty itself will find in such a government, with powers properly distributed and adjusted, its surest guardian. It is, indeed, little else than a name where the government is too feeble to withstand the enterprises of faction, to confine each member of the society within the limits prescribed by the laws, and to maintain all in the secure and tranquil enjoyment of the rights of person and property.

I have already intimated to you the danger of parties in the State, with particular reference to the founding of them on geographical discriminations. Let me now take a more comprehensive view, and warn you in the most solemn manner against the baneful effects of the spirit of party generally.

This spirit, unfortunately, is inseparable from our nature, having its root in the strongest passions of the human mind. It exists under different shapes in all governments, more or less stifled, controlled, or repressed; but in those of the popular form it is seen in its greatest rankness and is truly their worst enemy.

The alternative domination of one faction over another, sharpened by the spirit of revenge natural to party dissension, which in different ages and countries has perpetrated the most horrid enormities, is itself a frightful despotism. But this leads at length to a more formal and permanent despotism. The disorders and miseries which result gradually incline the minds of men to seek security and repose in the absolute power of an individual, and sooner or later the chief of some prevailing faction, more able or more fortunate than his competitors, turns this disposition to the purposes of his own elevation on the ruins of public liberty.

Without looking forward to an extremity of this kind (which nevertheless ought not to be entirely out of sight), the common and continual mischiefs of the spirit of party are sufficient to make it the interest and duty of a wise people to discourage and restrain it.

It serves always to distract the public councils and enfeeble the public administration. It agitates the community with ill-founded jealousies and false alarms; kindles the animosity of one part against another; foments occasionally riot and insurrection. It opens the door to foreign influence and corruption, which find a facilitated access to the government itself through the channels of party passion. Thus the policy and the will of one country are subjected to the policy and will of another.

There is an opinion that parties in free countries are useful checks upon the administration of the government, and serve to keep alive the spirit of liberty. This within certain limits is probably true; and in governments of a monarchical cast patriotism may look with indulgence, if not with favor, upon the spirit of party. But in those of the popular character, in governments purely elective, it is a spirit not to be encouraged. From their natural tendency it is certain there will always be enough of that spirit for every salutary purpose; and there being constant danger of excess, the effort ought to be by force of public opinion to mitigate and assuage it. A fire not to be quenched, it demands a uniform vigilance to prevent its bursting into a flame, lest, instead of warming, it should consume.

It is important, likewise, that the habits of thinking in a free country should inspire caution in those intrusted with its administration to confine themselves within their respective constitutional spheres, avoiding in the exercise of the powers of one department to encroach upon another. The spirit of encroachment tends to consolidate the powers of all the departments in one, and thus to create, whatever the form of government, a real despotism. A just estimate of that love of power and proneness to abuse it which predominates in the human heart is sufficient to satisfy us of the truth of this position. The necessity of reciprocal checks in the exercise of political power, by dividing and distributing it into different depositories, and constituting each the guardian of the public weal against invasions by the others, has been evinced by experiments ancient and modern, some of them in our country and under our own eyes. To preserve them must be as necessary as to institute them. If in the opinion of the people the distribution or modification of the constitutional powers be in any particular wrong, let it be corrected by an amendment in the way which the Constitution designates. But let there be no change by usurpation; for though this in one instance may be the instrument of good, it is the customary weapon by which free governments are destroyed. The precedent must always greatly overbalance in permanent evil any partial or transient benefit which the use can at any time yield.

Of all the dispositions and habits which lead to political prosperity, religion and morality are indispensable supports. In vain would that man claim the tribute of patriotism who should labor to subvert these great pillars of human happiness—these firmest props of the duties of men and citizens. The mere politician, equally with the pious man, ought to respect and to cherish them. A volume could not trace all their connections with private and public felicity. Let it simply be asked, Where is the security for property, for reputation, for life, if the sense of religious obligation *desert* the oaths which are the instruments of investigation in courts of justice? And let us with caution indulge the supposition that morality can be maintained without religion. Whatever may be conceded to the influence of refined education on minds of peculiar structure, reason and experience both forbid us to expect that national morality can prevail in exclusion of religious principle.

It is substantially true that virtue or morality is a necessary spring of popular government. The rule indeed extends with more or less force to every species of free government. Who that is a sincere friend to it can look with indifference upon attempts to shake the foundation of the fabric? Promote, then, as an object of primary importance, institutions for the general diffusion of knowledge. In proportion as the structure of a government gives force to public opinion, it is essential that public opinion should be enlightened.

As a very important source of strength and security, cherish public credit. One method of preserving it is to use it as sparingly as possible, avoiding occasions of expense by cultivating peace, but remembering also that timely disbursements to prepare for danger frequently prevent much greater disbursements to repel it; avoiding likewise the accumulation of debt, not only by shunning occasions of expense, but by vigorous exertions in time of peace to discharge the debts which unavoidable wars have occasioned, not ungenerously throwing upon posterity the burthen which we ourselves ought to bear. The execution of these maxims belongs to your representatives; but it is necessary that public opinion should cooperate. To facilitate to them the performance of their duty it is essential that you should practically bear in mind that toward the payment of debts there must be revenue; that to have revenue there must be taxes; that no taxes can be devised which are not more or less inconvenient and unpleasant; that the intrinsic embarrassment inseparable from the selection of the proper objects (which is always a choice of difficulties), ought to be a decisive motive for a candid construction of the conduct of the Government in making it, and for a spirit of acquiescence in the measures for obtaining revenue which the public exigencies may at any time dictate.

Observe good faith and justice toward all nations. Cultivate peace and harmony with all. Religion and morality enjoin this conduct. And can it be that good policy does not equally enjoin it? It will be worthy of a free, enlightened, and at no distant period a great nation to give to mankind the magnanimous and too novel example of a people always guided by an exalted justice and benevolence. Who can doubt that in the course of time and things the fruits of such a plan would richly repay any temporary advantages which might be lost by a steady adherence to it? Can it be that Providence has not connected the permanent felicity of a nation with its virtue? The experiment, at least, is recommended by every sentiment which ennobles human nature. Alas! is it rendered impossible by its vices?

In the execution of such a plan nothing is more essential than that permanent, inveterate antipathies against particular nations and passionate attachments for others should be excluded, and that in place of them just and amicable feelings toward all should be cultivated. The nation which indulges toward another an habitual hatred or an habitual fondness is in some degree a slave. It is a slave to its animosity or to its affection, either of which is sufficient to lead it astray from its duty and its interest. Antipathy in one nation against another disposes each more readily to offer insult and injury, to lay hold of slight causes of umbrage, and to be haughty and intractable when accidental or trifling occasions of dispute occur.

Hence frequent collisions, obstinate, envenomed, and bloody contests. The nation prompted by ill will and resentment sometimes impels to war the government contrary to the best calculations of policy. The government sometimes participates in the national propensity, and adopts through passion what reason would reject. At other times it makes the animosity of the nation subservient to projects of hostility, instigated by pride, ambition, and other sinister and pernicious motives. The peace often, sometimes perhaps the liberty, of nations has been the victim.

So, likewise, a passionate attachment of one nation for another produces a variety of evils. Sympathy for the favorite nation, facilitating the illusion of an imaginary common interest in cases where no real common interest exists, and infusing into one the enmities of the other, betrays the former into a participation in the quarrels and wars of the latter without adequate inducement or justification. It leads also to concessions to the favorite nation of privileges denied to others, which is apt doubly to injure the nation making the concessions by unnecessarily parting with what ought to have been retained, and by exciting jealousy, ill will, and a disposition to retaliate in the parties from whom equal privileges are withheld; and it gives to ambitious, corrupted, or deluded citizens (who devote themselves to the favorite nation) facility to betray or sacrifice the interests of their own country without odium, sometimes even with popularity, gilding with the appearances of a virtuous sense of obligation, a commendable deference for public opinion, or a laudable zeal for public good the base or foolish compliances of ambition, corruption, or infatuation.

As avenues to foreign influence in innumerable ways, such attachments are particularly alarming to the truly enlightened and independent patriot. How many opportunities do they afford to tamper with domestic factions, to practice the arts of seduction, to mislead public opinion, to influence or awe the public councils! Such an attachment of a small or weak toward a great and powerful nation dooms the former to be the satellite of the latter. Against the insidious wiles of foreign influence (I conjure you to believe me, fellow-citizens) the jealousy of a free people ought to be *constantly* awake, since history and experience prove that foreign influence is one of the most baneful foes of republican government. But that jealousy, to be useful, must be impartial, else it becomes the instrument of the very influence to be avoided, instead of a defense against it. Excessive partiality for one foreign nation and excessive dislike of another cause those whom they actuate to see danger only on one side, and serve to veil and even second the arts of influence on the other. Real patriots who may resist the intrigues of the favorite are liable to become suspected and odious, while its tools and dupes usurp the applause and confidence of the people to surrender their interests.

The great rule of conduct for us in regard to foreign nations is, in extending our commercial relations to have with them as little *political* connection as possible. So far as we have already formed engagements let them be fulfilled with perfect good faith. Here let us stop.

Europe has a set of primary interests which to us have none or a very remote relation. Hence she must be engaged in frequent controversies, the causes of which are essentially foreign to our concerns. Hence, therefore, it must be unwise in us to implicate ourselves by artificial ties in the ordinary vicissitudes of her politics or the ordinary combinations and collisions of her friendships or enmities.

Our detached and distant situation invites and enables us to pursue a different course. If we remain one people, under an efficient government, the period is not far off when we may defy material injury from external annoyance; when we may take such an attitude as will cause the neutrality we may at any time resolve upon to be scrupulously respected; when belligerent nations, under the impossibility of making acquisitions upon us, will not lightly hazard the giving us provocation; when we may choose peace or war, as our interest, guided by justice, shall counsel.

Why forego the advantages of so peculiar a situation? Why quit our own to stand upon foreign ground? Why, by interweaving our destiny with that of any part of Europe, entangle our peace and prosperity in the toils of European ambition, rivalship, interest, humor, or caprice?

It is our true policy to steer clear of permanent alliances with any portion of the foreign world, so far, I mean, as we are now at liberty to do it; for let me not be understood as capable of patronizing infidelity to existing engagements. I hold the maxim no less applicable to public than to private affairs that honesty is always the best policy. I repeat, therefore, let those engagements be observed in their genuine sense. But in my opinion it is unnecessary and would be unwise to extend them.

Taking care always to keep ourselves by suitable establishments on a respectable defensive posture, we may safely trust to temporary alliances for extraordinary emergencies.

Harmony, liberal intercourse with all nations are recommended by policy, humanity, and interest. But even our commercial policy should hold an equal and impartial hand, neither seeking nor granting exclusive favors or preferences; consulting the natural course of things; diffusing and diversifying by gentle means the streams of commerce, but forcing nothing; establishing with powers so disposed, in order to give trade a stable course, to define the rights of our merchants, and to enable the Government to support them, conventional rules of intercourse, the best that present circumstances and mutual opinion will permit, but temporary and liable to be from time to time abandoned or varied as experience and circumstances shall dictate; constantly keeping in view that it is folly in one nation to look for disinterested favors from another; that it must pay with a portion of its independence for whatever it may accept under that character; that by such acceptance it may place itself in the condition of having given equivalents for nominal favors, and yet of being reproached with ingratitude for not giving more. There can be no greater error than to expect or calculate upon real favors from nation to nation. It is an illusion which experience must cure, which a just pride ought to discard.

In offering to you, my countrymen, these counsels of an old and affectionate friend I dare not hope they will make the strong and lasting impression I could wish—that they will control the usual current of the passions or prevent our nation from running the course which has hitherto marked the destiny of nations. But if I may even flatter myself that they may be productive of some partial benefit, some occasional good—that they may now and then recur to moderate the fury of party spirit, to warn against the mischiefs of foreign intrigue, to guard against the impostures of pretended patriotism—this hope will be a full recompense for the solicitude for your welfare by which they have been dictated.

How far in the discharge of my official duties I have been guided by the principles which have been delineated the public records and other evidences of my conduct must witness to you and to the world. To myself, the assurance of my own conscience is that I have at least believed myself to be guided by them.

In relation to the still subsisting war in Europe my proclamation of the 22d of April, 1793, is the index to my plan. Sanctioned by your approving voice and by that of your representatives in both Houses of Congress, the spirit of that measure has continually governed me, uninfluenced by any attempts to deter or divert me from it.

After deliberate examination, with the aid of the best lights I could obtain, I was well satisfied that our country, under all the circumstances of the case, had a right to take, and was bound in duty and interest to take, a neutral position. Having taken it, I determined as far as should depend upon me to maintain it with moderation, perseverance, and firmness.

The considerations which respect the right to hold this conduct it is not necessary on this occasion to detail. I will only observe that, according to my understanding of the matter, that right, so far from being denied by any of the belligerent powers, has been virtually admitted by all.

The duty of holding a neutral conduct may be inferred, without anything more, from the obligation which justice and humanity impose on every nation, in cases in which it is free to act, to maintain inviolate the relations of peace and amity toward other nations.

The inducements of interest for observing that conduct will best be referred to your own reflections and experience. With me a predominant motive has been to endeavor to gain time to our country to settle and mature its yet recent institutions, and to progress without interruption to that degree of strength and consistency which is necessary to give it, humanly speaking, the command of its own fortunes.

Though in reviewing the incidents of my Administration I am unconscious of intentional error, I am nevertheless too sensible of my defects not to think it probable that I may have committed many errors. Whatever they may be, I fervently beseech the Almighty to avert or mitigate the evils to which they may tend. I shall also carry with me the hope that my country will never cease to view them with indulgence, and that, after forty-five years of my life dedicated to its service with an upright zeal, the faults of incompetent abilities will be consigned to oblivion, as myself must soon be to the mansions of rest.

Relying on its kindness in this as in other things, and actuated by that fervent love toward it which is so natural to a man who views in it the native soil of himself and his progenitors for several generations, I anticipate with pleasing expectation that retreat in which I promise myself to realize without alloy the sweet enjoyment of partaking in the midst of my fellow-citizens the benign influence of good laws under a free government—the ever-favorite object of my heart, and the happy reward, as I trust, of our mutual cares, labors, and dangers.

GO. WASHINGTON

8
Opposition to the Alien and Sidition Acts

The First Kentucky Resolutions

John Adams, a Federalist, succeeded George Washington to the presidency in 1797. American politics continued in an agitated state owing to the persisting tendency of the Hamiltonians and Jeffersonians to side with the two major warring European nations, England and France. Fearing the growth of the Jeffersonians, perhaps because of European immigration to the United States, the Federalists in 1798 passed a series of measures—the Naturalization, the Alien, the Alien Enemies, and Sedition Acts—designed to lengthen the period before aliens could be made citizens and thus participate in elections and to curb criticism of the Adams administration. The thinly disguised object of the Federalists was to bridle Jeffersonian critics (many recruited from recent immigrants) of Federalist policies in domestic and foreign affairs. Jefferson regarded the Alien and Sedition Acts as unconstitutional as if Congress had ordered Americans to bow down and worship a golden image. Compared with these iniquitous laws, the Bank of the United States, the Report on Manufactures, and Jay's Treaty seemed "unconsequential, timid things." Nevertheless, the Virginian moved with his customary circumspection to alert the American people to the threat to civil liberty posed by these laws and to propose a constitutional method of resistance. He and Madison drew a series of resolutions which their friends submitted to the Kentucky and Virginia legislatures in 1798–1799. These resolutions contended that the Sedition Act went beyond the

Thomas Jefferson, "The First Kentucky Resolutions," in Albert Bushnell Hart and Edward Channing, eds., *The Virginia and Kentucky Resolutions With the Alien, Sedition, and Other Acts, 1798–1799*. "American History Leaflets," no. 15 (New York: A Lovell and Company, 1894), pp. 10–17. EDITOR'S NOTE. The first Kentucky Resolutions approved by the State legislature in November, 1799 proved too strong for several Northern States and a second set (not reproduced here) was later enacted by the Kentucky legislature.

enumerated powers granted Congress and violated the Fifth Amendment prohibiting any laws "abridging the freedom of speech or of the press." To prevent what they considered to be a palpable violation of the constitution, Jefferson and Madison urged the States to interpose their authority. Both the Virginia (written by Madison) and the Kentucky (written anonymously by Jefferson) Resolutions called upon the State governments to take a concerted stand against the Acts. To this end, the Resolutions were transmitted to all the State legislatures. If Jefferson's and Madison's theory were accepted, the Federal government would have had no power to punish in Federal courts libellous and seditious utterances and writings. The Virginians had no intention, however, of removing all restraints upon freedom of the press and of speech. On the contrary, they would give the State courts full jurisdiction over the rights of individuals to seek legal redress and to punish seditious speech or writings. In the minds of their projectors, the Virginia and Kentucky Resolutions furnished an answer not only to the Alien and Sedition Acts but also to the reports of Alexander Hamilton on such matters as the public credit, a bank, and the tariff. Against the permissive or loose interpretation of the constitution favored by Hamilton, the collaborators opposed a strict interpretation and a theory of the origin and nature of the constitution that would forever preclude the the exercise by the Federal government of many of the powers it uses today as a matter of course. Later, Southern leaders found support in the Virginia and Kentucky Resolutions for nullification in 1832 (see the next volume in this series, Charles M. Wiltse, ed., *Expansion and Reform, 1815–1850*) and secession in 1860 (see volume five in this series, Robert W. Johannsen, ed., *The Union in Crisis, 1850–1865*).

For the part played by Jefferson and Madison in these proceedings see the book by Adrienne Koch cited in Chapter 6, **Jefferson and Madison: The Great Collaboration*. An older study by a scholar interested in constitutional history, which deals with the loose *v.* strict interpretation debate, is Andrew C. McLaughlin's "Social Compact and Constitutional Construction," in *The American Historical Review*, V (1900), 467–90. John C. Miller's **Crisis in Freedom: The Alien and Sedition Acts* (Boston: Little, Brown and Company, 1951) gives details of cases arising out of the operation of the acts. One might also consult James Morton Smith, **Freedom's Fetters: The Alien and Sedition Laws and American Civil Liberties* (Ithaca: Cornell University Press, 1956).

In reading this selection note (1) Jefferson's theory concerning the nature of the union and of the constitution of the United States; (2) what agency in his opinion constituted the final judge of the constitutionality of acts of the Federal government; (3) the acts of the central government he thought were void and of no force; (4) how he used the first, the fifth, and the tenth amendments to the constitution to support his contentions; (5) on what grounds he opposed the Federal government's exercise of power under the constitution to lay and collect taxes, duties, imposts and excises; to pay the debts, and so on; (6) the remedy he proposed for dealing with unconstitutional acts of the Federal government; (7) the action he thought the Commonwealth of Kentucky should take; (8) what charges he levelled at the Adams administration respecting its presumed intentions; and (9) the character and quality of the rhetoric Jefferson employed.

I N THE HOUSE OF REPRESENTATIVES, NOVEMBER 10TH, 1798

I. Resolved, that the several states composing the United States of America, are not united on the principle of unlimited submission to their General Government; but that by compact under the style and title of a Constitution for the United States and of amendments thereto, they constituted a General Government for special purposes, delegated to that Government certain definite powers, reserving each state to itself, the residuary mass of right to their own self Government; and that whensoever the General Government assumes undelegated powers, its acts are unauthoritative, void, and are of no force: That to this compact each state acceded as a state, and is an integral party, its co-states forming as to itself, the other party: That the Government created by this compact was not made the exclusive or final judge of the extent of the powers delegated to itself; since that would have made its discretion, and not the constitution, the measure of its powers; but that as in all other cases of compact among parties having no common judge, each party has an equal right to judge for itself, as well of infractions as of the mode and measure of redress.

II. Resolved, that the Constitution of the United States having delegated to Congress a power to punish treason, counterfeiting the securities and current coin of the United States, piracies and felonies committed on the High Seas, and offences against the laws of nations, and no other crimes whatever, and it being true as a general principle, and one of the amendments to the Constitution having also declared, "that the powers not delegated to the United States by the Constitution, nor prohibited by it to the states, are reserved to the states respectively, or to the people," therefore also the same act of Congress passed on the 14th day of July, 1798, and entitled "An act in addition to the act entitled an act for the punishment of certain crimes against the United States;" as also the act passed by them on the 27th of June, 1798, entitled "An act to punish frauds committed on the Bank of the United States" (and all other their acts which assume to create, define, or punish crimes other than those enumerated in the constitution) are altogether void and of no force, and that the power to create, define, and punish such other crimes is reserved, and of right appertains solely and exclusively to the respective states, each within its own Territory.

III. Resolved, that it is true as a general principle, and is also expressly declared by one of the amendments to the Constitution that "the powers not delegated to the United States by the Constitution, nor prohibited by it to the states, are reserved to the states respectively or to the people;" and that no power over the freedom of religion, freedom of speech, or freedom of the press being delegated to the United States by the Constitution, nor prohibited by it to the states, all lawful powers respecting the same did of right remain, and were reserved to the states, or to the people: That thus was manifested their determination to retain to themselves the right of judging how far the licentiousness of speech and of the press may be abridged without lessening their useful freedom, and how far those abuses which cannot be separated from their use, should be tolerated, rather than the use be destroyed; and thus also they guarded against all abridgment by the United States of the freedom of religious opinions and exercises, and retained to themselves the right of protecting the same, as this state by a Law passed on the general demand of its Citizens, had already protected them from all human restraint or interference; and that in addition to this general principle and express declaration, another and more special provision has been made by one of the amendments to the Constitution which expressly declares that "Congress shall make no law respecting an Establishment of religion, or prohibiting the free exercise thereof, or abridging the freedom of speech, or of the press," thereby guarding in the same sentence, and under the same same words, the freedom of religion, of speech, and of the press, insomuch, that whatever violates either, throws down the sanctuary which covers the others, and that libels, falsehoods, and defamation, equally with heresy and false religion, are withheld from the cognizance of federal tribunals. That therefore the act of the Congress of the United States passed on the 14th day of July, 1798, entitled "An act in addition to the act for the punishment of certain crimes against the United States," which does abridge the freedom of the press, is not law, but is altogether void and of no effect.

IV. Resolved, that alien friends are under the jurisdiction and protection of the laws of the state wherein they are; that no power over them has been delegated to the United States, nor prohibited to the individual states distinct from their power over citizens; and it being true as a general principle, and one of the amendments to the Constitution having also declared, that "the powers not delegated to the United States by the Constitution nor prohibited by it to the states are reserved to the states respectively or to the people," the act of the Congress of the United States passed on the 22d day of June, 1798, entitled "An act concerning aliens," which assumes power over alien friends not delegated by the Constitution, is not law, but is altogether void and of no force.

V. Resolved, that in addition to the general principle as well as the express declaration, that powers not delegated are reserved, another and more special provision inserted in the Constitution from abundant caution has declared, "that the migration or importation of such persons as any of the states now existing shall think proper to admit, shall not be prohibited by the Congress prior to the year 1808." That this Commonwealth does admit the migration of alien friends described as the subject of the said act concerning aliens; that a provision against prohibiting their migration, is a provision against all acts equivalent thereto, or it would be nugatory; that to remove them when migrated is equivalent to a prohibition of their migration, and is therefore contrary to the said provision of the Constitution, and void.

VI. Resolved, that the imprisonment of a person under the protection of the Laws of this Commonwealth on his failure to obey the simple order of the President to depart out of the United States, as is undertaken by the said act entitled "An act concerning aliens," is contrary to the Constitution, one amendment to which has provided, that "no person shall be deprived of liberty without due process of law," and that another having provided "that in all criminal prosecutions the accused shall enjoy the right to a public trial by an impartial jury, to be informed of the nature and cause of the accusation, to be confronted with the witnesses against him, to have compulsory process for obtaining witnesses in his favour, and to have the assistance of counsel for his defence," the same act undertaking to authorize the President to remove a person out of the United States who is under the protection of the Law, on his own suspicion, without accusation, without jury, without public trial, without confrontation of the witnesses against him, without having witnesses in his favour, without defence, without counsel, is contrary to these provisions also of the Constitution, is therefore not law but utterly void and of no force.

That transferring the power of judging any person who is under the protection of the laws, from the Courts to the President of the United States, as is undertaken by the same act concerning Aliens, against the article of the Constitution which provides, that "the judicial power of the United States shall be vested in Courts, the Judges of which shall hold their offices during good behaviour," and that the said act is void for that reason also; and it is further to be noted, that this transfer of Judiciary power is to that magistrate of the General Government who already possesses all the Executive, and a qualified negative in all the Legislative powers.

VII. Resolved, that the construction applied by the General Government (as is evinced by sundry of their proceedings) to those parts of the Constitution of the United States which delegate to Congress a power to lay and collect taxes, duties, imposts, and excises; to pay the debts, and provide for the common defence, and general welfare of the United States, and to make all laws which shall be necessary and proper for carrying into execution the powers vested by the Constitution in the Government of the United States, or any department thereof, goes to the destruction of all the limits prescribed to their power by the Constitution—That words meant by that instrument to be subsidiary only to the execution of the limited powers, ought not to be so construed as themselves to give unlimited powers, nor a part so to be taken, as to destroy the whole residue of the instrument: That the proceedings of the General Government under colour of these articles, will be a fit and necessary subject for revisal and correction at a time of greater tranquility, while those specified in the preceding resolutions call for immediate redress.

VIII. Resolved, that the preceding Resolutions be transmitted to the Senators and Representatives in Congress from this Commonwealth, who are hereby enjoined to present the same to their respective Houses, and to use the best endeavours to procure at the next session of Congress, a repeal of the aforesaid unconstitutional and obnoxious acts.

IX. Resolved lastly, that the Governor of this Commonwealth be, and is hereby authorised and requested to communicate the preceding Resolutions to the Legislatures of the several States, to assure them that this Commonwealth considers Union for specified National purposes, and particularly for those specified in their late Federal compact, to be friendly to the peace, happiness, and prosperity of all the states: that faithful to the compact, according to the plain intent and meaning in which it was understood and acceded to by the several parties, it is sincerely anxious for its preservation: that it does also believe, that to take from the states all the powers of self government, and transfer them to a general and consolidated Government, without regard to the special delegations and reservations solemnly agreed to in that compact, is not for the peace, happiness, or prosperity of these states: And that therefore, this Commonwealth is determined, as it doubts not its Co-states are, tamely to submit to undelegated and consequently unlimited powers in no man or body of men on earth: that if the acts before specified should stand, these conclusions would flow from them; that the General Government may place any act they think proper on the list of crimes and punish it themselves, whether enumerated or not enumerated by the Constitution as cognizable by them: that they may transfer its cognizance to the President or any other person, who may himself be the accuser, counsel, judge, and jury, whose suspicions may be the evidence, his order the sentence, his officer the executioner, and his breast the sole record of the transaction: that a very numerous and valuable description of the inhabitants of these states, being by this precedent reduced as outlaws to the absolute dominion of one man and the barrier of the Constitution thus swept away from us all, no rampart now remains against the passions and the power of a majority of Congress, to protect from a like exportation or other more grievous punishment the minority of the same body, the Legislatures, Judges, Governors, and Counsellors of the states, nor their other peaceable inhabitants who may venture to reclaim the constitutional rights and liberties of the states and people, or who for other causes, good or bad, may be obnoxious to the views or marked by the suspicions of the President, or be thought dangerous to his or their elections or other interests public or personal: that the friendless alien has indeed been selected as the safest subject of a first experiment: but the citizen will soon follow, or rather has already followed; for already has a Sedition Act marked him as its prey: that these and successive acts of the same character, unless arrested on the threshold, may tend to drive these states into revolution and blood, and will furnish new calumnies against Republican Governments, and new pretexts for those who wish it to be believed that man cannot be governed but by a rod of iron: that it would be a dangerous delusion were a confidence in the men of our choice to silence our fears for the safety of our rights: that confidence is everywhere the parent of despotism: free government is founded in jealousy and not in confidence; it is jealousy and not confidence which prescribes limited Constitutions to bind down those whom we are obliged to trust with power: that our Constitution has accordingly fixed the limits to which and no further our confidence may go; and let the honest advocate of confidence read the Alien and Sedition Acts, and say if the Constitution has not been wise in fixing limits to the Government it created, and whether we should be wise in destroying those limits? Let him say what the Government is if it be not a tyranny, which the men of our choice have conferred on the President, and the President of our choice has assented to and accepted over the friendly strangers, to whom the mild spirit of our Country and its laws had pledged hospitality and protection: that the men of our choice have more respected the bare suspicions of the President than the solid rights of innocence, the claims of justification, the sacred force of truth, and the forms and subsistance of law and justice. In questions of power then let no more be heard of confidence in man, but bind him down from mischief by the chains of the Constitution. That this Commonwealth does therefore call on its Co-states for an expression of their sentiments on the acts concerning Aliens, and for the punishment of certain crimes hereinbefore specified, plainly declaring whether these acts are or are not authorized by the Federal Compact? And it doubts not that their sense will be so announced as to prove their attachment unaltered to limited Government, whether general or particular, and that the rights and liberties of their Co-states will be exposed to no dangers by remaining embarked on a common bottom with their own: That they will concur with this Commonwealth in considering the said acts so palpably against the Constitution as to amount to an undisguised declaration, that the Compact is not meant to be the measure of the powers of the General Government, but that it will proceed in the exercise over these states of all powers whatsoever: That they will view this as seizing the rights of the states and consolidating them in the hands of the General Government with a power assumed to bind the states (not merely in cases made federal) but in all cases whatsoever, by laws made, not with their consent, but by others against their consent: That this would be to surrender the form of Government we have chosen, and to live under one deriving its powers from its own will, and not from our authority; and that the Co-states recurring to their natural right in cases not made federal, will concur in declaring these acts void and of no force, and will each unite with this Commonwealth in requesting their repeal at the next session of Congress.

EDMUND BULLOCK, S. H. R.

JOHN CAMPBELL, S. S. P. T.

Passed the House of Representatives, Nov. 10th, 1798.

Attest: THOMAS TODD, C. H. R.

In Senate, November 13th, 1798, unanimously concurred in.

Attest: B. THURSTON, CLK. SEN.

Approved, November 16th, 1798.

JAMES GARRARD, G. K.

By the Governor,

HARRY TOULMIN,

Secretary of State

9

The Jeffersons Come to Power

Jefferson's First Inaugural Address

Thomas Jefferson was elected President in 1800 following a campaign that pitted the Virginian against the incumbent, John Adams of Massachusetts. Campaign issues included the Alien and Sedition Acts, taxation, and foreign policy.

President Jefferson made his first inaugural a major exposition of his political philosophy. In the spirit of Washington's Farewell Address, he called upon Americans to abate their political passions and to display the "harmony and affection" without which, the President asserted, "liberty and even life are but dreary things." He told his auditors (few could hear him because he spoke in such a low tone of voice) that every difference of opinion was not a difference of principle and that Americans enjoyed the inestimable felicity, if they would but see it, of being in agreement upon fundamentals—an agreement that made republican government possible in the United States. He called upon the minority to accept the outcome of the election with good grace and he pledged in turn that the victorious majority would not oppress the defeated party. Only by accepting the principle of majority rule and minority rights, he said, could the American people realize the ideals of equal justice, peace, and good will among men.

Recognizing the intimate connection between partisan politics and foreign affairs, President Jefferson promised to preserve strict neutrality in the European war: "peace, commerce and honest friendship with all nations, entangling alliances with none" became the guiding principle of his administration. Finally, he promised the payment of the national debt, the "sacred preservation of the public faith"—obviously intended to reassure the Federalists—and to conduct a "wise and frugal government, which

Thomas Jefferson, "First Inaugural Address, Washington, D.C., March 4, 1801," in James D. Richardson, ed., *A Compilation of the Messages and Papers of the Presidents* (Washington, D.C.: Government Printing Office, 1898, I, pp. 321-24.

shall restrain men from injuring one another, which shall leave them otherwise free to regulate their own pursuits of industry and improvement, and shall not take from the mouth of labor the bread it has earned. This is the sum of good government, and this is all that is necessary to close the circle of our felicities."

One of the great masterpieces of American historiography is the monumental work of one of President John Adams's great grandsons, Henry Adams. His *History of the United States of America During the First Administration to the Second Administration of James Madison*, 9 vols. (New York: Charles Scribner's Sons, 1889–1890) is not only informative, but it is written with zest and grace. The dean of American Progressive historians of the early years of the twentieth century, Charles A. Beard, after writing *An Economic Interpretation of the Constitution of the United States* (1913), published *The Economic Origins of Jeffersonian Democracy* (New York: The Macmillan Company, 1915), in which he explored some of the possibilities of an economic interpretation of American history. Charles M. Wiltse in *The Jeffersonian Tradition in American Democracy* (Chapel Hill: The University of North Carolina Press, 1935) examined the origins of the tradition, then proceeded to trace the history of its use by statesmen and politicians and others from the time of Jefferson to the New Deal.

In reading Jefferson's address note (1) evidences of his attempt to allay the fears of his political antagonists; (2) where, apparently, he thought the path of duty lay for him; (3) the basic principles he believed both Republicans and Federalists shared; (4) the advantages he thought Americans possessed for the pursuit of happiness; (5) what he believed were the ends or objectives of good government; (7) his guiding policy for the conduct of relations with foreign powers; and (8) the nature of the rhetoric employed by Jefferson in this address.

F RIENDS AND FELLOW-CITIZENS

Called upon to undertake the duties of the first executive office of our country, I avail myself of the presence of that portion of my fellow-citizens which is here assembled to express my grateful thanks for the favor with which they have been pleased to look toward me, to declare a sincere consciousness that the task is above my talents, and that I approach it with those anxious and awful presentiments which the greatness of the charge and the weakness of my powers so justly inspire. A rising nation, spread over a wide and fruitful land, traversing all the seas with the rich productions of their industry, engaged in commerce with nations who feel power and forget right, advancing rapidly to destinies beyond the reach of mortal eye—when I contemplate these transcendent objects, and see the honor, the happiness, and the hopes of this beloved country committed to the issue and the auspices of this day, I shrink from the contemplation, and humble myself before the magnitude of the undertaking. Utterly, indeed, should I despair did not the presence of many whom I here see remind me that in the other high authorities provided by our Constitution I shall find resources of wisdom, of virtue, and of zeal on which to rely under all difficulties. To you, then, gentlemen, who are charged with the sovereign functions of legislation, and to those associated with you, I look with encouragement for that guidance and support which may enable us to steer with safety the vessel in which we are all embarked amidst the conflicting elements of a troubled world.

During the contest of opinion through which we have passed the animation of discussions and of exertions has sometimes worn an aspect which might impose on strangers unused to think freely and to speak and to write what they think; but this being now decided by the voice of the nation, announced according to the rules of the Constitution, all will, of course, arrange themselves under the will of the law, and unite in common efforts for the common good. All, too, will bear in mind this sacred principle, that though the will of the majority is in all cases to prevail, that will to be rightful must be reasonable; that the minority possess their equal rights, which equal law must protect, and to violate would be oppression· Let us, then, fellow-citizens, unite with one heart and one mind. Let us restore to social intercourse that harmony and affection without which liberty and even life itself are but dreary things. And let us reflect that, having banished from our land that religious intolerance under which mankind so long bled and suffered, we have yet gained little if we countenance a political intolerance as despotic, as wicked, and capable of as bitter and bloody persecutions. During the throes and convulsions of the ancient world, during the agonizing spasms of infuriated man, seeking through blood and slaughter his long-lost liberty, it was not wonderful that the agitation of the billows should reach even this distant and peaceful shore; that this should be more felt and feared by some and less by others, and should divide opinions as to measures of safety. But every difference of opinion is not a difference of principle.

We have called by different names brethren of the same principle. We are all Republicans, we are all Federalists. If there be any among us who would wish to dissolve this Union or to change its republican form, let them stand undisturbed as monuments of the safety with which error of opinion may be tolerated where reason is left free to combat it. I know, indeed, that some honest men fear that a republican government can not be strong, that this Government is not strong enough; but would the honest patriot, in the full tide of successful experiment, abandon a government which has so far kept us free and firm on the theoretic and visionary fear that this Government, the world's best hope, may by possibility want energy to preserve itself? I trust not. I believe this, on the contrary, the strongest Government on earth. I believe it the only one where every man, at the call of the law, would fly to the standard of the law, and would meet invasions of the public order as his own personal concern. Sometimes it is said that man can not be trusted with the government of himself. Can he, then, be trusted with the government of others? Or have we found angels in the forms of kings to govern him? Let history answer this question.

Let us, then, with courage and confidence pursue our own Federal and Republican principles, our attachment to union and representative government. Kindly separated by nature and a wide ocean from the exterminating havoc of one quarter of the globe; too high-minded to endure the degradations of the others; possessing a chosen country, with room enough for our descendants to the thousandth and thousandth generation; entertaining a due sense of our equal right to the use of our own faculties, to the acquisitions of our own industry, to honor and confidence from our fellow-citizens, resulting not from birth, but from our actions and their sense of them; enlightened by a benign religion, professed, indeed, and practiced in various forms, yet all of them inculcating honesty, truth, temperance, gratitude, and the love of man; acknowledging and adoring an overruling Providence, which by all its dispensations proves that it delights in the happiness of man here and his greater happiness hereafter—with all these blessings, what more is necessary to make us a happy and a prosperous people? Still one thing more, fellow-citizens—a wise and frugal Government, which shall restrain men from injuring one another, shall leave them otherwise free to regulate their own pursuits of industry and improvement, and shall not take from the mouth of labor the bread it has earned. This is the sum of good government, and this is necessary to close the circle of our felicities.

About to enter, fellow-citizens, on the exercise of duties which comprehend everything dear and valuable to you, it is proper you should understand what I deem the essential principles of our Government, and consequently those which ought to shape its Administration. I will compress them within the narrowest compass they will bear, stating the general principle, but not all its limitations. Equal and exact justice to all men, of whatever state or persuasion, religious or political; peace, commerce, and honest friendship with all nations, entangling alliances with none; the support of the State governments in all their rights, as the most competent administrations for our domestic concerns and the surest bulwarks against antirepublican tendencies; the preservation of the General Government in its whole constitutional vigor, as the sheet anchor of our peace at home and safety abroad; a jealous care of the right of election by the people—a mild and safe corrective of abuses which are lopped by the sword of revolution where peaceable remedies are unprovided; absolute acquiescence in the decisions of the majority, the vital principle of republics, from which is no appeal but to force, the vital principle and immediate parent of despotism; a well-disciplined militia, our best reliance in peace and for the first moments of war, till regulars may relieve them; the supremacy of the civil over the military authority; economy in the public expense, that labor may be lightly burthened; the honest payment of our debts and sacred preservation of the public faith; encouragement of agriculture, and of commerce as its handmaid; the diffusion of information and arraignment of all abuses at the bar of the public reason; freedom of religion; freedom of the press, and freedom of person under the protection of the habeas corpus, and trial by juries impartially selected. These principles form the bright constellation which has gone before us and guided our steps through an age of revolution and reformation. The wisdom of our sages and blood of our heroes have been devoted to their attainment. They should be the creed of our political faith, the text of civic instruction, the touchstone by which to try the services of those we trust; and should we wander from them in moments of error or of alarm, let us hasten to retrace our steps and to regain the road which alone leads to peace, liberty, and safety.

I repair, then, fellow-citizens, to the post you have assigned me. With experience enough in subordinate offices to have seen the difficulties of this the greatest of all, I have learnt to expect that it will rarely fall to the lot of imperfect man to retire from this station with the reputation and the favor which bring him into it. Without pretensions to that high confidence you reposed in our first and greatest revolutionary character, whose preeminent services had entitled him to the first place in his country's love and destined for him the fairest page in the volume of faithful history, I ask so much confidence only as may give firmness and effect to the legal administration of your affairs. I shall often go wrong through defect of judgment. When right, I shall often be thought wrong by those whose positions will not command a view of the whole ground. I ask your indulgence for my own errors, which will never be intentional, and your support against the errors of others, who may condemn what they would not if seen in all its parts. The approbation implied by your suffrage is a great consolation to me for the past, and my future solicitude will be to retain the good opinion of those who have bestowed it in advance, to conciliate that of others by doing them all the good in my power, and to be instrumental to the happiness and freedom of all.

Relying, then, on the patronage of your good will, I advance with obedience to the work, ready to retire from it whenever you become sensible how much better choice it is in your power to make. And may that Infinite Power which rules the destinies of the universe lead our councils to what is best, and give them a favorable issue for your peace and prosperity.

10

Jefferson on the State of the Union

Message to Congress, December 8, 1801

To signify the triumph of republicanism, President Jefferson abolished all the monarchical "pomp and parade" introduced by the Federalists. Among other things, he proscribed the wearing of wigs in the English fashion by justices of the Supreme Court (Jefferson wore his hair straight; but John Adams said that he thought that curled hair was as republican as straight); to the mortification of the ladies, he refused to hold levees, and, his wife having predeceased him, the capital was spared what Republicans called "the burlesque of a female levee"; he used his chariot drawn by four horses only when his daughters were visiting him—the rest of the time he rode horseback, often unattended, into the wildest and most remote parts of the District of Columbia; and in place of personal appearances before Congress reminiscent of the Speech from the Throne, Jefferson sent written messages to the legislature. This practice, begun in 1801 in Jefferson's first Message to Congress, was followed by all subsequent presidents until Woodrow Wilson went before Congress in April, 1913, to recommend a revision of the tariff laws of the nation.

One can find detailed descriptions and discussions of the events which Jefferson mentioned in his message to Congress in Henry Adams's *History of the United States*, cited in Chapter 9. Leonard D. White continued his ground-breaking studies in administrative history with his * *The Jeffersonians: A Study in Administrative History, 1801–1829* (New York: The Macmillan Company, 1951); for one concerned with the extent to which Jefferson altered the procedures of administration following the so-called "Jeffersonian revolution" this volume is indispensable. A very stimulating study of the sources of Jefferson's amazing collection and integration of ideas is to be

Thomas Jefferson, "First Annual Message," in James D. Richardson, ed., *A Compilation of the Messages and Papers of the Presidents* (Washington, D.C.: Government Printing Office, 1898), I, pp. 326–32.

found in Gilbert Chinard's *Thomas Jefferson, the Apostle of Americanism* (Boston: Little, Brown and Company, 1929).

In reading this selection note (1) the hopes Jefferson envisaged for Americans as a result of the cessation of hostilities in the European war; (2) the facts he laid before the Congress respecting the Tripolitan war (1805–1805); (3) evidence of the President's scruples over the exercise of authority in the developing war with Tripoli; (4) intimations of his humanitarianism; (5) possibilities concerning taxes he envisaged; (6) implications revealing his attitudes toward war; (7) evidences of his attachment to the doctrine of a diminished state as against a strong central state; (8) his views concerning the advisability of maintaining a large standing army and a large, far-ranging navy; (9) his observations relating to what is called "the free enterprise system"; (10) intimations he gave of his wish to see the Federal judiciary diminished; (11) the proposals and the reasons therefor he made concerning the problem of naturalization of foreign born seeking American citizenship; and (12) his expectations for the conduct of public affairs.

December 8, 1801

FELLOW-CITIZENS OF THE SENATE AND HOUSE OF REPRESENTATIVES:

It is a circumstance of sincere gratification to me that on meeting the great council of our nation I am able to announce to them on grounds of reasonable certainty that the wars and troubles which have for so many years afflicted our sister nations have at length come to an end, and that the communications of peace and commerce are once more opening among them.* Whilst we devoutly return thanks to the beneficent Being who has been pleased to breathe into them the spirit of conciliation and forgiveness, we are bound with peculiar gratitude to be thankful to Him that our own peace has been preserved through so perilous a season, and ourselves permitted quietly to cultivate the earth and to practice and improve those arts which tend to increase our comforts. The assurances, indeed, of friendly disposition received from all the powers with whom we have principal relations had inspired a confidence that our peace with them would not have been disturbed. But a cessation of irregularities which had affected the commerce of neutral nations and of the irritations and injuries produced by them can

---

* Editor's Note: England, France, and Spain in the Peace of Amiens (1802) confirmed the cessation of hostilities noted here by the President.

not but add to this confidence, and strengthens at the same time the hope that wrings committed on unoffending friends under a pressure of circumstances will now be reviewed with candor, and will be considered as founding just claims of retribution for the past and new assurance for the future.

Among our Indian neighbors also a spirit of peace and friendship generally prevails, and I am happy to inform you that the continued efforts to introduce among them the implements and the practice of husbandry and of the household arts have not been without success; that they are becoming more and more sensible of the superiority of this dependence for clothing and subsistence over the precarious resources of hunting and fishing, and already we are able to announce that instead of that constant diminution of their numbers produced by their wars and their wants, some of them begin to experience an increase of population.

To this state of general peace with which we have been blessed, one only exception exists. Tripoli, the least considerable of the Barbary States, had come forward with demands unfounded either in right or in compact, and had permitted itself to denounce war on our failure to comply before a given day. The style of the demand admitted but one answer. I sent a small squadron of frigates into the Mediterranean, with assurances to that power of our sincere desire to remain in peace, but with orders to protect our commerce against the threatened attack. The measure was seasonable and salutary. The Bey had already declared war. His cruisers were out. Two had arrived at Gibraltar. Our commerce in the Mediterranean was blockaded and that of the Atlantic in peril. The arrival of our squadron dispelled the danger. One of the Tripolitan cruisers having fallen in with and engaged the small schooner *Enterprise*, commanded by Lieutenant Sterret, which had gone as a tender to our larger vessels, was captured, after a heavy slaughter of her men, without the loss of a single one on our part. The bravery exhibited by our citizens on that element will, I trust, be a testimony to the world that it is not the want of that virtue which makes us seek their peace, but a conscientious desire to direct the energies of our nation to the multiplication of the human race, and not to its destruction. Unauthorized by the Constitution, without the sanction of Congress, to go beyond the line of defense, the vessel, being disabled from committing further hostilities, was liberated with its crew. The

Legislature will doubtless consider whether, by authorizing measures of offense also, they will place our force on an equal footing with that of its adversaries. I communicate all material information on this subject, that in the exercise of this important function confided by the Constitution to the Legislature exclusively their judgment may form itself on a knowledge and consideration of every circumstance of weight.

I wish I could say that our situation with all the other Barbary States was entirely satisfactory. Discovering that some delays had taken place in the performance of certain articles stipulated by us, I thought it my duty, by immediate measures for fulfilling them, to vindicate to ourselves the right of considering the effect of departure from stipulation on their side. From the papers which will be laid before you you will be enabled to judge whether our treaties are regarded by them as fixing at all the measure of their demands or as guarding from the exercise of force our vessels within their power, and to consider how far it will be safe and expedient to leave our affairs with them in their present posture.

I lay before you the result of the census lately taken of our inhabitants, to a conformity with which we are now to reduce the ensuing ratio of representation and taxation. You will perceive that the increase of numbers during the last ten years, proceeding in geometrical ratio, promises a duplication in little more than twenty-two years. We contemplate this rapid growth and the prospect it holds up to us, not with a view to the injuries it may enable us to do others in some future day, but to the settlement of the extensive country still remaining vacant within our limits to the multiplication of men susceptible of happiness, educated in the love of order, habituated to self-government, and valuing its blessings above all price.

Other circumstances, combined with the increase of numbers, have produced an augmentation of revenue arising from consumption in a ratio far beyond that of population alone; and though the changes in foreign relations now taking place so desirably for the whole world may for a season affect this branch of revenue, yet weighing all probabilities of expense as well as of income, there is reasonable ground of confidence that we may now safely dispense with all the internal taxes, comprehending excise, stamps, auctions, licenses, carriages, and refined sugars, to which the postage on newspapers may be added to facilitate the progress of information, and that the remaining sources of revenue will be sufficient to provide for the support of Government, to pay the interest the of public debts, and to discharge the principals within shorter periods than the laws or the general expectation had contemplated. War, indeed, and untoward events may change this prospect of things and call for expenses which the imposts could not meet; but sound principles will not justify our taxing the industry of our fellow-citizens to accumulate treasure for wars to happen we know not when, and which might not, perhaps, happen but from the temptations offered by that treasure.

These views, however, of reducing our burthens are formed on the expectation that a sensible and at the same time a salutary reduction may take place in our habitual expenditures. For this purpose those of the civil Government, the Army, and Navy will need revisal.

When we consider that this Government is charged with the external and mutual relations only of these States; that the States themselves have principal care of our persons, our property, and our reputation, constituting the great field of human concerns, we may well doubt whether our organization is not too complicated, too expensive; whether offices and officers have not been multiplied unnecessarily and sometimes injuriously to the service they were meant to promote. I will cause to be laid before you an essay toward a statement of those who, under public employment of various kinds, draw money from the Treasury or from our citizens. Time has not permitted a perfect enumeration, the ramifications of office being too multiplied and remote to be completely traced in a first trial. Among those who are dependent on Executive discretion I have begun the reduction of what was deemed unnecessary. The expenses of diplomatic agency have been considerably diminished. The inspectors of internal revenue who were found to obstruct the accountability of the institution have been discontinued. Several agencies created by Executive authority, on salaries fixed by that also, have been suppressed, and should suggest the expediency of regulating that power by law, so as to subject its exercises to legislative inspection and sanction. Other reformations of the same kind will be pursued with that caution which is requisite in removing useless things, not to injure what is retained. But the great mass of public offices is established by law, and therefore by law alone can be abolished. Should the Legislature think it expedient to pass this roll in review and try all its parts by the test of public utility, they may be assured of every aid and light which Executive information can yield. Considering the general tendency to multiply offices and dependencies and to increase expense to the ultimate term of burthen which the citizen can bear, it behooves us to avail ourselves of every occasion which presents itself for taking off the surcharge, that it never may be seen here that after leaving to labor the smallest portion of its earnings on which it can subsist, Government shall itself consume the whole residue of what it was instituted to guard.

In our care, too, of the public contributions intrusted to our direction it would be prudent to multiply barriers against their dissipation by appropriating specific sums to every specific purpose susceptible of definition; by disallowing all applications of money varying from the appropriation in object or transcending it in amount; by reducing the undefined field of contingencies and thereby circumscribing discretionary powers over money, and by bringing back to a single department all accountabilities for money, where the examinations may be prompt, efficacious, and uniform.

An account of the receipts and expenditures of the last year, as prepared by the Secretary of the Treasury, will, as usual, be laid before you. The success which has attended the late sales of the public lands shews that with attention they may be made an important source of receipt. Among the payments those made in discharge of the principal and interest of the national debt will shew that the public faith has been exactly maintained. To these will be added an estimate of appropriations necessary for the ensuing year. This last will, of course, be affected by such modifications of the system of expense as you shall think proper to adopt.

A statement has been formed by the Secretary of War, on mature consideration, of all the posts and stations where garrisons will be expedient and of the number of men requisite for each garrison. The whole amount is considerably short of the present military establishment. For the surplus no particular use can be pointed out. For defense against invasion their number is as nothing, nor is it conceived needful or safe that a standing army should be kept up in time of peace for that purpose. Uncertain as we must ever be of the particular point in our circumference where an enemy may choose to invade us, the only force which can be ready at every point and competent to oppose them is the body of neighboring citizens as formed into a militia. On these, collected from the parts most convenient in numbers proportioned to the invading force, it is best to rely not only to meet the first attack, but if it threatens to be permanent to maintain the defense until regulars may be engaged to relieve them. These considerations render it important that we should at every session continue to amend the defects which from time to time shew themselves in the laws for regulating the militia until they are sufficiently perfect. Nor should we now or at any time separate until we can say we have done everything for the militia which we could do were an enemy at our door.

The provision of military stores on hand will be laid before you, that you may judge of the additions still requisite.

With respect to the extent to which our naval preparations should be carried some difference of opinion may be expected to appear, but just attention to the circumstances of every part of the Union will doubtless reconcile all. A small force will probably continue to be wanted for actual service in the Mediterranean. Whatever annual sum beyond that you may think proper to appropriate to naval preparations would perhaps be better employed in providing those articles which may be kept without waste or consumption, and be in readiness when any exigence calls them into use. Progress has been made, as will appear by papers now communicated, in providing materials for 74-gun ships as directed by law.

How far the authority given by the Legislature for procuring and establishing sites for naval purposes has been perfectly understood and pursued in the execution admits of some doubt. A statement of the expenses already incurred on that subject is now laid before you. I have in certain cases suspended or slackened these expenditures, that the Legislature might determine whether so many yards are necessary as have been contemplated. The works at this place are among those permitted to go on, and five of the seven frigates directed to be laid up have been brought and laid up here, where, besides the safety of their position, they are under the eye of the Executive Administration, as well as of its agents, and where yourselves also will be guided by your own view in the legislative provisions respecting them which may from time to time be necessary. They are preserved in such condition, as well the vessels as whatever belongs to them, as to be at all times ready for sea on a short warning. Two others are yet to be laid up so soon as they shall have received the repairs requisite to put them also into sound condition. As a superintending officer will be necessary at each yard, his duties and emoluments, hitherto fixed by the Executive, will be a more proper subject for legislation. A communication will also be made of our progress in the execution of the law respecting the vessels directed to be sold.

The fortifications of our harbors, more or less advanced, present considerations of great difficulty. While some of them are on a scale sufficiently proportioned to the advantages of their position, to the efficacy of their protection, and the importance of the points within it, others are so extensive, will cost so much in their first erection, so much in their maintenance, and require such a force to garrison them as to make it questionable what is best now to be done. A statement of those commenced or projected, of the expenses already incurred, and estimates of their future cost, as far as can be foreseen, shall be laid before you, that you may be enabled to judge whether any alteration is necessary in the laws respecting this subject.

Agriculture, manufactures, commerce, and navigation, the four pillars of our prosperity, are then most thriving when left most free to individual enterprise. Protection from casual embarrassments, however, may sometimes be seasonably interposed. If in the course of your observations or inquiries they should appear to need any aid within the limits of our constitutional powers, your sense of their importance is a sufficient assurance they will occupy your attention. We can not, indeed, but all feel an anxious solicitude for the difficulties under which our carrying trade will soon be placed. How far it can be relieved, otherwise than by time, is a subject of important consideration.

The judiciary system of the United States, and especially that portion of it recently erected, will of course present itself to the contemplation of Congress, and, that they may be able to judge of the proportion which the institution bears to the business it has to perform, I have caused to be procured from the several States and now lay before Congress an exact statement of all the causes decided since the first establishment of the courts, and of those which were depending when additional courts and judges were brought in to their aid.

And while on the judiciary organization it will be worthy your consideration whether the protection of the inestimable institution of juries has been extended to all the cases involving the security of our persons and property. Their impartial selection also being essential to their value, we ought further to consider whether that is sufficiently secured in those States where they are named by a marshal depending on Executive will or designated by the court or by officers dependent on them.

I can not omit recommending a revisal of the laws on the subject of naturalization. Considering the ordinary chances of human life, a denial of citizenship under a residence of fourteen years is a denial to a great proportion of those who ask it, and controls a policy pursued from their first settlement by many of these States, and still believed of consequence to their prosperity; and shall we refuse to the unhappy fugitives from distress that hospitality which the savages of the wilderness extended to our fathers arriving in this land? Shall oppressed humanity find no asylum on this globe? The Constitution indeed has wisely provided that for admission to certain offices of important trust a residence shall be required sufficient to develop character and design. But might not the general character and capabilities of a citizen be safely communicated to everyone manifesting a bona fide purpose of embarking his life and fortunes permanently with us, with restrictions, perhaps, to guard against the fraudulent usurpation of our flag, an abuse which brings so much embarrassment and loss on the genuine citizen and so much danger to the nation of being involved in war that no endeavor should be spared to detect and suppress it?

These, fellow-citizens, are the matters respecting the state of the nation which I have thought of importance to be submitted to your consideration at this time. Some others of less moment or not yet ready for communication will be the subject of separate messages. I am happy in this opportunity of committing the arduous affairs of our Government to the collected wisdom of the Union. Nothing shall be wanting on my part to inform as far as in my power the legislative judgment, nor to carry that judgment into faithful execution. The prudence and temperance of your discussions will promote within your own walls that conciliation which so much befriends rational conclusion, and by its example will encourage among our constituents that progress of opinion which is tending to unite them in object and in will. That all should be satisfied with any one order of things is not to be expected; but I indulge the pleasing persuasion that the great body of our citizens will cordially concur in honest and disinterested efforts which have for their object to preserve the General and State Governments in their constitutional form and equilibrium; to maintain peace abroad, and order and obedience to the laws at home; to establish principles and practices of administration favorable to the security of liberty and property, and to reduce expenses to what is necessary for the useful purposes of Government.

TH: JEFFERSON

11

The Louisiana Purchase

Jefferson Explains His Views

The cessation of hostilities (1801–1803) confirmed by the Peace of Amiens (1802) afforded Napoleon an opportunity to effectuate his Grand Design in the western hemisphere: a new French colonial empire based upon the twin pillars of Louisiana and Santo Domingo. Santo Domingo was a French possession, but since 1763 Louisiana had been Spanish territory. Napoleon settled the difficulty by compelling the King of Spain in the secret convention of San Ildefonso (October, 1801) to retrocede Louisiana to France in exchange for territory in the Italian peninsula.

The "secret" of San Ildefonso was soon making the rounds of all the whispering galleries in Europe. Reports reached the United States early in 1802 that the French would soon be in Louisiana in force. Napoleon did not disguise his intentions. Two expeditions were prepared for duty in the western hemisphere: a fleet and army were sent to Santo Domingo and a second expeditionary force, destined for Louisiana, was held in readiness in Holland.

Americans' worst fears of French intentions were realized when, in October, 1802, the Spanish Intendant at New Orleans suspended the right of deposit guaranteed United States citizens by the Treaty of San Lorenzo (Pinckney's treaty, 1795). Unable to tranship their farm products to Europe by way of New Orleans, westerners vowed to force a passage with the aid of their rifles. President Jefferson, unwilling to appeal to arms until all the resources of diplomacy had been exhausted, sent James Monroe (1758–1831) as minister plenipotentiary to back up Robert R. Livingston (1746–1813), the resident minister in Paris. The outcome of his mission, the President said, would decide "whether we are to be a people consigned

Paul Leicester Ford, ed., *The Writings of Thomas Jefferson* (New York: G. P. Putnam's Sons, 1897), VIII, pp. 144–47; 190–92; 209–10; 266–69; 271.

to peace with all nations, unmeddling in the affairs of Europe, or are to take part in their broils and become an unhappy nation."

Monroe and Livingston were instructed to offer France $2 million for New Orleans and the east bank of the Mississippi. The President anticipated that the United States might have to pay as much as $10 million for this small but highly strategic area. The administration's attention was riveted upon the mouth of the Mississippi—the French could have kept the rest of Louisiana without risk of war with the United States.

But French defeats in Santo Domingo and Napoleon's decision to resume the war with Great Britain compelled a radical change in French policy. To the astonishment of the American negotiators, they were offered the whole of Louisiana for $15 million. Livingston and Monroe joyfully signed the treaty on May 2 (but antedated April 30, 1803), hardly able to believe their good fortune. Nothing in the constitution provided for such a contingency as now arose; but the President, recognizing the incredible nature of the bargain struck, swallowed his strict constructionist views and urged ratification of the treaty. The Federalists, as might be suspected, suspended their loose constructionist attitude and opposed the Purchase on the grounds, among others, that the constitution gave the government no power to buy territory. The good sense of the country prevailed, however, and the Senate ratified the treaty on October 20, 1803, by a vote of 24 to 7.

Much has been written on the subject of the Louisiana Purchase—the events and considerations leading up to it and some of the implications and consequences flowing from it. For a study of the relationships of the United States and Great Britain during these years, consult Bradford Perkins, *The First Rapprochement: England and the United States, 1795–1805* (Philadelphia: The University of Pennsylvania Press, 1955). Charles C. Tansill in *The United States and Santo Domingo, 1798–1873: A Chapter in Caribbean Diplomacy* (Baltimore: The Johns Hopkins Press, 1938) explores the role played by that unhappy island in the affair. On the French side, E. Wilson Lyon's *The Man Who Sold Louisiana: The Career of Francois Barbé-Marbois* (Norman: The University of Oklahoma Press, 1942) is informative. For the debates on the constitutionality of the Purchase one should read Everett S. Brown's *The Constitutional History of the Louisiana Purchase, 1803–1812* (Berkeley: The University of California Press, 1920). Again, Henry Adams, *History of the United States* should be cited.

In reading Jefferson's letter to Livingston note (1) the impact upon American foreign relations the President foresaw resulting from the transfer of sovereignty of Louisiana and the Floridas to France; (2) the reasons he gave for arriving at the foregoing conclusion; (3) why he wanted to avoid war with France; (4) the pressures from Americans he sensed as the news of the impending shift in sovereignty spread and the reasons therefor; and (5) his instructions for Livingston. In reading Jefferson's letter to

Monroe note (1) any significant change in tone; (2) what political capital Jefferson saw the Federalists exploiting in the Louisiana affair; (3) why Jefferson wanted Monroe to go to Paris; (4) the means of persuasion he used; and (5) the consequences he envisioned should the United States fail to acquire New Orleans. In reading Jefferson's second letter to minister Livingston note (1) evidences of changes in his sense of urgency; and (2) his explanation of why he was sending Monroe to Paris. In reading the President's message to Congress note (1) his explanation of why France was willing to sell all of Louisiana to the United States; (2) to what extent Jefferson discussed the constitutionality of the Purchase; and (3) how he proposed financing the Purchase.

Jefferson to Robert R. Livingston

Washington, April 18, 1802

THE SESSION OF LOUISIANA AND THE FLORIDAS by Spain to France works most sorely on the U.S. On this subject the Secretary of State has written to you fully. Yet I cannot forbear recurring to it personally, so deep is the impression it makes in my mind. It compleatly reverses all the political relations of the U.S. and will form a new epoch in our political course. Of all nations of any consideration France is the one which hitherto has offered the fewest points on which we could have any conflict of right, and the most points of a communion of interests. From these causes we have ever looked to her as our *natural friend,* as one with which we never could have an occasion of difference. Her growth therefore we viewed as our own, her misfortunes ours. There is on the globe one single spot, the possessor of which is our natural and habitual enemy. It is New Orleans, through which the produce of three-eighths of our territory must pass to market, and from its fertility it will ere long yield more than half of our whole produce and contain more than half our inhabitants. France placing herself in that door assumes to us the attitude of defiance. Spain might have retained it quietly for years. Her pacific dispositions, her feeble state, would induce her to increase our facilities there, so that her possession of the place would be hardly felt by us, and it would not perhaps be very long before some circumstance might arise which might make the cession of it to us the price of something of more worth to her. Not so can it ever be in the hands of France. The impetuosity of her temper, the energy and restlessness of her character, placed in a point of eternal friction with us . . . render it impossible that France and the U.S. can continue long friends when they meet in so irritable a position. They as well as we must be blind if they do not see this; and we must be very improvident if we do not begin to make arrangements on that hypothesis. The day that France takes possession of N. Orleans fixes the sentence which is to restrain her forever within her low water mark. It seals the union of two nations who in conjunction can maintain exclusive possession of the ocean. From that moment we must marry ourselves to the British fleet and nation. We must turn all our attentions to a maritime force, for which our resources place us on very high grounds: and having formed and cemented together a power which may render reinforcement of her settlements here impossible to France, make the first cannon, which shall be fired in Europe the signal for tearing up any settlement she may have made, and for holding the two continents of America in sequestration for the common purposes of the united British and American nations. This is not a state of things we seek or desire. It is one which this measure, if adopted by France, forces on us, as necessarily as any other cause, by the laws of nature, brings on its necessary effect. It is not from a fear of France that we deprecate this measure proposed by her. . . . But it is from a sincere love of peace, and a firm persuasion that bound to France by the interests and the strong sympathies still existing in the minds of our citizens, and holding relative positions which ensure their continuance we are secure of a long course of peace. Whereas the change of friends, which will be rendered necessary if France changes that position, embarks us necessarily as a belligerent power in the first war of Europe. . . .

If France considers Louisiana however as indispensable for her views she might perhaps be willing to look about for arrangements which might reconcile it to our interests. If anything could do this it would be the ceding to us the island of New Orleans and the Floridas. This would certainly in a great degree remove the causes of jarring and irritation between us, and perhaps for such a length of time as might produce other means of making the measure permanently conciliatory to our interests and friendships. It would at any rate relieve us from the necessity of taking immediate measures for countervailing such an operation by arrangements in another quarter. Still we should consider N. Orleans and the Floridas as equivalent for the risk of a quarrel with France produced by her vicinage.* I have no doubt you have urged these considerations on every proper occasion with the government where you are. They are such as must have effect if you can find the means of producing thorough reflection on them by that government. The idea here is that the troops sent to St. Domingo, were to proceed to Louisiana after finishing their work in that island. If this were the arrangement, it will give you time to return again and again to the charge, for the conquest of St. Domingo will not be a short work. It will take considerable time to wear down a great number of souldiers. Every eye in the U.S. is now fixed on this affair of Louisiana. Perhaps nothing since the revolutionary war has produced more uneasy sensations through the body of the nation. Notwithstanding temporary bickerings have taken place with France, she has still a strong hold on the affections of our citizens generally. I have thought it not amiss, by way of supplement to the letters of the Secretary of State to write you this private one to impress you with the importance we affix to this transaction. I pray you to cherish Dupont. He has the best dispositions for the continuance of friendship between the two nations, and perhaps you may be able to make a good use of him. Accept assurances of my affectionate esteem and high consideration.

Jefferson to James Monroe

Washington, Jan. 13, 1803

Dear Sir: I dropped you a line on the 10th informing you of a nomination I had made of you to the Senate, and yesterday I enclosed you their approbation not then having time to write. The agitation of the public mind on occasion of the late suspension of our right of deposit at N. Orleans is extreme. In the western country it is natural and grounded on honest motives. In the seaports it proceeds from a desire for war which increases the mercantile lottery; in the federalists generally and especially those of Congress the object is to force us into war if possible, in order to derange our

* Editor's Note: For "vicinage" read: by becoming a neighbor of the United States.

finances, or if this cannot be done, to attach the western country to them, as their best friends, and thus get again into power. Remonstrances memorials &c. are now circulating through the whole of the western country and signing by the body of the people. The measures we have been pursuing being invisible, do not satisfy their minds. Something sensible therefore was become necessary; and indeed our object of purchasing N. Orleans and the Floridas is a measure liable to assume so many shapes, that no instructions could be squared to fit them, it was essential then to send a minister extraordinary to be joined with the ordinary one, with discretionary powers, first however well impressed with all our views and therefore qualified to meet and modify to these every form of proposition which could come from the other party. This could be done only in full and frequent oral communications. Having determined on this, there could not be two opinions among the republicans as to the person. You possess the unlimited confidence of the administration and of the western people; and generally of the republicans everywhere; and were you to refuse to go, no other man can be found who does this. The measure has already silenced the Feds. here. Congress will no longer be agitated by them: and the country will become calm as fast as the information extends over it. All eyes, all hopes, are now fixed on you; and were you to decline, the chagrin would be universal, and would shake under your feet the high ground on which you stand with the public. Indeed I know nothing which would produce such a shock, for on the event of this mission depends the future destinies of this republic. If we cannot by a purchase of the country insure to ourselves a course of perpetual peace and friendship with all nations, then as war cannot be distant, it behooves us immediately to be preparing for that course, without, however, hastening it, and it may be necessary (on your failure on the continent) to cross the channel.

We shall get entangled in European politics, and figuring more, be much less happy and prosperous. This can only be prevented by a successful issue to your present mission. I am sensible after the measures you have taken for getting into a different line of business, that it will be a great sacrifice on your part, and presents from the season and other circumstances serious difficulties. But some men are born for the public. Nature by fitting them for the service of the human race on a broad scale, has stamped with the evidences of her destination and their duty. . . .

As to the time of your going you cannot too much hasten it, as the moment in France is critical. St. Domingo delays their taking possession of Louisiana, and they are in the last distress for money for current purposes. You should arrange your affairs for an absence of a year at least, perhaps for a long one. It will be necessary for you to stay here some days on your way to New York. You will receive here what advance you chuse. Accept assurances of my constant and affectionate attachment.

Jefferson to Livingston

Washington, Feb. 3, 1803

Dear Sir: My last to you was by Mr. Dupont. Since that I received yours of May 22. Mr. [James] Madison [Secretary of State] supposes you have written a subsequent one which has never come to hand. A late suspension by the Intendant of N Orleans of our right of deposit there, without which the right of navigation is impracticable, has thrown this country into such a flame of hostile disposition as can scarcely be described. The western country was peculiarly sensible to it as you may suppose. Our business was to take the most effectual pacific measures in our power to remove the suspension, and at the some time to persuade our countrymen that pacific measures would be the most effectual and the most speedily so. The opposition caught it as a plank in a shipwreck, hoping it would enable them to tack the Western people to them. They raised the cry of war, were intriguing in all the quarters to exasperate the Western inhabitants to arm & go down on their own authority & possess themselves of New Orleans, and in the meantime were daily reiterating, in new shapes, inflammatory resolutions for the adoption of the House. As a remedy to all this we determined to name a minister extraordinary to go immediately to Paris & Madrid to settle this matter. This measure being a visible one, and the person named peculiarly proper with the Western country, crushed at once & put an end to all further attempts on the Legislature. From that moment all has become quiet; and the more readily in the Western country, as the sudden alliance of these new federal friends had of itself already began to make them suspect the wisdom of their own course. The measure was moreover proposed from another cause. We must know at once whether we can acquire N Orleans or not. We are satisfied nothing else will secure us against a war at no distant period; and we cannot press this reason without beginning those arrangements which will be necessary if war is hereafter to result. For this purpose it was necessary that the negotiators should be fully possessed of every idea we have on the subject, so as to meet the propositions of the opposite party, in whatever form they may be offered; and give them a shape admissible by us without being obliged to await new instructions hence, With this view, we have joined Mr. Monroe to yourself at Paris, & to Mr. Pinkney [*sic.*] at Madrid, altho' we believe it will be hardly necessary for him to go to this last place. Should we fail in this object of the mission, a further one will be superadded for the other side of the channel. On this subject you will be informed by the Secretary of State, & Mr. Monroe will be able also to inform you of all our views and purposes. By him I send another letter to Dupont, whose aid may be of the greatest service, as it will be divested of the shackles of form. The letter is left open for your perusal, after which I wish a wafer stuck on it before it be delivered. . . .

THIRD ANNUAL MESSAGE TO CONGRESS, OCTOBER 17, 1803 BY THOMAS JEFFERSON

In calling you together, fellow citizens, at an earlier day than was contemplated by the act of the last session of Congress, I have not been insensible to the personal inconvenience necessarily resulting from an unexpected change in your arrangements. But matters of great public concern have rendered this call necessary, and the interest you feel in these will supersede in our minds all private considerations.

Congress witnessed, at their last session, the extraordinary agitation produced in the public mind by the suspension of our right of deposit at the port of New-Orleans, no assignment of another place having been made according to treaty. They were sensible that the continuance of that privation would be more injurious to our nation than any consequences which could flow from any mode of redress, but reposing just confidence in the good faith of the government whose officer had committed the wrong, friendly and reasonable representations were resorted to, and the right of deposit was restored.

Previous, however, to this period, we had not been unaware of the danger to which our peace would be perpetually exposed while so important a key to the commerce of the western country remained under foreign power. Difficulties, too, were presenting themselves as to the navigation of other streams, which, arising within our territories, pass through those adjacent. Propositions had, therefore, been authorized for obtaining, on fair conditions, the sovereignty of New Orleans, and of other possessions in that quarter interesting to our quiet, to such extent as was deemed practicable; and the provisional appropriation of two millions of dollars, to be applied and accounted for by the president of the United States, intended as part of the price, was considered as conveying the sanction of Congress to the acquisition proposed. The enlightened government of France saw, with just discernment, the importance to both nations of such liberal arrangements as might best and permanently promote the peace, friendship, and interests of both; and the property and sovereignty of all Louisiana, which had been restored to them, have on certain conditions been transferred to the United States by instruments bearing date the 30th of April last. When these shall have received the constitutional sanction of the senate, they will without delay be communicated to the representatives also, for the exercise of their functions, as to those conditions which are within the powers vested by the constitution in Congress. While the property and sovereignty of the Mississippi and its waters secure an independent outlet for the produce of the western States, and an uncontrolled navigation through their whole course, free from collision with other powers and the dangers to our peace from that source, the fertility of the country, its climate and extent, promise in due season important aids to our treasury, an ample provision for our posterity, and a wide-spread field for the blessings of freedom and equal laws.

With the wisdom of Congress it will rest to take those ulterior measures which may be necessary for the immediate occupation and temporary government of the country; for its incorporation into our Union; for rendering the change of government a blessing to our newly-adopted brethren; for securing to them the rights of conscience and of property: for confirming to the Indian inhabitants their occupancy and self-government, establishing friendly and commercial relations with them, and for ascertaining the geography of the country acquired. Such materials for your information, relative to its affairs in general, as the short space of time has permitted me to collect, will be laid before you when the subject shall be in a state for your consideration. . . .

Should the acquisition of Louisiana be constitutionally confirmed and carried into effect, a sum of nearly thirteen millions of dollars will then be added to our public debt, most of which is payable after fifteen years; before which term the present existing debts will all be discharged by the established operation of the sinking fund. When we contemplate the ordinary annual augmentation of imposts from increasing population and wealth, the augmentation of the same revenue by its extension to the new acquisition, and the economies which may still be introduced into our public expenditures, I cannot but hope that Congress in reviewing their resources will find means to meet the intermediate interests of this additional debt without recurring to new taxes, and applying to this object only the ordinary progression of our revenue. Its extraordinary increase in times of foreign war will be the proper and sufficient fund for any measures of safety or precaution which that state of things may render necessary in our neutral position. . . .

12

The Burr Conspiracy

Reports by Thomas Jefferson and Washington Irving, 1807

Although Aaron Burr (1756–1836) had contributed to the victory of the Jeffersonian Republicans in the presidential election of 1800, Thomas Jefferson considered Burr to be a "crooked stick." By 1804, even though he was Vice-President, Burr had been stripped of his control over the patronage in New York and all but read out of the Republican party. The Federalists were eager to run Burr against President Jefferson, but after Burr killed Alexander Hamilton in a duel at Weehawken, New Jersey, in 1804, all prospect of Federalist support for Burr vanished; Burr was a man without a party. In this crisis of his fortunes, Burr embarked upon the most grandiose filibustering scheme ever conceived by an American adventurer. In order to enlist financial aid he told a variety of tales: that he intended to separate the West from the remainder of the union; that he planned to wrest control of Texas and the rest of Mexico from Spain; and that he had nothing more in view than to colonize a land grant west of the Mississippi River. He brought General James Wilkinson (1757–1825), commander of American forces in the region, into the conspiracy with the offer of $100,000 and a high military post in the new government Burr talked of establishing in Spanish territory. What Burr did not know was that General Wilkinson had been in the pay of the Spanish government for almost twenty years. Burr's expeditionary force rendezvoused at

Thomas Jefferson to the Senate and the House of Representatives of the United States, January 22, 1807, in James D. Richardson, ed., *A Compilation of the Messages and Papers of the Presidents* (Washington, D.C.: Government Printing Office, 1898), I, pp. 412–17; Washington Irving to Mrs. Hoffman, James K. Paulding, and Mary Fairlie, June–July, 1807, in James Parton, *The Life and Time of Aaron Burr, Lieutenant-Colonel in the Army of the Revolution, United States Senator, Vice-President of the United States, etc.*, 2 vols. (New York: Mason Brothers, 1858), II, pp. 372–75.

Blennerhasset's Island in the Ohio River in Virginia (now West Virginia) in August, 1806. About a hundred armed men began to descend the Ohio and Mississippi Rivers toward New Orleans. At this juncture, General Wilkinson informed President Jefferson that Burr was engaged in a treasonable plot against the union. The President immediately issued orders that Burr and his men be stopped forthwith. Burr was arrested in February, 1807 while fleeing toward Spanish Florida; he was brought to Richmond, Virginia for trial. At the time Jefferson expressed the conviction that Burr was guilty of treason, but later he admitted privately that the government's case was far from complete. And so, indeed, it proved. Standing trial before Chief Justice John Marshall (1755–1835) at Richmond, Burr was acquitted on the ground that his presence on Blennerhasset's Island was not proved by the testimony of two independent witnesses. Burr subsequently exiled himself to Europe (1808–1812) to escape further prosecution for the murder of Alexander Hamilton in New York and New Jersey and for treason in several western States. He later returned to New York to practice law.

Washington Irving (1783–1859), who later became one of America's most distinguished men of letters, had, despite his youth, commenced writing for publication in New York in 1802. In 1807–1808 he began contributing essays to *Salmagundi*, then in 1809 he brought out his *History of New York* (see Chapter 19), which among other things contains thinly disguised blasts launched against Thomas Jefferson and Jeffersonians in general. Irving, present at Burr's trial in Richmond, communicated some of his observations of the trial and of its principal actors in letters to his friends, three of which epistles are reprinted here.

In addition to Parton's biography of Burr from which Irving's letters are taken, the student might wish to consult the more recent life written by Nathan Schachner, *Aaron Burr, A Biography* (New York: Frederick A. Stokes Company, 1937). Two authoritative studies are available for those interested in a scholarly treatment of the conspiracy itself: Thomas P. Abernathy, *The Burr Conspiracy* (New York: Oxford University Press, 1954) and Walter F. McCaleb, *The Aaron Burr Conspiracy: A History Largely from Original and Hitherto Unused Sources* (New York: Dodd, Mead and Company, 1903). [Wilson-Erickson Inc. of New York in 1936 brought out an expanded edition of McCaleb's earlier volume.]

In reading Jefferson's message to Congress note (1) the reasons the President gave for reporting to the Congress; (2) his description of the kind of evidence he possessed which motivated him to act; (3) what the President thought respecting Burr's guilt or innocence; (4) his report of what action he had already taken; (5) what Jefferson had learned from General Wilkinson; (6) the extent to which the President put credence in General Wilkinson; (7) the President's report of what action he and others took following receipt of information from General Wilkinson; and (8) to what extent the President thought foreign powers were implicated in the plot. In reading Washington Irving's correspondence from Richmond note (1) his characterizations of Burr and General Wilkinson; (2) the extent to which the thought Burr guilty; (3) how fair a hearing he thought Burr received; and (4) evidence suggesting what he (Irving) believed Jefferson's role in the affair to be.

January 22, 1807

To THE SENATE AND HOUSE OF REPRESENTATIVES OF
THE UNITED STATES:

Agreeably to the request of the House of Representatives communicated in their resolution of the 16th instant, I proceed to state, under the reserve therein expressed, information received touching an illegal combination of private individuals against the peace and safety of the Union, and a military expedition planned by them against the territories of a power in amity with the United States, with the measures I have pursued for suppressing the same.

I had for some time been in the constant expectation of receiving such further information as would have enabled me to lay before the Legislature the termination as well as the beginning and progress of this scene of depravity so far as it has been acted on the Ohio and its waters. From this the state of safety of the lower country might have been estimated on probable grounds, and the delay was indulged the rather because no circumstance had yet made it necessary to call in the aid of the legislative functions. Information now recently communicated has brought us nearly to the period contemplated. The mass of what I have received in the course of these transactions is voluminous, but little has been given under the sanction of an oath so as to constitute formal and legal evidence. It is chiefly in the form of letters, often containing such a mixture of rumors, conjectures, and suspicions as renders it difficult to sift out the real facts and unadvisable to hazard more than general outlines, strengthened by concurrent information or the particular credibility of the relator. In this state of the evidence, delivered sometimes, too, under the restriction of private confidence, neither safety nor justice will permit the exposing names, except that of the principal actor, whose guilt is placed beyond question.

Some time in the latter part of September I received intimations
that designs were in agitation in the Western country unlawful and
unfriendly to the peace of the Union, and that the prime mover in
these was Aaron Burr, heretofore distinguished by the favor of his
country. The grounds of these intimations being inconclusive, the
objects uncertain, and the fidelity of that country known to be
firm, the only measures taken was to urge the informants to use
their best endeavors to get further insight into the designs and
proceedings of the suspected persons and to communicate them to
me.

It was not till the latter part of October that the objects of the
conspiracy began to be perceived, but still so blended and involved
in mystery that nothing distinct could be singled out for pursuit.
In this state of uncertainty as to the crime contemplated, the acts
done, and the legal course to be pursued, I thought it best to send
to the scene where these things were principally in transaction a
person in whose integrity, understanding, and discretion entire
confidence could be reposed, with instructions to investigate the
plots going on, to enter into conference (for which he had sufficient
credentials) with the governors and all other officers, civil and
military, and with their aid to do on the spot whatever should be
necessary to discover the designs of the conspirators, arrest their
means, bring their persons to punishment, and to call out the force
of the country to suppress any unlawful enterprise in which it
should be found they were engaged. By this time it was known that
many boats were under preparation, stores of provisions collecting,
and an unusual number of suspicious characters in motion on the
Ohio and its waters. Besides dispatching the confidential agent to that
quarter, orders were at the same time sent to the governors of the
Orleans and Mississippi Territories and to the commanders of the
land and naval forces there to be on their guard against surprise
and in constant readiness to resist any enterprise which might be
attempted on the vessels, posts, or other objects under their care;
and on the 8th of November instructions were forwarded to General
Wilkinson to hasten an accommodation with the Spanish commandant on the Sabine, and as soon as that was effected to fall
back with his principal force to the hither bank of the Mississippi
for the defense of the interesting points on that river. By a letter
received from that officer on the 25th of November, but dated

October 21, we learnt that a confidential agent of Aaron Burr had been deputed to him with communications, partly written in cipher and partly oral, explaining his designs, exaggerating his resources, and making such offers of emolument and command to engage him and the army in his unlawful enterprise as he had flattered himself would be successful. The General, with the honor of a soldier and fidelity of a good citizen, immediately dispatched a trusty officer to me with information of what had passed, proceeding to establish such an understanding with the Spanish commandant on the Sabine as permitted him to withdraw his force across the Mississippi and to enter on measures for opposing the projected enterprise.

The General's letter, which came to hand on the 25th of November, as has been mentioned, and some other information received a few days earlier, when brought together developed Burr's general designs, different parts of which only had been revealed to different informants. It appeared that he contemplated two distinct objects, which might be carried on either jointly or separately, and either the one or the other first, as circumstances should direct. One of these was the severance of the Union of these States by the Alleghany Mountains; the other an attack on Mexico. A third object was provided, merely ostensible, to wit, the settlement of a pretended purchase of a tract of country on the Washita claimed by a Baron Bastrop. This was to serve as the pretext for all his preparations, an allurement for such followers as really wished to acquire settlements in that country and a cover under which to retreat in the event of a final discomfiture of both branches of his real design.

He found at once that the attachment of the Western country to the present Union was not to be shaken; that its dissolution could not be effected with the consent of its inhabitants, and that his resources were inadequate as yet to effect it by force. He took his course then at once, determined to seize on New Orleans, plunder the bank there, possess himself of the military and naval stores, and proceed on his expedition to Mexico, and to this object all his means and preparations were now directed. He collected from all the quarters where himself or his agents possessed influence all the ardent, restless, desperate, and disaffected persons who were ready for any enterprise analogous to their characters. He seduced good and well-meaning citizens, some by assurances that he possessed the confidence of the Government and was acting under its secret patronage, a pretense which procured some credit from the state of our differences with Spain, and others by offers of land in Bastrop's claim on the Washita.

This was the state of my information of his proceedings about the last of November, at which time, therefore, it was first possible to take specific measures to meet them. The proclamation of November 27, two days after the receipt of General Wilkinson's information, was now issued. Orders were dispatched to every interesting point on the Ohio and Mississippi from Pittsburg to New Orleans for the employment of such force either of the regulars or of the militia and of such proceedings also of the civil authorities as might enable them to seize on all the boats and stores provided for the enterprise, to arrest the persons concerned, and to suppress effectually the further progress of the enterprise. A little before the receipt of these orders in the State of Ohio our confidential agent, who had been diligently employed in investigating the conspiracy, had acquired sufficient information to open himself to the governor of that State and apply for the immediate exertion of the authority and power of the State to crush the combination. Governor Tiffin and the legislature, with a promptitude, an energy, and patriotic zeal which entitle them to a distinguished place in the affection of their sister States, effected the seizure of all the boats, provisions, and other preparations within their reach, and thus gave a first blow, materially disabling the enterprise in its outset.

In Kentucky a premature attempt to bring Burr to justice without sufficient evidence for his conviction had produced a popular impression in his favor and a general disbelief of his guilt. This gave him an unfortunate opportunity of hastening his equipments. The arrival of the proclamation and orders and the application and information of our confidential agent at length awakened the authorities of that State to the truth, and then produced the same promptitude and energy of which the neighboring State had set the example. Under an act of their legislature of December 23 militia was instantly ordered to different important points, and measures taken for doing whatever could yet be done. Some boats (accounts vary from five to double or treble that number) and persons (differently estimated from 100 to 300) had in the meantime passed the Falls of Ohio to rendezvous at the mouth of Cumberland with others expected down that river.

Not apprised till very late that any boats were building on Cumberland, the effect of the proclamation had been trusted to for some time in the State of Tennessee; but on the 19th of December similar communications and instructions with those to the neighboring States were dispatched by express to the governor and a general officer of the western division of the State, and on the 23rd of December our confidential agent left Frankfort for Nashville to put into activity the means of that State also. But by information received yesterday I learn that on the 22d of December Mr. Burr descended the Cumberland with two boats merely of accommodation, carrying with him from that State no quota toward his unlawful enterprise. Whether after the arrival of the proclamation, of the orders, or of our agent any exertion which could be made by that State or the orders of the governor of Kentucky for calling out the militia at the mouth of Cumberland would be in time to arrest these boats and those from the Falls of Ohio is still doubtful.

On the whole, the fugitives from the Ohio, with their associates from Cumberland or any other place in that quarter, can not threaten serious danger to the city of New Orleans.

By the same express of December 19 orders were sent to the governors of Orleans and Mississippi, supplementary to those which had been given on the 25th of November, to hold the militia of their Territories in readiness to cooperate for their defense with the regular troops and armed vessels then under command of General Wilkinson. Great alarm, indeed, was excited at New Orleans by the exaggerated accounts of Mr. Burr, disseminated through his emissaries, of the armies and navies he was to assemble there. General Wilkinson had arrived there himself on the 24th of November, and had immediately put into activity the resources of the place for the purpose of its defense, and on the 10th of December he was joined by his troops from the Sabine. Great zeal was shewn by the inhabitants generally, the merchants of the place readily agreeing to the most laudable exertions and sacrifices for manning the armed vessels with their seamen, and the other citizens manifesting unequivocal fidelity to the Union and a spirit of determined resistance to their expected assailants.

Surmises have been hazarded that this enterprise is to receive aid from certain foreign powers; but these surmises are without proof or probability. The wisdom of the measures sanctioned by Congress at its last session has placed us in the paths of peace and justice with the only powers with whom we had any differences, and nothing has happened since which makes it either their interest or ours to pursue another course. No change of measures has taken place on our part; none ought to take place at this time. With the one, friendly arrangement was then proposed, and the law deemed necessary on the failure of that was suspended to give time for a fair trial of the issue. With the same power friendly arrangement is now proceeding under good expectations, and the same law deemed necessary on failure of that is still suspended, to give time for a fair trial of the issue. With the other, negotiation was in like manner then preferred, and provisional measures only taken to meet the event of rupture. With the same power negotiation is still preferred, and provisional measures only are necessary to meet the event of rupture. While, therefore, we do not deflect in the slightest degree from the course we then assumed and are still pursuing with mutual consent to restore a good understanding, we are not to impute to them practices as irreconcilable to interest as to good faith, and changing necessarily the relations of peace and justice between us to those of war. These surmises are therefore to be imputed to the vauntings of the author of this enterprise to multiply his partisans by magnifying the belief of his prospects and support.

By letters from General Wilkinson of the 14th and 18th of December, which came to hand two days after the date of the resolution of the House of Representatives—that is to say, on the morning of the 18th instant—I received the important affidavit a copy of which I now communicate, with extracts of so much of the letters as comes within the scope of the resolution. By these it will be seen that of three of the principal emissaries of Mr. Burr whom the General had caused to be apprehended, one had been liberated by habeas corpus, and two others, being those particularly employed in the endeavor to corrupt the general and army of the United States, have been embarked by him for ports in the Atlantic States, probably on the consideration that an impartial trial could not be expected during the present agitations of New Orleans, and that that city was not as yet a safe place of confinement. As soon as these persons shall arrive they will be delivered to the custody of the law and left to such course of trial, both as to place and process, as its functionaries may direct. The presence of the highest judicial authorities, to be assembled at this place within a few days, the means of pursuing a sounder course of proceedings here than elsewhere, and the aid of the Executive means, should the judges have occasion to use them, render it equally desirable for the criminals as for the public that, being already removed from the place where they were first apprehended, the first regular arrest should take place here, and the course of proceedings receive here its proper direction.

TH: JEFFERSON

To MRS. HOFFMAN, *June 4th, 1807* You can little conceive the talents for procrastination that have been exhibited in this affair. Day after day have we been disappointed by the non-arrival of the magnanimous Wilkinson; day after day have fresh murmurs and complaints been uttered; and day after day are we told that the next mail will probably bring his noble self, or at least some accounts when he may be expected. We are now enjoying a kind suspension of hostilities; the grand jury having been dismissed the day before yesterday for five or six days, that they might go home, see to their wives, get their clothes washed, and flog their negroes. As yet we are not even on the threshold of a trial; and, if the great hero of the South does not arrive, it is a chance if we have any trial this term. I am told the Attorney-General talks of moving the Court next Tuesday for a continuance and a special court, by which means the present grand jury (the most enlightened, perhaps, that was ever assembled in this country) will be discharged; the witnesses will be dismissed; many of whom live such a distance off that it is a chance if half of them will ever be again collected. The Government will again be subjected to immense expense, Col. Burr, besides being harassed and detained for an additional space of time, will have to repeat the enormous expenditures which the trial has already caused him. I am very much mistaken, if the most under-hand and ungenerous measures have not been observed towards him. He, however, retains his serenity and self-possession unshaken, and wears the same aspect in all times and situations. I am impatient for the arrival of this Wilkinson, that the whole matter may be put to rest; and I never was more mistaken in my calculations, if the whole will not have a most farcical termination as it respects the charges against Col. Burr.

Life and Letters of Washington Irving, I., 191.

To JAMES K. PAULDING—*Richmond, June 22, 1807* I can appoint no certain time for my return, as it depends entirely upon the trial. Wilkinson, you will observe, has arrived; the bets were against Burr that he would abscond, should W. come to Richmond; but he still maintains his ground, and still enters the court every morning with the same serene and placid air that he would show were he brought there to plead another man's cause, and not his own.

The lawyers are continually entangling each other in law points, motions, and authentics, and have been so crusty to each other, that there is a constant sparring going on. Wilkinson is now before the grand jury, and has such a mighty mass of *words* to deliver himself of, that he claims at least two days more to discharge the wondrous cargo. The jury are tired enough of his verbosity. The first interview between him and Burr was highly interesting, and I secured a good place to witness it. Burr was seated with his back to the entrance, facing the judge, and conversing with one of his counsel. Wilkinson strutted into court, and took his stand in a parallel line with Burr on his right hand. Here he stood for a moment swelling like a turkey-cock, and bracing himself up for the encounter of Burr's eye. The latter did not take any notice of him until the judge directed the clerk to swear Gen. Wilkinson; at the mention of the name Burr turned his head, looked him full in the face with one of his piercing regards, swept his eye over his whole person from head to foot, as if to scan its dimensions, and then coolly resumed his former position, and went on conversing with his counsel as tranquilly as ever. The whole look was over in an instant; but it was an admirable one. There was no appearance of study or constraint in it; no affectation of disdain or defiance; a slight expression of contempt played over his countenance, such as you would show on regarding any person to whom you were indifferent, but whom you considered mean and contemptible. Wilkinson did not remain in court many minutes.

Life and Letters of Washington Irving, I., 194.

To MISS MARY FAIRLIE—*Washington City, July 7, 1807* I have seen traits of female goodness while at Richmond, that have sunk deeply in my heart—not displayed in one or two individual instances, but frequently and generally manifested; I allude to the case of Col. Burr. Whatever may be his innocence or guilt, in respect to the charges alleged against him, (and God knows I do not pretend to decide thereon,) his situation is such as should appeal eloquently to the feelings of every generous bosom. Sorry am I to say, the reverse has been the fact—fallen, proscribed, prejudged, the cup of bitterness has been administered to him with an unsparing hand. It has almost been considered as culpable to evince towards him the least sympathy or support; and many a hollow-hearted caitiff have I seen, who basked in the sunshine of his bounty, when in power, who now skulked from his side, and even mingled among the most clamorous of his enemies. The ladies alone have felt, or at least had candor and independence sufficient to express, those feelings which do honor to humanity. They have been uniform in their expressions of compassion for his misfortunes, and a hope for his acquittal; not a lady, I believe, in Richmond, whatever may be her husband's sentiments on the subject, who would not rejoice at seeing Col. Burr at liberty. It may be said that Col. Burr has ever been a favorite with the sex; but I am not inclined to account for it in so illiberal a manner; it results from that merciful, that heavenly disposition, implanted in the female bosom, which ever inclines in favor of the accused and the unfortunate. You will smile at the high strain in which I have indulged; believe me, it is because I feel it; and I love your sex ten times better than ever. The last time I saw Burr was the day before I left Richmond. He was then in the Penitentiary, a kind of State prison. The only reason given for immuring him in this abode of thieves, cut-throats, and incendiaries, was that it would save the United States a couple of hundred dollars, (the charge of guarding him at his lodgings,) and it would insure the security of his person. This building stands about a mile and a half from town, situated in a solitary place among the hills. It will prevent his counsel from being as much with him as they deemed necessary. I found great difficulty in gaining admission to him for a few moments. The keeper had orders to admit none but his counsel and his witnesses—strange measures these! That it is not sufficient that a man against whom no certainty of crime is proved, should be confined by bolts, and bars, and massy walls, in a criminal prison; but he is likewise to be cut off from all intercourse with society, deprived of all the kind offices of friendship, and made to suffer all the penalties and deprivations of a condemned criminal. I was permitted to enter for a few moments as a special favor, contrary to orders. Burr seemed in lower spirits than formerly; he was composed and collected as usual; but there was not the same cheerfulness that I have hitherto remarked. He said it was with difficulty his very servant was allowed occasionally to see him; he had a bad cold, which I suppose was occasioned by the dampness of his chamber, which had lately been whitewashed. I bid him farewell with a heavy heart, and he expressed with peculiar warmth and feeling his sense of the interest I had taken in his fate. I never felt in a more melancholy mood than when I rode from his solitary prison. Such is the last interview I had with poor Burr, and I shall never forget it. I have written myself into a sorrowful kind of a mood, so I will at once desist, begging you to receive this letter with indulgence, and regard, with an eye of Christian charity, its many imperfections.

Life and Letters of Washington Irving, I., 201.

13

The Embargo

A Defence and an Attack

Caught between the upper and nether millstones of the belligerents' war machines, neutral rights were ground exceedingly small. Neither France nor Great Britain would permit neutral trade to benefit its adversary and each power sought to control the commerce of the neutrals in its own interest. In the Berlin and Milan Decrees of 1806–1807, Napoleon declared the British Isles to be in a state of blockade and ordered the confiscation of every neutral ship that touched at a British port or carried British merchandise. The British government retaliated with the Orders in Council of 1807, which required all neutral ships carrying cargoes to French-controlled Europe to touch first at a British port, there to pay taxes, port duties, handling charges and re-exportation duties and finally, to buy a license that permitted them to proceed to their European destinations.

Unofficial reports of the Order in Council of November 11, 1807, reached President Jefferson late in December. His immediate conclusion was that the British intended to lay claim to absolute dominion of the sea and to prescribe the terms and conditions under which other nations might navigate upon it. By the President's reckoning, Great Britain had challenged the United States to war, yet he did not pick up the gauntlet. Instead, he saw in the crisis a providential opportunity to put into effect his long-cherished plan of coercing Great Britain into showing a decent respect for the rights of neutrals by depriving the island kingdom of the

[William Branch] Giles, *Speech on the Resolution of Mr. Hillhouse, to Repeal the Embargo Laws, November 24, 1808* (Boston, [1808]), pp. 4–15, in Albert Bushnell Hart, ed., *American History Told by Contemporaries* (New York: The Macmillan Company, 1901), III, pp. 403–06; William Cullen Bryant, *The Embargo; Or, Sketches of the Times, a Satire* . . . 2nd ed. (Boston: E. G. House, 1809), pp. 7–20, in Thomas O. Mabbott, ed., *The Embargo by William Cullen Bryant, Facsimile Reproductions of the Editions of 1808 and 1809 With an Introduction and Notes* (Gainesville, Fla.: Scholars' Facsimiles and Reprints, 1955), pp. 35–48.

economic and financial sustenance it drew from trade with the United States. The President therefore recommended to Congress the adoption of an embargo confining American merchant ships to port and prohibiting foreign ships from carrying away any cargo grown or produced in the United States. Congress promptly carried out the President's plan. The United States thereby undertook to ascertain "by a fair experiment . . . the power of this great weapon, the embargo." Senator William Branch Giles (1762–1830) of Virginia was a close friend and ardent supporter of President Jefferson. His speeches usually reflected the thinking of the administration and the address delivered in 1808 in defense of the embargo was no exception.

Politically, the embargo benefited the Federalist party. Just at the moment it seemed headed for oblivion, President Jefferson's efforts to establish American rights at sea by means of a self-imposed blockade rejuvenated the party. In the elections of 1808, Federalism gained strength in New England, New York, New Jersey, and Delaware. With some important exceptions, the mercantile interests which President Jefferson had seemed to be on the point of detaching from the Federalists and incorporating into the Republican party were now arrayed against him. Despite this political reverse, President Jefferson consoled himself with the reflection that war would have been even more disastrous in its consequences to the United States. The abhorrence in which the embargo and President Jefferson himself were held by New England Federalists clearly emerges in William Cullen Bryant's poem, *The Embargo* (1808). Bryant (1794–1878), later to be acclaimed as the greatest poet of his generation, enjoined President Jefferson to

> Go, scan, Philosophist, thy Sally's charms,
> And sink supinely in her sable arms;
> But quit to abler hands the helm of state.

The Sally of the poem was one of Jefferson's slaves by whom he was alleged to have had several children. As Bryant was at the time only thirteen years old, obviously he was knowledgeable beyond his years upon matters not usually considered fit to mention in a New England parlor or poem. But in Federalist circles, when the morals of President Jefferson were under discussion, the proprieties were cheerfully dispensed with.

Again, one might consult Henry Adams's *History of the United States* for both the domestic and overseas aspects of Jefferson's experiment in economic sanctions. Louis M. Sears has written the standard account in his *Jefferson and the Embargo* (Durham: Duke University Press, 1927). For Giles's part in the politics of the period see Dice Robins Anderson, *William Branch Giles: A Study in the Politics of Virginia and the Nation from 1790 to 1830* (Menasha, Wisc.: George Banta Publishing Company, 1914). A satisfactory life of Bryant is Parke Godwin, *A Biography of William Cullen Bryant, with Extracts from His Private Correspondence,* 2 vols. (New York: D. Appleton and Company, 1883).

In reading Senator Giles's speech note (1) the choices he thought the United States faced in dealing with the depredations of the European belligerents; (2) what effects, in his judgment, the embargo had had in protecting American property and American seamen; (3) his response to the charge that American seamen had been driven from the country by the embargo; (4) what he thought the embargo had preserved for the United States; (5) the effects he thought the embargo had had upon England and France; (6) why, in his opinion, the British had refused to revoke the hated Orders in Council; and (7) the consequences he envisaged should the United States attempt to protect its commerce by force. In reading Bryant's poem note (1) the form and style employed; (2) his characterization of President Jefferson; (3) his description of the effects of the embargo upon various economic sectors; (4) the foreign interests he implies Jefferson is serving; (5) the purport of the call to action he sounds; (6) his suggestions for Jefferson's future occupation; (7) the views of democracy he expresses; (8) his proposals for meeting the emergency; and (9) the promise he voices for the future once America's foreign and domestic enemies are laid low.

MR. PRESIDENT, I HAVE ALWAYS UNDERSTOOD THAT there were two objects contemplated by the embargo laws—The first, precautionary, operating upon ourselves—The second, coercive, operating upon the aggressing belligerents. Precautionary, in saving our seamen, our ships and our merchandize from the plunder of our enemies, and avoiding the calamities of war. Coercive, by addressing strong appeals to the interests of both the belligerents. The first object has been answered beyond my most sanguine expectations. To make a fair and just estimate of this measure, reference should be had to our situation at the time of its adoption. At that time, the aggressions of both the belligerents were such, as to leave the United States but a painful alternative in the choice of one of three measures, to wit, the embargo, war, or submission. . . .

It was found that merchandize to the value of one hundred millions of dollars was actually afloat, in vessels amounting in value to twenty millions more—That an amount of merchandize and vessels equal to fifty millions more, was expected to be shortly put afloat, and that it would require fifty thousand seamen to be employed in the navigation of that enormous amount of property. The administration was informed of the hostile edicts of France previously issued, and then in a state of execution, and of an intention on the part of Great Britain to issue her orders, the character and object of which were also known. The object was, to sweep this valuable commerce from the ocean.—The situation of this commerce was as well known to Great Britain, as to ourselves, and her inordinate cupidity could not withstand the temptation of the rich booty, she vainly thought within her power. This was the state of information at the time this measure was recommended.

The President of the United States ever watchful and anxious for the preservation of the persons and property of all our fellow citizens, but particularly of the merchants, whose property is most exposed to danger, and of the seamen whose persons are also most exposed, recommended the embargo for the protection of both; and it has saved and protected both. . . . It is admitted by all, that the embargo laws have saved this enormous amount of property, and this number of seamen, which, without them, would have forcibly gone into the hands of our enemies, to pamper their arrogance, stimulate their injustice, and increase their means of annoyance.

I should suppose, Mr. President, this saving worth some notice. But, Sir, we are told that instead of protecting our seamen, it has driven them out of the country, and into foreign service. I believe, Sir, that this fact is greatly exaggerated. But, Sir, suppose for a moment that it is so, the government has done all, in this respect, it was bound to do. It placed these seamen in the bosoms of their friends and families, in a state of perfect security; and if they have since thought proper to abandon these blessings, and emigrate from their country, it was an act of choice, not of necessity. . . .

. . . But, Sir, these are not the only good effects of the embargo. It has *preserved our peace—it has saved our honor—it has saved our national independence*. Are these savings not worth notice? Are these blessings not worth preserving? . . .

The gentleman next triumphantly tells us that the embargo laws have not had their expected effects upon the aggressing belligerents. That they have not had their complete effects; that they have not caused a revocation of the British orders and French decrees, will readily be admitted; but they certainly have not been without beneficial effects upon those nations. . . .

The first effect of the embargo, upon the aggressing belligerents, was to lessen their inducements to war, by keeping out of their way, the rich spoils of our commerce, which had invited their cupidity, and which was saved by those laws. . . .

The second effect, which the embargo laws have had on the aggressing belligerents, is to enhance [the] prices of all American produce, especially articles of the first necessity to them, to a considerable degree, and, if it be a little longer persisted in, will either banish our produce, (which I believe indispensable to them,) from their markets altogether, or increase the prices to an enormous amount—and, of course, we may hope will furnish irresistible inducements for a relaxation of their hostile orders & edicts. . . .

All these considerations must present strong inducements to Great Britain to revoke her hostile orders; but she has hitherto refused to do so.

Let a candid inquiry be now made into the actual causes of this refusal. The gentleman from Massachusetts, (Mr. Lloyd) informs us, that the British cabinet shewed some solicitude about the embargo laws, till some time between the 22d of June and the 29th of July last, within which time, information flowed in upon them, which relieved them from this solicitude . . .

What was the information that flowed in upon the British cabinet, from the 22d June to the 29th July? That period announced two events. First, the wonderful revolution in Spain; although this event must have been pretty well understood in London before even the 22d June, perhaps not to its full extent. The other event was, the paltry attempt at the resistance of the embargo laws in Vermont, magnified into a formidable insurrection against the government; and the unhappy discontents manifested in Boston and its neighborhood, together with the results of the elections in Massachusetts. All these circumstances were certainly greatly exaggerated, or perhaps, utterly misrepresented. Here, then sir, we clearly discern the real causes of the refusal of the British cabinet to meet the just and honorable proposition of the United States, and to revoke their orders in council. The Spanish revolution, no doubt, contributed to their determination; but the principal cause, was our [own] divisions and discontents, either wholly misrepresented or highly exaggerated. . . .

. . . The refusal of the British government, to revoke their hostile orders, therefore, appears not to have been founded upon a calculation of its interests upon correct information; but upon a miscalculation of its interests upon misinformation. . . .

It is asked, Sir, how do the embargo laws operate on France? It is readily admitted, that the commercial connection between the United States and France, is not of such a nature as to make a suspension of it operate as injuriously to France herself particularly in the interior, as on G. Britain. But our commerce cannot be deemed unimportant to France in the feeble state of her navy. . . .

The French West India islands too, have felt the pressure with great severity. . . .

I think . . . Sir, I am warranted in concluding, that if the embargo laws have failed of complete success, their failure has been owing to extraordinary causes which could neither have been foreseen nor anticipated at the time of the adoption of the measure, and therefore cannot furnish any imputation against its policy or wisdom.

. . . I have said, Sir, that there are no substitutes for the embargo, but *war or submission.* I will now proceed to prove this position—a repeal of the embargo without a substitute, is *submission*, if with a substitute, it is *war*. Gentlemen in the opposition, seem fully sensible of the delicacy and urgency of this part of the question. When pressed their substitute, they manifest vast reluctance in producing it. . . .

. . . the gentleman from Connecticut . . . intimates merely that he is in favor of an armed commerce. . . .

Would he extend it to acts of reprisal? If so, it is immediate war.—Would he stop short of that. It would still be war; but of a more inefficient kind. If our vessels are to arm, I presume their arms are to be used in self defence; they would be used against both the belligerents. In the present temper of Great-Britain, the first gun fired in a spirit of hostility, even with a blank cartridge; or if it were a popgun, would be instant war. It would be the signal to her navy to seize upon the whole of our commerce, which would be spread over the ocean, the moment of raising the embargo. The gentleman's substitute I, therefore, believe to be war, and war of the most inefficient kind. A repeal of the embargo, without a substitute, is submission.—Submis[s]ion to what! to colonization, to taxation, to tribute!!

The Embargo
William Cullen Bryant

When private faith and public trust are sold,
And traitors barter liberty for gold;
When fell corruption, dark, and deep, like fate,
Saps the foundation of a sinking state;
Then warmer numbers glow through satire's page,
And all her smiles are darken'd into rage;
Then keener indignation fires her eye,
Then flash her lightnings, and her thunders fly!

ESSAY ON SATIRE

LOOK where we will, and in whatever land,
Europe's rich soil, or Afric's barren sand,
Where the wild savage hunts his wilder prey,
Or art and science pour their brightest day,
The monster *Vice* appears before our eyes,
In naked impudence, or gay disguise.

But quit the meaner game indignant muse,
And to thy country turn thy nobler views;
Ill-fated clime! condemn'd to feel th' extremes,
Of a weak ruler's philosophic dreams;
Driven headlong on, to ruin's fateful brink,
When will thy country feel, when will she think!

Satiric muse, shall injured Commerce weep
Her ravish'd rights, and will thy thunders sleep;
Dart thy keen glances, knit thy threat'ning brows,
Call fire from heaven to blast thy country's foes.
Oh let a youth thine inspiration learn—
Oh give him "words that breathe and thoughts
    that burn!"

Curse of our nation, source of countless woes,
From whose dark womb unreckon'd misery flows;
Th' Embargo rages, like a sweeping wind,
Fear lowers before, and famine stalks behind.
What words, oh Muse! can paint the mournful scene,
The saddening street, the desolated green;
How hungry labourers leave their toil and sigh,
And sorrow droops in each desponding eye!

See the bold Sailor from the Ocean torn,
His element, sink friendless and forlorn!
His suffering spouse the tear of anguish shed,
His starving children cry in vain for bread!
On the rough billows of misfortune tost,
Resources fail, and all his hopes are lost;
To foreign climes, for that relief he flies,
His native land ungratefully denies.

In vain Mechanics ply their curious art,
And bootless mourn the interdicted mart;
While our sage *Ruler's* diplomatic skill,
Subjects our councils to his sovereign will;
His grand '*restrictive energies*' employs,
And wisely regulating trade—destroys.

The Farmer, since supporting trade is fled,
Leaves the rude joke, and cheerless hangs his head;
Misfortunes fall, an unremitting shower,
Debts follow debts, on taxes, taxes pour,—
See in his stores his hoarded produce rot,
Or Sheriff sales his profits bring to naught;
Disheartening cares in thronging myriads flow,
Till down he sinks to poverty and woe!

Ye, who rely on Jeffersonian skill;
And say that fancy paints ideal ill;
Go, on the wings of observation fly,
Cast o'er the land a scrutinizing eye;
States, counties, towns, remark with keen review,
Let *facts* convince and own the picture true!

Oh, ye bright pair! the blessing of mankind,
Whom time has sanction'd, and whom fate has join'd,
COMMERCE, that bears the trident of the main,
And AGRICULTURE, empress of the plain;
Who hand in hand, and heav'n-directed, go
Diffusing gladness through the world below;
Whoe'er the wretch, would hurl the flaming brand

Of dire disunion, palsied be his hand!
Like 'Cromwell damn'd to everlasting fame,'
Let unborn ages execrate his name!

How foul a blot Columbia's glory stains!
How dark the scene! infatuation reigns!
For French intrigue which wheedles to devour,
Threatens to fix us in Napoleon's power;
Anon within th' insatiate vortex whirl'd,
Whose wide periphery involves the world.

Oh, heaven defend, as future seasons roll,
These western climes from Bonaparte's control;
Preserve our freedom, and our rights secure,
While truth subsists, and virtue shall endure!
Lo Austria crouches to the tyrant's stroke,
And bends proud Rome beneath his galling yoke;
Infuriate, reeking with the spoils of war,
O'er prostrate kingdoms rolls his blood-stain'd car;
Embattled hosts in vain his fury meet,
Sceptres and crowns he treads beneath his feet.

Aspiring Belgia, once the patriot's pride,
When barbarous Alva, her brave sons defied;
The nurse of arts, th' advent'rous merchant's boast,
Whose wide-spread commerce whiten'd every coast.
Humbled, degraded, by the vilest arts,
Beneath his iron scourge, succumbing smarts;
The crowded city, the canal's green shore,
Fair haunts of free-born opulence, no more!

Ah, hapless land! where freedom lov'd to dwell,
Helvetia's fall, what weeping bard shall tell!
Warn'd too by Lusitania's fate, beware!—
Columbians wake! evade the deep laid snare!
Insensate! shall we ruin court, and fall,
Slaves to the proud autocrator of Gaul?
Our laws laid prostrate by his ruthless hand,
And independence banish'd from our land!

We who seven years erst brav'd Britannia's power,
By Heaven supported in the gloomiest hour;
For whom our Sages plann'd, our Heroes bled,
Whom WASHINGTON, our pride, and glory led;
Till heaven propitious did our efforts crown
With freedom, commerce, plenty, and renown.

When shall this land, some courteous angel say,
Throw off a weak, and erring ruler's sway?
Rise, injured people, vindicate your cause!
And prove your love of liberty and laws;
Oh wrest, sole refuge of a sinking land,
The sceptre from the slave's imbecile hand!
Oh ne'er consent, obsequious, to advance,
The *willing vassal* of imperious France!
Correct that suffrage you misus'd before,
And lift your voice above a congress roar.

And thou, the scorn of every patriot name,
Thy country's ruin, and her council's shame!
Poor servile thing! derision of the brave!
Who erst from Tarleton fled to Carter's cave;
Thou, who, when menac'd by perfidious Gaul,
Didst prostrate to her whisker'd minion fall;
And when our cash her empty bags supply'd,
Didst meanly strive the foul disgrace to hide;
Go, wretch, resign the presidential chair,
Disclose thy secret measures, foul or fair.
Go, search with curious eye, for horned frogs,
Mid the wild wastes of Louisianian bogs;
Or, where Ohio rolls his turbid stream,
Dig for huge bones, thy glory and thy theme.
Go, scan, Philosophist, thy ****** charms
And sink supinely in her sable arms;
But quit to abler hands the helm of state,
Nor image ruin on thy country's fate!

Ah hapless State! with wayward councils curst,
Blind to thy weal, and to thy laws unjust;—
For, where their blasting '*energies*' extend,
Foes undermine and dire divisions rend;—
Who shall sustain thy gradual sinking form,
And guide thee safely through the gathering storm?
What guardian Angel shall conduct thee o'er
Misfortune's ocean to a peaceful shore?—
Remove the source whence all thy troubles rose,
And shield from foreign and domestic foes!

Oh for a WASHINGTON, whose boundless mind,
Infolds his friends, his country, and mankind;
He might restore our happy state again,
And roll our Navy o'er the billowy main;
From all our shores bid lawless pirates fly,
And lift our wond'ring Eagle to the sky!

But vain are reason, eloquence, and art,
And vain the warm effusions of the heart.
E'en while I sing, see Faction urge her claim,
Mislead with falsehood, and with zeal inflame;
Lift her black banner, spread her empire wide,
And stalk triumphant with a fury's stride.
She blows her brazen trump, and at the sound,
A motley throng, obedient, flock around;
A mist of changing hue, o'er all she flings,
And darkness perches on her dragon wings!

As Johnson deep, as Addison refin'd,
And skill'd to pour conviction o'er the mind,
Oh, might some patriot rise! the gloom dispel,
Chase error's mist, and break her magic spell!

But vain the wish, for hark! the murmuring meed
Of hoarse applause from yonder shed proceed;
Enter, and view the thronging concourse there,
Intent, with gaping mouth, and stupid stare;
While in the midst their supple leader stands,
Harangues aloud, and flourishes his hands;
To adulation tunes his servile throat,
And sues successful for each blockhead's vote.

"The advocate of *liberty* I stand,—
Oh were I made a ruler in the land!
Your interests none more cherishes than I,
In your sweet service, may I live and die!
For the dear *people*, how my bowels yearn!—
That *such* may govern be your chief concern;
Then *federalism*, and all its lordling train,
Shall fall disgrac'd before our *equal* reign;
Dismay'd, diminish'd, our fair presence shun,
As shadows shorten to the rising sun;

Spontaneous banquests shall succeed to want,
No tax shall vex you, and no sheriff haunt."

The powerful influence of the knave's address,
In capers droll, the foolish dupes express;
With *horrid* shouts th' affrighted sky is rent,
And high in air their tatter'd hats are sent.

But should truth shine distinguishingly bright,
And lay his meanness naked to the sight;
He tries new arts to blind their willing eyes,
Feeds with new flatt'ries, hammers out new lies,
Exerts his influence, urges all his weight,
To blast the laurels of the good and great;
Till reconfirm'd, the fools uphold him still,
Their creed his *dictum*, and their law his will.

Now morning rises borne on golden wings,
And fresh to toil the waking post-boy springs;
Lo, trudging on his raw bon'd steed he hies,
Dispersing Suns, and Chronicles, and Spys.
Men uninform'd, in rage for something new,
Howe'er unprincipled, howe'er untrue,
Suck in with greedy throat the gilded pill,
Whose fatal sweetness pleases but to kill.
Wide, and more wide the dire contagion flies,
Till half the town is overwhelm'd with lies.
Hence that delusion, hence that furious zeal,
Which wrong-heads cherish, and which hot-heads feel.

Oh, snatch me heaven! to some sequester'd spot,
Where Jefferson, and faction, are forgot;
Where never 'Suns' nor 'Chronicles' molest,
Duane and Colvin unregarded rest.
Sick of the tumult, where the noisy throng,
In wild disorder, roar of right and wrong;
Where lying pamphlets round the town are sped,
And knowing politicians talk you dead!

In vain *Italia* boats her genial clime,
Her Rome's proud towers, and palaces sublime;
In vain the hardy Swiss, inur'd to toil,

Draw scant subsistence from a stubborn soil;
Both doom'd alike, to feel, in evil hour,
The giant grasp of huge despotic power!
Touch not their shores, fair freedom dwells not there,
But far remote, she breathes Columbian air;
Yet here, her temple totters to its fall,
Shook from its centre by gigantic Gaul!

Oh, let not prating *History* proclaim,
The foul disgrace, the scandal of our name!
Write not the deed my hand! Oh may it lie,
Plung'd deep, and mantled in obscurity!
Forbid it heaven! that while true honour reigns,
And ancient valour glows within our veins,
(Our standard justice, and our shield our God,)
We e'er should tremble at a despot's nod!

Oh, may the laurels of unrival'd fame,
For ever flourish round your honour'd name!
Ye, who unthrall'd by prejudice, or power,
Determin'd stood in that eventful hour;
Tore the dire secret from the womb of night,
And brought your country's infamy to light!
Go boldly on the deep-laid plot unfold,
Though much is known, yet much remains untold.
But chief to thee our gratitude belongs,
Oh Pickering!* who hast scan'd thy country's wrongs,
Whose ardent mind, and keen discerning eye,
Trac'd out the true Embargo policy;
Shew'd that our Chief, unable to control,
The alien yearnings of his dastard soul;
And curst with feelings hostile to our trade,
At beck of France, the dire restriction laid!

Hail first of Statesmen! Massachusetts' pride!
Fam'd in her wars, and in her councils try'd;
Long to thy friends by private worth endear'd,

* Editor's Note: Timothy Pickering (1745–1829) of Massachusetts, one-time
  Secretary of War in Washington's second administration, Secretary of State
  from 1795 to 1800, and United States Senator from Massachusetts, 1803–
  1811. Anti-French Federalist to the core, Pickering at the time of the Louisiana
  Purchase proposed establishing a northern confederacy. During the controversy arising out of the embargo he suggested calling a New England
  convention to nullify the embargo.

"In pure majestic poverty rever'd;"
At thy rebuke, (though late so monstrous grown,)
Corruption trembles on her venal throne!
Oh, may the people, with attentive eyes,
Peruse thy well-tim'd warnings and be wise!

Mournful reverse! the muse with grief would trace,
The painful scene of thy colleague's disgrace,
Unhappy he, by glare of *office* lur'd,
Renounc'd the truth, and federal faith abjur'd!
With fine spun sophisms, and inflated style,
Strove to mislead, bewilder, and beguile;
O'er presidential error gently spread
The flimsy veil, perverted reason made,
Virtue abash'd beheld th' apostate's zeal,
And freedom trembled for the public weal;
Till Coleman rose, by honest anger led,
And at his touch the gay delusion fled;
The veil disparts, the painted bubbles burst,
The splendid fabric crumbles into dust!

Go on, ye pimps of France! intriguers fell!
Wind your dark ways, and aid the work of hell!
Go, rouse dire *faction* from her gloomy den,
Wake the worst passions in the breasts of men;
O'er a once free, once heaven-protected land,
Impel the tempest with infuriate hand;
Go, lure the simple, with unfaithful views,
To paths where error her wild way pursues;
But soon from heaven, shall justice wing her way,
Arrest your course, and immolate her prey!

So prays the muse;—while bursting on the sight,
Hope's torch diffuses an enlivening light;
And scenes, prophetic of Columbia's rise
To former glory, greet the gladden'd eyes.

Rous'd by the murmurs of the coming storm,
Lo, freedom's genius lifts her radiant form!
Rolls her keen eye, and hovering o'er the land,
Calls in loud thunders to her slumbering band.

Far o'er the realm, electric, unconfin'd,
Flies the quick flame, and runs from mind to mind.
Wak'd from her stupid lethargy, at length
Old Massachusetts, feels returning strength;
Her sons, reflecting, break the baneful league,
With factious zeal, and popular intrigue;
No more they hug delusion's magic chain,
Nor grasp at objects, fleeting, and inane;
But break the charm, false, flatt'ring error binds,
The pleasing mania, that enchain'd their minds.

And now as *Truth* with growing lustre shines,
Before her beams Democracy declines;
Vain are all arts her baffled leaders try,
And vain alike, to flatter or to lie.
From their long sleep alarm'd the people rise,
And spite of sophisms, learn to trust their eyes.

Rise then, Columbians! heed not France's wiles,
Her bullying mandates, her seductive smiles;
Send home Napoleon's slave, and bid him say
No arts can lure us, and no threats dismay;
Determin'd yet to war with whom we will,
Choose our allies, or dare be 'neutral' still.

Ye merchants arm! the tyrant Gaul repel,
Your prowess shall the naval triumph swell;
Send the marauders shatter'd whence they came,
And Gallia's cheed suffuse with crimson shame.
But first select, our councils to direct,
One whose true worth entitles to respect:
In whom concentrates all that men admire,
The Sage's prudence, and the Soldier's fire;
Who scorns ambition, and the venal tribe,
And neither offers, nor receives a bribe;
Who firmly guards his country's every right,
And shines alike, in council, or in fight.

Then on safe seas, the merchant's barque shall fly,
Our waving flag, shall kiss the polar sky;
On canvass wings our thunders shall be borne,
Far to the west, or tow'rd the rising morn;
Then may we dare a haughty tyrant's rage,
And gain the blessings of an unborn age.

'Tis done, behold, the cheerful prospects rise!
And splendid scenes the startled eye surprize;
Lo! busy Commerce courts the prosperous main,
And peace and plenty glad our shores again!
Th' industrious swain sees nature smile around,
His fields with fruit, with flocks, his pastures crown'd.

Thus, in a fallen tree, from sprouting roots,
With sudden growth, a tender sapling shoots,
Improves from day to day, delights the eyes,
With strength, and beauty, stateliness, and size,
Puts forth robuster arms, and broader leaves,
And high in air its branching head upheaves.

Turn now our views to Europe's ravag'd plains,
Where murderous war, with grim oppression reigns;
There long, and loud, the storm of battle roars,
With direful portent to our distant shores;
The regal robber, rages uncontrol'd,
No law restrains him, and no faith can hold;
Before his steps, lo! cowering terror flies,
And pil'd behind him, heaps of carnage rise!
With fraud, or force, he spreads his iron sway,
And blood, and rapine, mark his frightful way!

Thus some huge rock of ice, on Greenland's shore,
When bound in frost, the surges cease to roar,
Breaks loosen'd from its base, with mighty sweep,
And thunders horrid o'er the frozen deep.

While thus, all Europe rings with his alarms,
Say, shall we rush, unthinking, to his arms?
No; let us dauntless all his fury brave,
Our fluttering flag, in freedom's gale shall wave,
Our guardian Sachem's errless shafts shall fly,
And terrors lighten from our eagle's eye!

Hear then I cease, rewarded, if my song,
Shall prompt one honest mind, though guided wrong,
To pause from party, view his country's state,
And lend his aid to stem approaching fate.

Written, April, 1808

14

The Coming of the War of 1812

Three Speeches before Congress

The view that only by war could American rights on the high seas, and security in the West be achieved gained ground simultaneously in Congress, the administration, and the popular mind. Disenchantment with embargoes, nonimportation, nonintercourse, and all other measures short of war as a means of vindicating American rights had the effect of enhancing the attractions of war. Americans' stock of forbearance was about exhausted; even Thomas Jefferson, in retirement at Monticello, admitted that the policy of palliating and enduring no longer held out hope of redress of grievances. On the contrary, he feared that if Americans continued to submit to British exactions they would lose their sense of national identity and pride. For this reason John Adams advocated war: "[I]t is," he said, "necessary against England; necessary to convince France that we are something; and above all necessary to convince ourselves, that we are not-Nothing."

The outcome of the Congressional elections of 1810–1811 reflected this new commitment to militancy. Although the Republicans, as usual, scored a sweeping victory, over 60 of the incumbent Republicans were replaced by new members, many of whom were impatient with the Jeffersonian-Madisonian policy of economic coercion. They conceived war, not economic reprisals, to be the natural outcome of diplomacy particularly when it had become clear, as it had to them, that American rights, security, and honor could be preserved in no other way. As orators, parliamentarians, and leaders of men these newcomers—soon to be called

John Randolph, December 10, 1811; John C. Calhoun, December 12, 1811 in *The Debates and Proceedings in the Congress of the United States, First to Eighteenth Congress, March 3, 1789, to May 27, 1824, Inclusive* (Washington, D.C.: Gales and Seaton, 1854), XXIII, pp. 445–50; 454–55; 476–83. Henry Clay, January 8, 1813 in *Annals of Congress*, 12 Cong., 2 sess. (Washington, D.C.: Gales and Seaton, 1853), pp. 667–75.

War Hawks by John Randolph (1773–1833) of Virginia—were as talented as any who have sat in Congress. Chief among them were John C. Calhoun (1782–1850) of South Carolina, Felix Grundy (1777–1840) of Tennessee, and Henry Clay (1777–1852) of Kentucky.

Although the War Hawks were in a minority in Congress, the peace party represented by John Randolph was overborne by the course of events. By November, 1811, even President Madison's faith in peaceful coercion as a means of bringing Great Britain to terms had begun to erode. The repeal of the Orders in Council seemed as far away as ever; the British government stood firm upon all its claims of right including that of impressing British seamen from American merchant ships. On June 1, 1812, despairing of ever coercing the British government by commercial reprisals, President Madison delivered a message to Congress recommending that Congress consider the advisability of declaring war. Despite the War Hawks' assertion that a vote against war was "a vote for England against America," Congress was not stampeded into declaring war. The declaration did not pass the House of Representatives until June 18, 1812. The vote was 79 to 49; in the Senate, 19 votes were cast in favor, 13 were opposed.

Julius W. Pratt in his *The Expansionists of 1812* (New York: The Macmillan Company, 1925), writing in the debunking era of the 1920s, explored other causes of the War of 1812 than the violations of American maritime rights traditionally held to be the primary cause of the conflict. Two recent studies of the origins of the war worth consulting are Albert C. Carr's *The Coming of the War: An Account of the Remarkable Events Leading to the War of 1812* (Garden City: Doubleday and Company, 1960) and Bradford Perkins's *Prologue to War: England and the United States, 1805–1812* (Berkeley: The University of California Press, 1961). John Randolph, responding to remarks made by Felix Grundy advocating war against Great Britain, addressed the House of Representatives on December 10, 1811 and rehearsed the views of those opposing a war policy. In reading Randolph's speech note (1) his response to the charge that the British had encouraged the Indian massacres on the frontier; (2) what he thought was the real cause of the Indian uprisings; (3) what, in his judgment, motivated the war party; (4) who would profit and who would lose in a war against England; (5) what he thought of Napoleon's treatment of the United States and its citizens; (6) the fears he expressed should the armed forces of the United States move against Canada; (7) what he thought would be the response of the American people to war; and (8) the nature of his rhetoric. In the December, 1811 debate over military preparedness in the Congress, John C. Calhoun answered Randolph and the peace party who advocated a cautious, conciliatory policy toward Great Britain. In reading Calhoun's speech note (1) what he thought was the only means of seeking redress of American grievances against Great Britain; (2) how he answered the charges that the nation was unprepared for war and that it could not or would not pay for a war; (3) how he answered the contention that war would be unconstitutional; (4) his estimate of the spiritual impact of war upon the people; (5) his answer to the charge that America had as much reason to go to war against France as against England; and (6) what the response of the United States should be in the issue of the balance of power in Europe.

On June 23, 1812, the Orders in Council were revoked by the British government on the condition that the United States repeal the nonintercourse act forbidding American trade with Great Britain. The sailing ships carrying the news of the declaration of war by the United States and the revocation of the British Orders in Council passed each other in mid-Atlantic. President Madison rejected the British peace overtures. From his point of view, the repeal of the Orders in Council had not put an end to Great Britain's maritime despotism. Upon the subject of impressment, on which the Americans were very sensitive, the British government said not a word nor did it promise satisfaction for American shipping losses. It was equally silent upon the issue of paramount concern to western Americans—the depredations of the Indians presumably as a result of British encouragement. In reading Clay's speech note (1) what, in his opinion, was the real cause of the war; (2) the views he voiced respecting Canada; (3) his response to those who wanted to terminate the war because of the failure of American arms; (4) what he thought of the administration's handling of the issues outstanding between the United States and Great Britain; (5) how he planned to conclude the war; and (6) the character of Clay's rhetoric.

M̲R. RANDOLPH ROSE. . . .

It was a question, as it has been presented to the House, of peace or war. In that light it had been argued; in no other light could he consider it, after the declarations made by members of the Committee of Foreign Relations. . . .

An insinuation had fallen from the gentleman from Tennessee, (Mr. Grundy,) that the late [Indian] massacre of our brethren on the Wabash [River] had been instigated by the British Government. Has the President given any such information? has the gentleman received any such, even informally, from any officer of this Government? Is it so believed by the Administration? He had cause to think the contrary to be the fact; that such was not their opinion. This insinuation was of the grossest kind—a presumption the most rash, the most unjustifiable. Show but good ground for it, he would

give up the question at the threshold—he was ready to march to
Canada. It was indeed well calculated to excite the feelings of the
Western people particularly, who were not quite so tenderly
attached to our red brethren as some modern philosophers; but it
was destitute of any foundation, beyond mere surmise and
suspicion. . . .

He was sorry to say that for this signal calamity and disgrace the
House was, in part, at least, answerable. Session after session, their
table had been piled up with Indian treaties, for which the appropriations had been voted as a matter of course, without examination.
Advantage had been taken of the spirit of the Indians, broken by
the war which ended in the Treaty of Greenville [August 3, 1795].
Under the ascendency then acquired over them, they had been
pent up by subsequent treaties into nooks, straightened in their
quarters by a blind cupidity, seeking to extinguish their title to
immense wildernesses, for which, (possessing, as we do already, more
land than we can sell or use) we shall not have occasion, for half a
century to come. It was our own thirst for territory, our own want
of moderation, that had driven these sons of nature to desperation,
of which we felt the effects. . . .

He could but smile at the liberality of the gentleman, in giving
Canada to New York, in order to strengthen the Northern balance
of power, while at the same time he forwarned her that the Western
scale must preponderate. Mr. R. [Randolph] said he could almost
fancy that he saw the Capitol in motion towards the falls of Ohio—
after a short sojourn taking its flight to the Mississippi, and finally
alighting on Darien [Colombia, now Panama]; which, when the
gentleman's dreams are realized, will be a most eligible seat of
Government for the new Republic (or Empire) of the two
Americas! . . .

This war of conquest, a war for the acquisition of territory and
subjects, is to be a new commentary on the doctrine that Republics
are destitute of ambition—that they are addicted to peace, wedded
to the happiness and safety of the great body of their people. But
it seems this is to be a holiday campaign—there is to be no expense
of blood, or treasure, on our part—Canada is to conquer herself—
she is to be subdued by the principles of fraternity. The people of
that country are first to be seduced from their allegiance, and
converted into traitors, as preparatory to the making them good

citizens. Although he must acknowledge that some of our flaming patriots were thus manufactured, he did not think the process would hold good with a whole community. It was a dangerous experiment. We were to succeed in the French mode by the system of fraternization—all is French! but how dreadfully it might be retorted on the Southern and Western slave-holding States. He detested this subornation of treason. No—if he must have them, let them fall by the valor of our arms, by fair, legitimate conquest; not become the victims of treacherous seduction.

He was not surprised at the war spirit which was manifesting itself in gentlemen from the South. In the year 1805–6, in a struggle for the carrying trade of belligerent colonial produce, this country had been most unwisely brought into collision with the great Powers of Europe. By a series of most impolitic and ruinous measures, utterly incomprehensible to every rational, sober-minded man, the Southern planters, by their own votes, had succeeded in knocking down the price of cotton to seven cents, and of tobacco (a few choice crops excepted) to nothing—and in raising the price of blankets, (of which a few would not be amiss in a Canadian campaign,) coarse woolens, and every article of first necessity, three or four hundred per cent. And now that, by our own acts, we have brought ourselves into this unprecedented condition, we must get out of it in any way, but by an acknowledgement of our own want of wisdom and forecast. But is war the true remedy? Who will profit by it? Speculators—a few lucky merchants, who draw prizes in the lottery—commissaries and contractors. Who must suffer by it? The people. It is their blood, their taxes, that must flow to support it. . . .

He was gratified to find gentlemen acknowledging the demoralizing and destructive consequences of the non-importation law—confessing the truth of all that its opponents foretold when it was enacted. And will you plunge yourselves in war, because you have passed a foolish and ruinous law, and are ashamed to repeal it?

"But our good friend the French Emperor [Napoleon] stands in the way of its repeal," and as we cannot go too far in making sacrifices to him who has given such demonstration of his love for the Americans, we must, in point of fact, become parties to his war. "Who can be so cruel as to refuse him this favor?" His imagination shrunk from the miseries of such a connexion. He called upon

the House to reflect whether they were not about to abandon all
reclamation for the unparalleled outrages, "insults and injuries"
of the French Government, to give up our claim for plundered
millions; and asked what reparation or atonement they could expect
to obtain in hours of future dalliance after they should have made a
tender of their person to this great deflowerer of the virginity of republics. . . . Go! march to Canada! leave the broad bosom of the
Chesapeake and her hundred tributary rivers—the whole line of
seacoast from Machias to St. Mary's unprotected! You have taken
Quebec—have you conquered England? Will you seek for the deep
foundations of her power in the frozen deserts of Labrador? . . .

Will you call upon her to leave your ports and harbors untouched,
only just till you can return from Canada, to defend them? The
coast is to be left defenceless, whilst men of the interior are revelling
in conquest and spoil. But grant for a moment, for mere argument's
sake, that in Canada you touched the sinews of her strength,
instead of removing a clog upon her resources—an encumbrance,
but one, which, from a spirit of honor, she will vigorously defend.
In what situation would you then place some of the best men of the
nation? As Chatham and Burke, and the whole band of her patriots,
prayed for her defeat in 1776, so must some of the truest friends
to their country deprecate the success of our arms against the only
Power that holds in check the archenemy of mankind [Napoleon]. . . .

Our people will not submit to be taxed for this war of conquest
and dominion. The Government of the United States was not
calculated to wage offensive foreign war—it was instituted for the
common defence and general welfare; and whosoever should
embark it in a war of offence, would put it to a test which it was by
no means calculated to endure. Make it out that Great Britain had
instigated the Indians on the late occasion, and he was ready for
battle; but not for dominion. He was unwilling, however, under
present circumstances, to take Canada, at the risk of the Constitution
—to embark in a common cause with France and be dragged at
the wheels of the car of some Burr or Bonaparte. For a gentleman
from Tennessee or Gennessee, or Lake Champlain, there may be
some prospect of advantage. Their hemp would bear a great
price by the exclusion of foreign supply. In that too the great
importers were deeply interested. The upper country on the
Hudson and the Lakes would be enriched by the supplies for the

troops, which they alone could furnish. They would have the exclusive market: to say nothing of the increased preponderance from the acquisition of Canada and that section of the Union, which the Southern and Western States had already felt so severely in the apportionment bill. . . .

And shall Republicans become the instruments of him who had effaced the title of Attila to the "Scourge of God!" Yet even Attila, in the falling fortunes of civilization, had, no doubt, his advocates, his tools, his minions, his parasites in the very countries that he overran— sons of that soil whereon his horse had trod; where grass could never after grow. . . . He could not give utterance to that strong detestation which he felt towards (above all other works of the creation) such characters as Zingis, Tamerlane, Kouli-Khan, or Bonaparte. His instincts involuntarily revolted at their bare idea. Malefactors of the human race, who ground down man to a mere machine of their impious and bloody ambition. Yet under all the accumulated wrongs and insults and robberies of the last of these chieftains, are we not in point of fact about to become a party to his views, a partner in his wars? . . .

He called upon those professing to be Republicans to make good the promises held out by their Republican predecessors when they came into power—promises, which for years afterwards they had honestly, faithfully fulfilled. We had vaunted of paying off the national debt, of retrenching useless establishments; and yet had now become as infatuated with standing armies, loans, taxes, navies, and war, as ever were the Essex Junto. What Republicanism is this? . . .

MR. CALHOUN

Mr. Speaker: I understand the opinion of the Committee of Foreign Relations differently from what the gentleman from Virginia (Mr. Randolph) has stated to be his impression. . . . The report could mean nothing but war or empty menace. I hope no member of this House is in favor of the latter. A bullying, menacing system has everything to condemn and nothing to recommend it; in expense, it is almost as considerable as war; it excites contempt abroad, and destroys confidence at home. Menaces are serious things; and, if we expect any good from them, they ought to be resorted to with as much caution and seriousness as war itself, and should, if not successful, be invariably followed by it. It was not the gentleman from Tennessee (Mr. Grundy) that made this a war question. The resolve contemplates an additional regular force; a measure confessedly improper but as a preparation for war, but undoubtedly necessary in that event. . . .

Sir, I might prove the war, should it ensue, justifiable, by the express admission of the gentleman from Virginia; and necessary, by facts undoubted and universally admitted, such as that gentleman did not pretend to controvert. The extent, duration, and character of the injuries received; the failure of those peaceful means heretofore resorted to for the redress of our wrongs, is my proof that it is necessary. Why should I mention the impressment of our seamen; depredation on every branch of our commerce, including the direct export trade, continued for years, and made under laws which professedly undertake to regulate our trade with other nations; negotiation resorted to time after time, till it is become hopeless; the restrictive system persisted in to avoid war, and in the vain expectation of returning justice? The evil still grows, and in each succeeding year swells in extent and pretension beyond the preceding. The question, even in the opinion and admission of our opponents, is reduced to this single point—which shall we do, abandon or defend our own commercial and maritime rights, and the personal liberties of our citizens employed in exercising them? These rights are essentially attacked, and war is the only means of redress. The gentleman from Virginia has suggested none—unless we consider the whole of his speech as recommending patient and resigned submission as the best remedy. Sir, which alternative this House ought to embrace, it is not for me to say. I hope the decision is made already, by a higher authority than the voice of any man. It is not for the human tongue to instill the sense of independence and honor. This is the work of nature—a generous nature, that disdains tame submission to wrongs. . . .

The first argument of the gentleman which I shall notice, is the unprepared state of the country. Whatever weight this argument might have, in a question of immediate war, it surely has little in that of preparation for it. If our country is unprepared, let us remedy the evil as soon as possible. Let the gentleman submit his plan; and, if a reasonable one, I doubt not it will be supported by the House. But, sir, let us admit the fact and the whole force of the argument, I ask whose is the fault? Who has been a member for many years past, and has seen the defenceless state of his country even near home, under his own eyes, without a single endeavor to remedy so serious an evil? Let him not say "I have acted in a minority." It is no less the duty of the minority than a majority to endeavor to serve our country. For that purpose we are sent here and not for that of opposition. We are next told of the expenses of the war, and that the people will not pay taxes. Why not? Is it a want of capacity? What, with one million tons of shipping, a trade of near $100,000,000, manufactures of $150,000,000, and agriculture of thrice that amount, shall we be told the country wants capacity to raise and support ten thousand or fifteen thousand additional regulars? No; it has the ability, that is admitted; but will it not have the disposition? Is not the course a just and necessary one? Shall we, then, utter this libel on the nation? Where will proof be found of a fact so disgraceful? It is said, in the history of the country twelve or fifteen years ago. The case is not parallel. The ability of the country is greatly increased since. The object of that tax was unpopular. But on this, as well as my memory and almost infant observation at that time serve me, the objection was not to the tax, or its amount, but the mode of collection. The eye of the nation was frightened by the number of officers; its love of liberty shocked with the multiplicity of regulations. We, in the vile spirit of imitation, copied from the most oppressive part of European laws on that subject, and imposed on a young and virtuous nation all the severe provisions made necessary by corruption and long growing chicane. If taxes should become necessary, I do not hesitate to say the people will pay cheerfully. It is for their Government and their cause, and would be their interest and duty to pay. But it may be, and I believe was said, that the nation will not pay taxes, because the rights violated are not worth defending, or that the defence will cost more than the profit. Sir, I here enter my solemn protest against this low and "calculating avarice" entering this hall of legislation. It is only fit for shops and counting-houses, and ought not to disgrace the seat of sovereignty by its squalid and vile appearance. Whenever it touches sovereign power, the nation is ruined. It is too short-sighted to defend itself. It is an unpromising spirit, always ready to yield a part to save the balance. It is too timid to have in itself the laws of self-preservation. It is never safe but under the shield of honor. Sir, I only know of one principle to make a nation great, to produce in this country not the form but real spirit of union, and that is, to protect every citizen in the lawful pursuit of his business. He will then feel that he is backed by the Government; that its arm is his arms; and will rejoice in its increased strength and prosperity. Protection and patriotism are reciprocal. This is the road that all great nations have trod. Sir, I am not versed in this calculating policy; and will not, therefore, pretend to estimate in dollars and cents the value of national independence, or national affection. I cannot dare to measure, in shillings and pence, the misery, the stripes, and the slavery of our impressed seamen; nor even to value our shipping, commercial, and agricultural losses, under the Orders in Council and the British system of blockade. I hope I have not condemned any prudent estimate of the means of a country, before it enters on a war. This is wisdom, the other folly. Sir, the gentleman from Virginia has not failed to touch on the calamity of war; that fruitful source of declamation, by which pity becomes the advocate of cowardice; but I know not what we have to do with that subject. If the genetleman desires to repress the gallant ardor of our countrymen by such topics, let me inform him, that true courage regards only the cause—that it is just and necessary—and that it despises the pain and danger of war. If he really wishes to promote the cause of humanity, let his eloquence be addressed to Lord Wellesley or Mr. Percival, and not the American Congress. Tell them, if they persist in such daring insult and injury to a neutral nation, that, however inclined to peace, it will be bound in honor and interest to resist; that their patience and benevolence, however great, will be exhausted; that the calamity of war will ensue; and that they, in the opinion of wounded humanity, will be answerable for all its devastation and misery. Let melting pity, a regard to the interest of humanity, stay the hand of injustice, and, my life on it, the gentleman will not find it difficult to call off his country from the bloody scenes of war. . . .

But we have not yet come to the end of the chapter of dangers. The gentleman's imagination, so fruitful on this subject, conceives that our Constitution is not calculated for war, and that it cannot stand its rude shock. This is rather extraordinary—we must depend upon the pity or contempt of other nations, for our existence. The Constitution, it seems, has failed in its essential part, "to provide for the common defence." No, says the gentleman from Virginia, it is competent for a defensive, but not an offensive war. It is not necessary for me to expose the error of this opinion. Why make the distinction in this instance? Will he pretend to say, that this is an offensive war; a war of conquest? Yes, the gentleman has dared to make this assertion; and for reasons no less extraordinary than the assertion itself. He says, our rights are violated on the ocean, and that these violations affect our shipping, and commercial rights, to which the Canadas have no relation. The doctrine of retaliation has been much abused of late by an unnatural extension; we have now to witness a new abuse. The gentleman from Virginia has limited it down to a point. By his system, if you receive a blow on the breast, you dare not return it on the head; you are obliged to measure and return it on the precise point on which it was received. If you do not proceed with mathematical accuracy, it ceases to be just self-defence; it becomes an unprovoked attack. . . .

Sir, said Mr. C. [Calhoun], the gentleman from Virginia attributes preparation for war to everything but its true cause. He endeavored to find it in the probable rise of the price of hemp. He represents the people of the Western States as willing to plunge our country into war for such base and precarious motives. I will not reason on this point. I see the cause of their ardor, not in such base motives, but in their known patriotism and disinterestedness. No less mercenary is the reason which he attributes to the Southern States. He says, that the non-importation act has reduced cotton to nothing, which has produced a feverish impatience. Sir, I acknowledge the cotton of our farms is worth but little; but not for the cause assigned by the gentleman from Virginia. The people of that section do not reason as he does; they do not attribute it to the efforts of their Government to maintain the peace and independence of their country; they see in the low price of the produce, the hand of foreign injustice; they know well, without the market to the Continent, the deep and steady current of supply will glut that of Great Britain; they are not prepared for the colonial state to which again that Power is endeavoring to reduce us. The manly spirit of that section of our country will not submit to be regulated by any foreign Power. The love of France and the hatred of England has also been assigned as the cause of the present measure. France has not done us justice, says the gentleman from Virginia, and how can we without partiality resist the aggressions of England? I know, sir, we have still cause of complaint against France; but it is of a different character from those against England. She professes now to respect our rights, and there cannot be a reasonable doubt but that the most objectionable parts of her decrees, as far as they respect us, are repealed. We have already formally acknowledged this to be a fact. I, however, protest against the whole of the principles on which this doctrine is founded. It is a novel doctrine, and nowhere to be found out of this House, that you cannot select your antagonist without being guilty of partiality. Sir, when two invade your rights you may resist both or either, at your pleasure. It is regulated by prudence and not by right. The stale imputation of partiality to France is better calculated for the columns of a newspaper than for the walls of this House. . . .

The balance of power has also been introduced as an argument for submission. England is said to be a barrier against the military despotism of France. There is, sir, one great error in our legislation. We are ready enough to protect the interest of the States; and it should seem from this argument to watch over those of a foreign nation, while we grossly neglect our own immediate concerns. This argument of the balance of power is well calculated for the British Parliament, but not at all fitted to the American Congress. Tell them that they have to contend with a mighty Power, and that if they persist in insult and injury to the American people, they will compel them to throw the whole weight of their force into the scale of their enemy. Paint the danger to them, and if they desist from injury, we, I answer for it, will not disturb the balance. But it is absurd for us to talk of the balance of power, while they by their conduct smile with contempt at our simple good-natured policy. If, however, in the contest, it should be found that they underrate us, which I hope and believe, and that we can affect the balance of power, it will not be difficult for us to obtain such terms as our rights demand. . . .

CLAY

The war was declared because Great Britain arrogated to herself the pretension of regulating foreign trade, under the delusive name of retaliatory Orders in Council—a pretension by which she undertook to proclaim to American enterprise, "Thus far shalt thou go, and no farther." Orders which she refused to revoke after the alleged cause of their enactment had ceased; because she persisted in the act of impressing American seamen; because she had instigated the Indians to commit hostilities against us; and because she refused indemnity for her past injuries upon our commerce. . . .

But it is said, that the Orders in Council are done away, no matter from what cause; and, that having been the sole motive for declaring the war, the relations of peace ought to be restored. . . .

I have no hesitation then in saying, that I have always considered the impressment of American seamen as much the most serious aggression. But, sir, how have those orders at last been repealed? Great Britain, it is true, has intimated a willingness to suspend their practical operation, but she still arrogates to herself the right to revive them upon certain contingencies, of which she constitutes herself the sole judge. She waives the temporary use of the rod, but she suspends it *in terrorem* over our heads. Supposing it was conceded to gentlemen that such a repeal of the Orders in Council, as took place on the 23d of June last, exceptionable as it is, being known before the war, would have prevented the war, does it follow that it ought to induce us to lay down our arms without the redress of any other injury? Does it follow, in all cases, that that which would have prevented the war in the first instance should terminate the war? By no means. It requires a great struggle for a nation, prone to peace as this is, to burst through its habits and encounter the difficulties of war. Such a nation ought but seldom to go to war. When it does, it should be for clear and essential rights alone, and it should firmly resolve to extort, at all hazards, their recognition. . . . And who is prepared to say that American seamen shall be surrendered the victims to the British principle of impressment? . . . It is in vain to assert the inviolability of the obligation of allegiance. It is in vain to set up the plea of necessity, and to allege that she cannot exist without the impressment of her seamen. The truth is, she comes, by her press gangs, on board of our vessels, seizes our native seamen, as well as naturalized, and drags them into her service. It is the case, then, of the assertion of an erroneous principle, and a practice not conformable to the principle—a principle which, if it were theoretically right, must be forever practically wrong. . . . If Great Britain desires a mark by which she can know her own subjects, let her give them an ear mark. The colors that float from the mast-head should be the the credentials of our seamen. There is no safety to us, and the gentlemen have shown it, but in the rule that all who sail under the flag (not being enemies) are protected by the flag. It is impossible that this country should ever abandon the gallant tars who have won for us such splendid trophies. . . .

The gentleman from Delaware sees in Canada no object worthy of conquest. . . . Other gentlemen consider the invasion of that country as wicked and unjustifiable. Its inhabitants are represented as unoffending, connected with those of the bordering States by a thousand tender ties, interchanging acts of kindness, and all the offices of good neighborhood. Canada innocent! Canada unoffending! Is it not in Canada that the tomahawk of the savage has been moulded into its deathlike form? From Canadian magazines, Malden, and others, that those supplies have been issued which nourish and sustain the Indian hostilities? . . . What does a state of war present? The united energies of one people arrayed against the combined energies of another; a conflict in which each party aims to inflict all the injury it can, by sea and land, upon the territories, property, and citizens of the other, subject only to the rules of mitigated war practised by civilized nations. The gentlemen would not touch the continental provinces of the enemy, nor I presume, for the same reason, her possessions in the West Indies. The same humane spirit would spare the seamen and soldiers of the enemy. The sacred person of His Majesty must not be attacked, for the learned gentlemen on the other side are quite familiar with the maxim, that the King can do no wrong. Indeed, sir, I know of no person on whom we may make war, upon the principles of the honorable gentlemen, except Mr. Stephen, the celebrated author of the Orders in Council, or the Board of Admiralty, who authorize and regulate the practice of impressment.

The disasters of the war admonish us, we are told, of the necessity of terminating the contest. If our achievements upon the land have been less splendid than those of our intrepid seamen, it is not because the American soldier is less brave. On the one element, organization, discipline, and a thorough knowledge of their duties, exist on the part of the officers and their men. On the other, almost everything is yet to be acquired. We have, however, the consolation that our country abounds with the richest materials, and that, in no instance, when engaged in an action, have our arms been tarnished. . . . It is true, that the disgrace of Detroit remains to be wiped off. . . . With the exception of that event, the war, even upon the land, had been attended by a series of the most brilliant exploits, which, whatever interest they may inspire on this side of the mountains, have given the greatest pleasure on the other. . . .

What cause, Mr. Chairman, which existed for declaring the war has been removed? We sought indemnity for the past and security for the future. The Orders in Council are suspended, not revoked; no compensation for spoliations; Indian hostilities, which were before secretly instigated, now openly encouraged; and the practice of impressment unremittingly persevered in and insisted upon. Yet Administration has given the strongest demonstrations of its love of peace. On the 29th June, less than ten days after the declaration of war, the Secretary of State writes to Mr. Russell, authorizing him to agree to an armistice, upon two conditions only; and what are they? That the Orders in Council should be repealed, and the practice of impressing American seamen cease, those already impressed being released. . . . When Mr. Russell renews the overture, in what was intended as a more agreeable form to the British Government, Lord Castlereagh is not content with a simple rejection, but clothes it in the language of insult. . . . The honorable gentleman from North Carolina (Mr. PEARSON) supposes, that if Congress would pass a law; prohibiting the employment of British seamen in our service, upon condition of a like prohibition on their part, and repeal the act of non-importation, peace would immediately follow. Sir, I have no doubt if such a law were passed, with all the requisite solemnities, and the repeal to take place, Lord Castlereagh would laugh at our simplicity. No, sir, Administration has erred in the steps which it has taken to restore peace, but its error has been not in doing too little but in betraying too great a solicitude for that event. An honorable peace is attainable only by an efficient war. My plan would be to call out the ample resources of the country, give them a judicious direction, prosecute the war with the utmost vigor, strike wherever we can reach the enemy, at sea or on land, and negotiate the terms of a peace at Quebec or Halifax. We are told that England is a proud and lofty nation that disdaining to wait for danger, meets it half-way. Haughty as she is, we once triumphed over her, and if we do not listen to the councils of timidity and despair we shall again prevail. In such a cause, with the aid of Providence, we must come out crowned with success; but if we fail, let us fail like men—lash ourselves to our gallant tars, and expire together in one common struggle, fighting for "seamen's rights and free trade."

15

The Hartford Convention
December 15, 1814—January 5, 1815
Report of the Convention

The New England Federalists staked the future of their party upon opposition to the War of 1812. In their opinion, Great Britain was fighting the battles of the United States against Napoleonic France yet the United States had perversely chosen to go to war with Great Britain at the very time that Napoleon seemed on the point of conquering the entire European continent. They condemned the invasion of Canada as "cruel, wanton, senseless and wicked"—a war without hope of either plunder or glory unless, as Josiah Quincy of Massachusetts said, "[I]t is the glory of the tiger which lifts its jaws, all foul and bloody from the bowels of his victim, and roars for his companion of the wood to come and witness his prowess and his spoil." In actuality, however, when Quincy spoke, the American tiger had never appeared more like a paper cutout of that fearsome animal.

Yet the ill-success of the war merely intensified the Federalist leaders' opposition to it; they viewed American defeats merely as a vindication of their prophesies, not as calls to action to save the country. Some New England State officials carried their dislike of the war to the point of sabotaging the war effort. Several State governors refused to place detachments of their militia under the command of United States Army officers; the governor of Massachusetts did not even condescend to answer President Madison's requisition for artillery and men from the militia; and in 1813, the governor of New Hampshire called home the militia of his State serving under United States command. As a result, the trained reserves

"Report," in Theodore Dwight, *The History of the Hartford Convention: With a Review of the Policy of the United States Government which Led to the War of 1812* (New York: N. & J. White; Boston: Russell, Odiorne, & Co., 1833), pp. 352–79. Dwight (1764–1846) was secretary of the convention.

of the New England States were jealously kept at home at a time when their fighting prowess might have turned the tables in Canada.

And yet not all New Englanders were antiwar Federalists. Fifteen regiments of volunteers were raised in the New England States, more than in any other section of the union. The entire South contributed only ten regiments. Moreover, thousands of New England seamen, made jobless by the British blockade, served on board privateers and the ships of the United States Navy.

The most strenuous and effective opposition to the war came from the Federalist elite—the merchants, bankers, politicians, lawyers, and clergymen. These men held the purse-strings in New England and they made sure that the financial resources of their section were not placed at the disposal of the government. Because New England, as a result of its relatively large manufacturing capacity and its long exemption from the effects of the British blockade (not until 1814 was the British blockade extended to New England), had become the financial center of the United States—for American dollars, all roads seemed to lead to Boston—the refusal to aid in financing the war proved to be as severe a reverse to the Madison administration as any defeat suffered in battle.

Although the Federalists steadily strengthened their position in Congress from 1812 to 1814, to a small group of Federalist leaders, New England's plight did not admit of a political remedy; after long calculating the value of the union they came to the conclusion that it was worthless to their section. Their grievances were political rather than economic in nature. Primarily they were in revolt against the shift in political power that had occurred since 1800. The war brought to the surface all the discontents, jealousies, and animosities that had been rankling New Englanders for many years: the three-fifths rule; the succession of Virginia-born presidents; the Louisiana Purchase and the admission of Louisiana as a State; the "jealousy and hatred of commerce" manifested by the government in Washington; a war for free trade and sailors' rights that compelled Americans to abandon the sea and to forego all the profits derived from commerce. As the New England Federalists saw it, the "slaveholders' power bestrode the Union as the Old Man of the Sea did the shoulders of Sinbad the Sailor." To Josiah Quincy, Timothy Pickering, John Lowell, and others, the break-up of the union was the only way to cast off the incubus of Southern rule.

The idea of a solemn convocation of delegates from the New England States for the purpose of issuing an ordinance of secession was originally advocated by Pickering and his fellow-extremists. But by the summer of 1814 they had come to look with disfavor upon such a convention, for the sufficient reason that it seemed likely to fall under the control of moderates. As for the moderates themselves—chief among whom were George Cabot

(1752–1823) and Harrison Gray Otis (1765–1848)—a convention appeared to be the surest means of heading off a secessionist plot. New England, they admitted, had grievances that must be redressed—but within the union. The majority of people wanted peace with Great Britain by a treaty and it seemed necessary to the moderate Federalists to prod the government into accelerating negotiations. A convention therefore had the merit of being the only peaceable way of registering New England's objections to the war and to assert its right of dissociating itself from that war. When the Convention assembled at Hartford, Connecticut on December 15, 1814—only Massachusetts, Connecticut, and Rhode Island were officially represented by delegates elected by their State legislatures; delegates from New Hampshire and Vermont had been selected by county conventions—it was clear that the fire-eaters were in a minority. Under the leadership of George Cabot and Harrison Gray Otis, the Convention adopted a series of resolutions intended to become amendments to the Constitution of the United States. Anticlimactic as was the Report, it did afford some measure of satisfaction to the radicals. If the constitution were not amended and if it should appear that the causes of New England's ills were deep and permanent, a separation of the States by equable arrangements might have to be considered. In the meantime, however, the Report cautioned against precipitate action. Early in January, 1815, the Massachusetts legislature, after reviewing the proceedings of the Convention, appointed three commissioners headed by Otis to go to Washington to press for the adoption of the recommended constitutional amendments. The commissioners reached Washington to be greeted by the news that peace had been made and a great victory won at New Orleans. The delegation folded its tents and silently stole away to New England. But nothing could undo the damage the Federalist party inflicted upon itself at Hartford. In the hour of the republic's trial, the party leaders had thought not of how they might serve their country but of how they might convert the crisis into sectional and partisan advantage.

An excellent biography of Otis is to be found in Samuel Eliot Morison's *The Life and Letters of Harrison Gray Otis, Federalist, 1765–1848*, 2 vols. (Boston and New York: Houghton, Mifflin Company, 1913). The student concerned with politics will find Henry Adams, ed., *Documents Relating to New England Federalism, 1800–1815* (Boston: Little, Brown and Company, 1877) quite useful. One might also consult Frank Maloy Anderson, "A Forgotten Phase of the New England Opposition to the War of 1812," in Mississippi Valley Historical Association, *Proceedings*, VI (1912–1913), pp. 176–88.

In reading this report note (1) what prompted the delegates to convene their sessions; (2) what they thought had happened to the United States following the administrations of George Washington and John Adams;

(3) the hopes the delegates expressed involving the Southern States; (4) what justification might exist for dissolving the union; (5) the set of grievances compiled against the central government; (6) the reasons for opposing the calling of the State militias and other measures to augment the armed services of the United States; (7) evidences of views reminiscent of the Virginia and Kentucky Resolutions (see Chapter 8); (8) the proposals they advanced for their own defense against the enemy; (9) items in the bill of indictment brought against the Jefferson and Madison administrations; (10) the amendments to the Constitution of the United States they proposed and the reasons given for the suggested changes; (11) the contents of the resolutions adopted by the convention; and (12) the form and style of the Report as a political document.

R EPORT, &c.

The delegates from the legislatures of the states of Massachusetts, Connecticut, and Rhode-Island, and from the counties of Grafton and Cheshire in the state of New-Hampshire and the county of Windham in the state of Veront, assembled in convention, beg leave to report the following result of their conference.

The Convention is deeply impressed with a sense of the arduous nature of the commission which they were appointed to execute, of devising the means of defence against dangers, and of relief from oppressions proceeding from the acts of their own government, without violating constitutional principles, or disappointing the hopes of a suffering and injured people. To prescribe patience and firmness to those who are already exhausted by distress, is sometimes to drive them to despair, and the progress towards reform by the regular road, is irksome to those whose imaginations discern, and whose feelings prompt, to a shorter course. But when abuses, reduced to a system, and accumulated through a course of years, have pervaded every department of government, and spread corruption through every region of the state; when these are clothed with the forms of law, and enforced by an executive whose will is their source, no summary means of relief can be applied without recourse to direct and open resistance. This experiment, even when justifiable, cannot fail to be painful to the good citizen; and the success of the effort will be no security against the danger of the example. Precedents of resistance to the worst administration, are eagerly seized by those who are naturally hostile to the best. Necessity alone can sanction a resort to this measure; and it should never be extended in duration or degree beyond the exigency, until the people, not merely in the fervour of sudden excitement, but after full deliberation, are determined to change the constitution.

It is a truth, not to be concealed, that a sentiment prevails to no inconsiderable extent, that administration have given such constructions to that instrument, and practised so many abuses under colour of its authority, that the time for a change is at hand. Those who so believe, regard the evils which surround them as intrinsic and incurable defects in the constitution. They yield to a persuasion, that no change, at any time, or on any occasion, can aggravate the misery of their country. This opinion may ultimately prove to be correct. But as the evidence on which it rests is not yet conclusive, and as measures adopted upon the assumption of its certainty might be irrevocable, some general considerations are submitted, in the hope of reconciling all to a course of moderation and firmness, which may save them from the regret incident to sudden decisions, probably avert the evil, or at least insure consolation and success in the last resort.

The constitution of the United States, under the auspices of a wise and virtuous administration, proved itself competent to all the objects of national prosperity comprehended in the views of its framers. No parallel can be found in history, of a transition so rapid as that of the United States from the lowest depression to the highest felicity—from the condition of weak and disjointed republics, to that of a great, united, and prosperous nation.

Although this high state of public happiness has undergone a miserable and afflicting reverse, through the prevalence of a weak and profligate policy, yet the evils and afflictions which have thus been induced upon the country, are not peculiar to any form of government. The lust and caprice of power, the corruption of patronage, the oppression of the weaker interests of the community by the stronger, heavy taxes, wasteful expenditures, and unjust and ruinous wars, are the natural offspring of bad administrations, in all ages and countries. It was indeed to be hoped, that the rulers of these states would not make such disastrous haste to involve their infancy in the embarrassments of old and rotten institutions. Yet all this have they done; and their conduct calls loudly for their dismission and disgrace. But to attempt upon every abuse of power to change the constitution, would be to perpetuate the evils of revolution.

Again, the experiment of the powers of the constitution to regain its vigour, and of the people to recover from their delusions, has been hitherto made under the greatest possible disadvantages arising from the state of the world. The fierce passions which have convulsed the nations of Europe, have passed the ocean, and finding their way to the bosoms of our citizens, have afforded to administration the means of perverting public opinion, in respect to our foreign relations, so as to acquire its aid in the indulgence of their animosities, and the increase of their adherents. Further, a reformation of public opinion, resulting from dear-bought experience, in the southern Atlantic states, at least, is not to be despaired of. They will have felt, that the eastern states cannot be made exclusively the victims of a capricious and impassioned policy. They will have seen that the great and essential interests of the people are common to the south and to the east. They will realize the fatal errors of a system which seeks revenge for commercial injuries in the sacrifice of commerce, and aggravates by needless wars, to an immeasurable extent, the injuries it professes to redress. They may discard the influence of visionary theorists, and recognize the benefits of a practical policy. Indications of this desirable revolution of opinion, among our brethren in those states, are already manifested. While a hope remains of its ultimate completion, its progress should not be retarded or stopped, by exciting fears which must check these favourable tendencies, and frustrate the efforts of the wisest and best men in those states, to accelerate this propitious change.

Finally, if the Union be destined to dissolution, by reason of the multiplied abuses of bad administrations, it should, if possible, be the work of peaceable times, and deliberate consent. Some new form of confederacy should be substituted among those states which shall intend to maintain a federal relation to each other. Events may prove that the causes of our calamities are deep and permanent. They may be found to proceed, not merely from the blindness of prejudice, price of opinion, violence of party spirit, or the confusion of the times; but they may be traced to implacable combinations of individuals, or of states, to monopolize power and office, and to trample without remorse upon the rights and interests of commercial sections of the Union. Whenever it shall appear that these causes are radical and permanent, a separation, by equitable arrangement, will be preferable to an alliance by constraint, among nominal friends, but real enemies, inflamed by mutual hatred and jealousy, and inviting, by intestine divisions, contempt and aggression from abroad. But a severance of the Union by one or more states, against the will of the rest, and especially in a time of war, can be justified only by absolute necessity. These are among the principal objections against precipitate measures tending to disunite the states, and when examined in connection with the farewell address of the Father of his country, they must, it is believed, be deemed conclusive.

Under these impressions, the convention have proceeded to confer and deliberate upon the alarming state of public affairs, especially as affecting the interests of the people who have appointed them for this purpose, and they are naturally led to a consideration, in the first place, of the dangers and grievances which menace an immediate or speedy pressure, with a view of suggesting means of present relief; in the next place, of such as are of a more remote and general description, in the hope of attaining future security.

Among the subjects of complaint and apprehension, which might be comprised under the former of these propositions, the attention of the convention has been occupied with the claims and pretensions advanced, and the authority exercised over the militia, by the executive and legislative departments of the national government. Also, upon the destitution of the means of defence in which the eastern states are left; while at the same time they are doomed to heavy requisitions of men and money for national objects.

The authority of the national government over the militia is derived from those clauses in the constitution which give power to Congress "to provide for calling forth the militia to execute the laws of the Union, suppress insurrections and repel invasions;"— Also "to provide for organizing, arming, and disciplining the militia, and for governing such parts of them as may be employed in the service of the United States, reserving to the states respectively the appointment of the officers, and the authority of training the militia according to the discipline prescribed by Congress." Again, "the President shall be commander in chief of the army and navy of the United States, and of the militia of the several states, *when called into the actual service of the United States.*" In these specified cases only, has the national government any power over the militia; and it follows conclusively, that for all general and ordinary purposes, this power belongs to the states respectively, and to them alone. It is not only with regret, but with astonishment, the convention perceive that under colour of an authority conferred with such plain and precise limitations, a power is arrogated by the executive government, and in some instances sanctioned by the two houses of congress, of control over the militia, which if conceded will render nugatory the rightful authority of the individual states over that class of men, and by placing at the disposal of the national government the lives and services of the great body of the people, enable it at pleasure to destroy their liberties, and erect a military despotism on the ruins.

An elaborate examination of the principles assumed for the basis of these extravagant pretensions, of the consequences to which they lead, and of the insurmountable objections to their admission, would transcend the limits of this report. A few general observations, with an exhibition of the character of these pretensions, and a recommendation of a strenuous opposition to them, must not, however, be omitted.

It will not be contended that by the terms used in the constitutional compact, the power of the national government to call out the militia is other than a power expressly limited to three cases. One of these must exist, as a condition precedent to the exercise of that power—Unless the laws shall be opposed, or an insurrection shall exist, or an invasion shall be made, congress, and of consequence the President as their organ, has no more power over the militia than over the armies of a foreign nation.

But if the declaration of the President should be admitted to be an unerring test of the existence of these cases, this important power would depend, not upon the truth of the fact, but upon executive infallibility. And the limitation of the power would consequently be nothing more than merely nominal, as it might always be eluded. It follows therefore that the decision of the President in this particular cannot be conclusive. It is as much the duty of the state authorities to watch over the rights *reserved*, as of the United States to exercise the powers which are *delegated*.

The arrangement of the United States into military districts, with a small portion of the regular force, under an officer of high rank of the standing army, with power to call for the militia, as circumstances in his judgment may require; and to assume the command of them, is not warranted by the constitution or any law of the United States. It is not denied that Congress may delegate to the President of the United States the power to call forth the militia in the cases which are within their jurisdiction—But he has no authority to substitute military prefects throughout the Union, to use their own discretion in such instances. To station an officer of the army in a military district without troops corresponding to his rank, for the purpose of taking command of the militia that may be called into service, is a manifest evasion of that provision of the constitution which expressly reserves to the states the appointment of the officers of the militia; and the object of detaching such officer cannot be well concluded to be any other than that of superseding the governor or other officers of the militia in their right to command.

The power of dividing the militia of the states into classes, and obliging such classes to furnish by contract or draft, able-bodied men, to serve for one or more years for the defence of the frontier, is not delegated to Congress. If a claim to draft the militia for one year for such general object be admissible, no limitation can be assigned to it, but the discretion of those who make the law. Thus, with a power in Congress to authorize such a draft or conscription, and in the Executive to decide conclusively upon the existence and continuance of the emergency, the whole militia may be converted into a standing army disposable at the will of the President of the United States.

The power of compelling the militia, and other citizens of the United States, by a forcible draft or conscription, to serve in the regular armies as proposed in a late official letter of the Secretary of War, is not delegated to Congress by the constitution, and the exercise of it would be not less dangerous to their liberties, than hostile to the sovereignty of the states. The effort to deduce this power from the right of raising armies, is a flagrant attempt to pervert the sense of the clause in the constitution which confers that right, and is incompatible with other provisions in that instrument. The armies of the United States have always been raised by contract, never by conscription, and nothing more can be wanting to a government possessing the power thus claimed to enable it to usurp the entire control of the militia, in derogation of the authority of the state, and to convert it by impressment into a standing army.

It may be here remarked, as a circumstance illustrative of the determination of the Executive to establish an absolute control over all descriptions of citizens, that the right of impressing seamen into the naval service is expressly asserted by the Secretary of the Navy in a late report. Thus a practice, which in a foreign government has been regarded with great abhorrence by the people, finds advocates among those who have been the loudest to condemn it.

The law authorising the enlistment of minors and apprentices into the armies of the United States, without the consent of parents and guardians, is also repugnant to the spirit of the constitution. By a construction of the power to raise armies, as applied by our present rulers, not only persons capable of contracting are liable to be impressed into the army, but those who are under legal disabilities to make contracts, are to be invested with the capacity, in order to enable them to annul at pleasure contracts made in their behalf by legal guardians. Such an interference with the municipal laws and rights of the several states, could never have been contemplated by the framers of the constitution. It impairs the salutary control and influence of the parent over his child—the master over his servant—the guardian over his ward—and thus destroys the most important relations in society, so that by the conscription of the father, and the seduction of the son, the power of the Executive over all the effective male population of the United States is made complete.

Such are some of the odious features of the novel system proposed by the rulers of a free country, under the limited powers derived from the constitution. What portion of them will be embraced in acts finally to be passed, it is yet impossible to determine. It is, however, sufficiently alarming to perceive, that these projects emanate from the highest authority, nor should it be forgotten, that by the plan of the Secretary of War, the classification of the militia embraced the principle of direct taxation upon the white population only; and that, in the house of representatives, a motion to apportion the militia among the white population exclusively, which would have been in its operation a direct tax, was strenuously urged and supported.

In this whole series of devices and measures for raising men, this convention discern a total disregard for the constitution, and a disposition to violate its provisions, demanding from the individual states a firm and decided opposition. An iron despotism can impose no harder servitude upon the citizen, than to force him from his home and his occupation, to wage offensive wars, undertaken to gratify the pride or passions of his master. The example of France has recently shown that a cabal of individuals assuming to act in the name of the people, may transform the great body of citizens into soldiers, and deliver them over into the hands of a single tyrant. No war, not held in just abhorrence by the people, can require the aid of such stratagems to recruit an army. Had the troops already raised, and in great numbers sacrificed upon the frontier of Canada, been employed for the defence of the country, and had the millions which have been squandered with shameless profusion, been appropriated to their payment, to the protection of the coast, and to the naval service, there would have been no occasion for unconstitutional expedients. Even at this late hour, let government leave to New-England the remnant of her resources, and she is ready and able to defend her territory, and to resign the glories and advantages of the border war to those who are determined to persist in its prosecution.

That acts of Congress in violation of the constitution are absolutely void, is an undeniable position. It does not, however, consist with respect and forbearance due from a confederate state towards the general government, to fly to open resistance upon every infraction of the constitution. The mode and the energy of the opposition, should always conform to the nature of the violation, the intention of its authors, the extent of the injury inflicted, the determination manifested to persist in it, and the danger of delay. But in cases of deliberate, dangerous, and palpable infractions of the constitution, affecting the sovereignty of a state, and liberties of the people; it is not only the right but the duty of such a state to interpose its authority for their protection, in the manner best calculated to secure that end. When emergencies occur which are either beyond the reach of the judicial tribunals, or too pressing to admit of the delay incident to their forms, states which have no common umpire, must be their own judges, and execute their own decisions. It will thus be proper for the several states to await the ultimate disposal of the obnoxious measures recommended by the Secretary of War, or pending before Congress, and so to use their power according to the character these measures shall finally assume, as effectually to protect their own sovereignty, and the rights and liberties of their citizens.

The next subject which has occupied the attention of the convention, is the means of defence against the common enemy. This naturally leads to the inquiries, whether any expectation can be reasonably entertained, that adequate provision for the defence of the eastern states will be made by the national government? Whether the several states can, from their own resources, provide for self-defence and fulfil the requisitions which are to be expected for the national treasury? and, generally, what course of conduct ought to be adopted by those states, in relation to the great object of defence.

Without pausing at present to comment upon the causes of the war, it may be assumed as a truth, officially announced, that to achieve the conquest of Canadian territory, and to hold it as a pledge for peace, is the deliberate purpose of administration. This enterprize, commenced at a period when government possessed the advantage of selecting the time and occasion for making a sudden descent upon an unprepared enemy, now languishes in the third year of the war. It has been prosecuted with various fortune, and occasional brilliancy of exploit, but without any solid acquisition. The British armies have been recruited by veteran regiments. Their navy commands Ontario. The American ranks are thinned by the casualties of war. Recruits are discouraged by the unpopular character of the contest, and by the uncertainty of receiving their pay.

In the prosecution of this favourite warfare, administration have left the exposed and vulnerable parts of the country destitute of all the efficient means of defence. The main body of the regular army has been marched to the frontier. The navy has been stripped of a great part of its sailors for the service of the lakes. Meanwhile the enemy scours the sea-coast, blockades our ports, ascends our bays and rivers, makes actual descents in various and distant places, holds some by force, and threatens all that are assailable with fire and sword. The sea-board of four of the New-England states, following its curvatures, presents an extent of more than seven hundred miles, generally occupied by a compact population, and accessible by a naval force, exposing a mass of people and property to the devastation of the enemy, which bears a great proportion to the residue of the maritime frontier of the United States. This extensive shore has been exposed to frequent attacks, repeated contributions, and constant alarms. The regular forces detached by the national government for its defence are mere pretexts for placing officers of high rank in command. They are besides confined to a few places, and are too insignificant in number to be included in any computation.

These states have thus been left to adopt measures for their own defence. The militia have been constantly kept on the alert, and harassed by garrison duties, and other hardships, while the expenses, of which the national government decline the reimbursement, threaten to absorb all the resources of the states. The President of the United States has refused to consider the expense of the militia detached by state authority, for the indispensable defence of the state, as chargeable to the Union, on the ground of a refusal by the Executive of the state to place them under the command of officers of the regular army. Detachments of militia placed at the disposal of the general government, have been dismissed either without pay, or with depreciated paper. The prospect of the ensuing campaign is not enlivened by the promise of any alleviation of these grievances. From authentic documents, extorted by necessity from those whose inclination might lead them to conceal the embarrassments of the government, it is apparent that the treasury is bankrupt, and its credit prostrate. So deplorable is the state of the finances, that those who feel for the honour and safety of the country, would be willing to conceal the melancholy spectacle, if those whose infatuation has produced this state of fiscal concerns had not found themselves compelled to unveil it to public view.

If the war be continued, there appears no room for reliance upon the national government for the supply of those means of defence which must become indispensable to secure these states from desolation and ruin. Nor is it possible that the states can discharge this sacred duty from their own resources, and continue to sustain the burden of the national taxes. The administration, after a long

perseverance in plans to baffle every effort of commercial enterprize, had fatally succeeded in their attempts at the epoch of the
war. Commerce, the vital spring of New-England's prosperity, was
annihilated. Embargoes, restrictions, and the rapacity of revenue
officers, had completed its destruction. The various objects for the
employment of productive labour, in the branches of business
dependent on commerce, have disappeared. The fisheries have
shared its fate. Manufactures, which government has professed
an intention to favour and to cherish, as an indemnity for the failure
of these branches of business, are doomed to struggle in their infancy with taxes and obstructions, which cannot fail most seriously
to affect their growth. The specie is withdrawn from circulation.
The landed interest, the last to feel these burdens, must prepare to
become their principal support, as all other sources of revenue must
be exhausted. Under these circumstances, taxes, of a description
and amount unprecedented in this country, are in a train of
imposition, the burden of which must fall with the heaviest pressure
upon the states east of the Potomac. *The amount of these taxes for the
ensuing year cannot be estimated at less than five millions of dollars upon the
New-England states, and the expenses of the last year for defence, in
Massachusetts alone, approaches to one million of dollars.*

From these facts, it is almost superfluous to state the irresistible
inference that these states have no capacity of defraying the expense requisite for their own protection, and, at the same time, of
discharging the demands of the national treasury.

The last inquiry, what course of conduct ought to be adopted
by the aggrieved states, is in a high degree momentous. When a
great and brave people shall feel themselves deserted by their
government, and reduced to the necessity either of submission to a
foreign enemy, or of appropriating to their own use those means of
defence which are indispensable to self-preservation, they cannot
consent to wait passive spectators of approaching ruin, which it is
in their power to avert, and to resign the last remnant of their
industrious earnings to be dissipated in support of measures
destructive of the best interests of the nation.

This convention will not trust themselves to express their conviction of the catastrophe to which such a state of things inevitably
tends. Conscious of their high responsibility to God and their
country, solicitous for the continuance of the Union, as well as the

sovereignty of the states, unwilling to furnish obstacles to peace—resolute never to submit to a foreign enemy, and confiding in the Divine care and protection, they will, until the last hope shall be extinguished, endeavor to avert such consequences.

With this view they suggest an arrangement, which may at once be consistent with the honour and interest of the national government, and the security of these states. This it will not be difficult to conclude, if that government should be so disposed. By the terms of it these states might be allowed to assume their own defence, by the militia or other troops. A reasonable portion, also, of the taxes raised in each state might be paid into its treasury, and credited to the United States, but to be appropriated to the defence of such state, to be accounted for with the United States. No doubt is entertained that by such an arrangement, this portion of the country could be defended with greater effect, and in a mode more consistent with economy, and the public convenience, than any which has been practised.

Should an application for these purposes, made to Congress by the state legislatures, be attended with success, and should peace upon just terms appear to be unattainable, the people would stand together for the common defence, until a change of administration, or of disposition in the enemy, should facilitate the occurrence of that auspicious event. It would be inexpedient for this Convention to diminish the hope of a successful issue to such an application, by recommending, upon supposition of a contrary event, ulterior proceedings. Nor is it indeed within their province. In a state of things so solemn and trying as may then arise, the legislatures of the states, or conventions of the whole people, or delegates appointed by them for the express purpose in another Convention, must act as such urgent circumstances may then require.

But the duty incumbent on this Convention will not have been performed, without exhibiting some general view of such measures as they deem essential to secure the nation against a relapse into difficulties and dangers, should they, by the blessing of Providence, escape from their present condition, without absolute ruin. To this end a concise retrospect of the state of this nation under the advantages of a wise administration, contrasted with the miserable abyss into which it is plunged by the profligacy and folly of political theorists, will lead to some practical conclusions. On this subject, it will be recollected, that the immediate influence of the Federal Constitution upon its first adoption, and for twelve succeeding years, upon the prosperity and happiness of the nation, seemed to countenance a belief in the transcendency of its perfection over all other human institutions. In the catalogue of blessings which have fallen to the lot of the most favoured nations, none could be enumerated from which our country was excluded—a free Constitution, administered by great and incorruptible statesmen, realized the fondest hopes of liberty and independence—The progress of agriculture was stimulated by the certainty of value in the harvest—and commerce, after traversing every sea, returned with the riches of every clime. A revenue, secured by a sense of honour, collected without oppression, and paid without murmurs, melted away the national debt; and the chief concern of the public creditor arose from its too rapid diminution. The wars and commotions of the European nations, and their interruptions of the commercial intercourse afforded to those who had not promoted, but who would have rejoiced to alleviate their calamities, a fair and golden opportunity, by combining themselves to lay a broad foundation for national wealth. Although occasional vexations to commerce arose from the furious collisions of the powers at war, yet the great and good men of that time conformed to the force of circumstances which they could not control, and preserved their country in security from the tempests which overwhelmed the old world, and threw the wreck of their fortunes on these shores. Respect abroad, prosperity at home, wise laws made by honoured legislators, and prompt obedience yielded by a contented people, had silenced the enemies of republican institutions. The arts flourished—the sciences were cultivated—the comforts and conveniences of life were universally diffused—and nothing remained for succeeding administrations but to reap the advantages and cherish the resources flowing from the policy of their predecessors.

But no sooner was a new administration established in the hands of the party opposed to the Washington policy, than a fixed determination was perceived and avowed of changing a system which had already produced these substantial fruits. The consequences of this change, for a few years after its commencement, were not sufficient to counteract the prodigious impulse towards prosperity, which had been given to the nation. But a steady perseverance in the new plans of administration, at length developed their weakness and deformity, but not until a majority of the people had been deceived by flattery, and inflamed by passion, into blindness to their defects. Under the withering influence of this new system, the declension of the nation has been uniform and rapid. The richest advantages for securing the great objects of the constitution have been wantonly rejected. While Europe reposes from the convulsions that had shaken down her ancient institutions, she beholds with amazement this remote country, once so happy and so envied, involved in a ruinous war, and excluded from intercourse with the rest of the world.

To investigate and explain the means whereby this fatal reverse has been effected, would require a voluminous discussion. Nothing more can be attempted in this report than a general allusion to the principal outlines of the policy which has produced this vicissitude. Among these may be enumerated—

First.—A deliberate and extensive system for effecting a combination among certain states, by exciting local jealousies and ambition, so as to secure to popular leaders in one section of the Union, the controul of public affairs in perpetual succession. To which primary object most other characteristics of the system may be reconciled.

Secondly.—The political intolerance displayed and avowed in excluding from office men of unexceptionable merit, for want of adherence to the executive creed.

Thirdly.—The infraction of the judiciary authority and rights, by depriving judges of their offices in violation of the constitution.

Fourthly.—The abolition of existing taxes, requisite to prepare the country for those changes to which nations are always exposed, with a view to the acquisition of popular favour.

Fifthly.—The influence of patronage in the distribution of offices, which in these states has been almost invariably made among men the least entitled to such distinction, and who have sold themselves as ready instruments for distracting public opinion, and encouraging administration to hold in contempt the wishes and remonstrances of a people thus apparently divided.

Sixthly.—The admission of new states into the Union formed at pleasure in the western region, has destroyed the balance of power which existed among the original States, and deeply affected their interest.

Seventhly.—The easy admission of naturalized foreigners, to places

of trust, honour or profit, operating as an inducement to the mal-
content subjects of the old world to come to these States, in quest
of executive patronage, and to repay it by an abject devotion to
executive measures.

Eighthly.—Hostility to Great Britain, and partiality to the late
government of France, adopted as coincident with popular
prejudice, and subservient to the main object, party power. Connected with these must be ranked erroneous and distorted estimates
of the power and resources of those nations, of the probable results
of their controversies, and of our political relations to them
respectively.

Lastly and principally.—A visonary and superficial theory in regard
to commerce, accompanied by a real hatred but a feigned regard
to its interests, and a ruinous perseverance in efforts to render it an
instrument of coercion and war.

But it is not conceivable that the obliquity of any administration
could, in so short a period, have so nearly consummated the work
of national ruin, unless favoured by defects in the constitution.

To enumerate all the improvements of which that instrument is
susceptible, and to propose such amendments as might render it
in all respects perfect, would be a task which this convention has
not thought proper to assume. They have confined their attention
to such as experience has demonstrated to be essential, and even
among these, some are considered entitled to a more serious attention than others. They are suggested without any intentional dis-
respect to other states, and are meant to be such as all shall find
an interest in promoting. Their object is to strengthen, and if
possible to perpetuate, the union of the states, by removing the
grounds of existing jealousies, and providing for a fair and equal
representation, and a limitation of powers, which have been
misused.

The first amendment proposed, relates to the apportionment of
representatives among the slave holding states. This cannot be
claimed as a right. Those states are entitled to the slave representation, by a constitutional compact. It is therefore merely a
subject of agreement, which should be conducted upon principles
of mutual interest and accommodation, and upon which no sensibility on either side should be permitted to exist. It has proved
unjust and unequal in its operation. Had this effect been foreseen,

the privilege would probably not have been demanded; certainly not conceded. Its tendency in future will be adverse to that harmony and mutual confidence which are more conducive to the happiness and prosperity of every confederated state, than a mere preponderance of power, the prolific source of jealousies and controversy, can be to any one of them. The time may therefore arrive, when a sense of magnanimity and justice will reconcile those states to acquiesce in a revision of this article, especially as a fair equivalent would result to them in the apportionment of taxes.

The next amendment relates to the admission of new states into the Union.

This amendment is deemed to be highly important, and in fact indispensable. In proposing it, it is not intended to recognize the right of Congress to admit new states without the original limits of the United States, nor is any idea entertained of disturbing the tranquillity of any state already admitted into the Union. The object is merely to restrain the constitutional power of Congress in admitting new states. At the adoption of the constitution, a certain balance of power among the original parties was considered to exist, and there was at that time, and yet is among those parties, a strong affinity between their great and general interests.—By the admission of these states that balance has been materially affected, and unless the practice be modified must ultimately be destroyed. The southern states will first avail themselves of their new confederates to govern the east, and finally the western states, multiplied in number, and augmented in population, will control the interests of the whole. Thus for the sake of present power, the southern states will be common sufferers with the east, in the loss of permanent advantages. None of the old states can find an interest in creating prematurely an overwhelming western influence, which may hereafter discern (as it has heretofore) benefits to be derived to them by wars and commercial restrictions.

The next amendments proposed by the convention, relate to the powers of Congress, in relation to embargo and the interdiction of commerce.

Whatever theories upon the subject of commerce have hitherto divided the opinions of statesmen, experience has at last shown that it is a vital interest in the United States, and that its success is essential to the encouragement of agriculture and manufactures, and to the wealth, finances, defence, and liberty of the nation. Its welfare can never interfere with the other great interests of the state, but must promote and uphold them. Still those who are immediately concerned in the prosecution of commerce, will of necessity be always a minority of the nation. They are, however, best qualified to manage and direct its course by the advantages of experience, and the sense of interest. But they are entirely unable to protect themselves against the sudden and injudicious decisions of bare majorities, and the mistaken or oppressive projects of those who are not actively concerned in its pursuits. Of consequence, this interest is always exposed to be harassed, interrupted, and entirely destroyed, upon pretence of securing other interests. Had the merchants of this nation been permitted by their own government to pursue an innocent and lawful commerce, how different would have been the state of the treasury and of public credit! How short-sighted and miserable is the policy which has annihilated this order of men, and doomed their ships to rot in the docks, their capital to waste unemployed, and their affections to be alienated from the government which was formed to protect them! What security for an ample and unfailing revenue can ever be had, comparable to that which once was realized in the good faith, punctuality, and sense of honour, which attached the mercantile class to the interests of the government! Without commerce, where can be found the ailment for a navy; and without a navy, what is to constitute the defence, and ornament, and glory of this nation! No union can be durably cemented, in which every great interest does not find itself reasonably secured against the encroachment and combinations of other interests. When, therefore, the past system of embargoes and commercial restrictions shall have been reviewed —when the fluctuation and inconsistency of public measures, betraying a want of information as well as feeling in the majority, shall have been considered, the reasonableness of some restrictions upon the power of a bare majority to repeat these oppressions, will appear to be obvious.

The next amendment proposes to restrict the power of making offensive war. In the consideration of this amendment, it is not necessary to inquire into the justice of the present war. But one sentiment now exists in relation to its expediency, and regret for its declaration is nearly universal. No indemnity can ever be attained for this terrible calamity, and its only palliation must be found in obstacles to its future recurrence. Rarely can the state of this country call for or justify offensive war. The genius of our institutions is unfavourable to its successful prosecution; the felicity of our situation exempts us from its necessity. In this case, as in the former, those more immediately exposed to its fatal effects are a minority of the nation. The commercial towns, the shores of our seas and rivers, contain the population whose vital interests are most vulnerable by a foreign enemy. Agriculture, indeed, must feel at last, but this appeal to its sensibility comes too late. Again, the immense population which has swarmed into the west, remote from immediate danger, and which is constantly augmenting, will not be averse from the occasional disturbances of the Atlantic states. Thus interest may not unfrequently combine with passion and intrigue, to plunge the nation into needless wars, and compel it to become a military, rather than a happy and flourishing people. These considerations, which it would be easy to augment, call loudly for the limitation proposed in the amendment.

Another amendment, subordinate in importance, but still in a high degree expedient, relates to the exclusion of foreigners hereafter arriving in the United States from the capacity of holding offices of trust, honour, or profit.

That the stock of population already in these states is amply sufficient to render this nation in due time sufficiently great and powerful, is not a controvertible question. Nor will it be seriously pretended, that the national deficiency in wisdom, arts, science, arms, or virtue, needs to be replenished from foreign countries. Still, it is agreed, that a liberal policy should offer the rights of hospitality, and the choice of settlement, to those who are disposed to visit the country. But why admit to a participation in the government aliens who were no parties to the compact—who are ignorant of the nature of our institutions, and have no stake in the welfare of the country but what is recent and transitory? It is surely a privilege sufficient, to admit them after due probation to become citizens, for all but political purposes. To extend it beyond these limits, is to encourage foreigners to come to these states as candidates for preferment. The Convention forbear to express their opinion upon the inauspicious effects which have already resulted to the honour and peace of this nation, from this misplaced and indiscriminate liberality.

The last amendment respects the limitation of the office of

President to a single constitutional term, and his eligibility from the same state two terms in succession.

Upon this topic it is superfluous to dilate. The love of power is a principle in the human heart which too often impels to the use of all practicable means to prolong its duration. The office of President has charms and attractions which operate as powerful incentives to this passion. The first and most natural exertion of a vast patronage is directed towards the security of a new election. The interest of the country, the welfare of the people, even honest fame and respect for the opinion of posterity, are secondary considerations. All the engines of intrigue, all the means of corruption are likely to be employed for this object. A President whose political career is limited to a single election, may find no other interest than will be promoted by making it glorious to himself, and beneficial to his country. But the hope of re-election is prolific of temptations, under which these magnanimous motives are deprived of their principal force. The repeated election of the President of the United States from any one state, affords inducements and means for intrigues, which tend to create an undue local influence, and to establish the domination of particular states. The justice, therefore, of securing to every state a fair and equal chance for the election of this officer from its own citizens is apparent, and this object will be essentially promoted by preventing an election from the same state twice in succession.

Such is the general view which this Convention has thought proper to submit, of the situation of these states, of their dangers and their duties. Most of the subjects which it embraces have separately received an ample and luminous investigation, by the great and able assertors of the rights of their country, in the national legislature; and nothing more could be attempted on this occasion than a digest of general principles, and of recommendations suited to the present state of public affairs. The peculiar difficulty and delicacy of performing even this undertaking, will be appreciated by all who think seriously upon the crisis. Negotiations for peace are at this hour supposed to be pending, the issue of which must be deeply interesting to all. No measures should be adopted which might unfavourably affect that issue; none which should embarrass the administration, if their professed desire for peace is sincere; and none which on supposition of their insincerity, should afford them pretexts for prolonging the war, or relieving themselves from the responsibility of a dishonourable peace. It is also devoutly to be wished, that an occasion may be afforded to all friends of the country, of all parties, and in all places, to pause and consider the awful state to which pernicious counsels and blind passions have brought this people. The number of those who perceive, and who are ready to retrace errors, must, it is believed, be yet sufficient to redeem the nation. It is necessary to rally and unite them by the assurance that no hostility to the constitution is meditated, and to obtain their aid in placing it under guardians who alone can save it from destruction. Should this fortunate change be effected, the hope of happiness and honour may once more dispel the surrounding gloom. Our nation may yet be great, our union durable. But should this prospect be utterly hopeless, the time will not have been lost which shall have ripened a general sentiment of the necessity of more mighty efforts to rescue from ruin, at least some portion of our beloved country.

THEREFORE RESOLVED,

That it be and hereby is recommended to the legislatures of the several states represented in this Convention, to adopt all such measures as may be necessary effectually to protect the citizens of said states from the operation and effects of all acts which have been or may be passed by the Congress of the United States, which shall contain provisions, subjecting the militia or other citizens to forcible drafts, conscriptions, or impressments, not authorised by the constitution of the United States.

Resolved, That it be and hereby is recommended to the said Legislatures, to authorize an immediate and earnest application to be made to the government of the United States, requesting their consent to some arrangement, whereby the said states may, separately or in concert, be empowered to assume upon themselves the defence of their territory against the enemy; and a reasonable portion of the taxes, collected within said States, may be paid into the respective treasuries thereof, and appropriated to the payment of the balance due said states, and to the future defence of the same. The amount so paid into the said treasuries to be credited, and the disbursements made as aforesaid to be charged to the United States.

Resolved, That it be, and hereby is, recommended to the legislatures of the aforesaid states, to pass laws (where it has not already been done) authorizing the governors or commanders-in-chief of their militia to make detachments from the same, or to form voluntary corps, as shall be most convenient and conformable to their constitutions, and to cause the same to be well armed, equipped, and disciplined, and held in readiness for service; and upon the request of the governor of either of the other states to employ the whole of such detachment or corps, as well as the regular forces of the state, or such part thereof as may be required and can be spared consistently with the safety of the state, in assisting the state, making such request to repel any invasion thereof which shall be made or attempted by the public enemy.

Resolved, That the following amendments of the constitution of the United States be recommended to the states represented as aforesaid, to be proposed by them for adoption by the state legislatures, and in such cases as may be deemed expedient by a convention chosen by the people of each state.

And it is further recommended, that the said states shall persevere in their efforts to obtain such amendments, until the same shall be effected.

First. Representatives and direct taxes shall be apportioned among the several states which may be included within this Union, according to their respective numbers of free persons, including those bound to serve for a term of years, and excluding Indians not taxed, and all other persons.

Second. No new state shall be admitted into the Union by Congress, in virtue of the power granted by the constitution, without the concurrence of two thirds of both houses.

Third. Congress shall not have power to lay any embargo on the ships or vessels of the citizens of the United States, in the ports or harbours thereof, for more than sixty days.

Fourth. Congress shall not have power, without the concurrence of two thirds of both houses, to interdict the commercial intercourse between the United States and any foreign nation, or the dependencies thereof.

Fifth. Congress shall not make or declare war, or authorize acts of hostility against any foreign nation, without the concurrence of two thirds of both houses, except such acts of hostility be in defence of the territories of the United States when actually invaded.

Sixth. No person who shall hereafter be naturalized, shall be eligible as a member of the senate or house of representatives of the United States, nor capable of holding any civil office under the authority of the United States.

Seventh. The same person shall not be elected president of the United States a second time; nor shall the president be elected from the same state two terms in succession.

Resolved, That if the application of these states to the government of the United States, recommended in a foregoing resolution, should be unsuccessful, and peace should not be concluded, and the defence of these states should be neglected, as it has been since the commencement of the war, it will, in the opinion of this convention, be expedient for the legislatures of the several states to appoint delegates to another convention, to meet at Boston in the state of Massachusetts, on the third Thursday of June next, with such powers and instructions as the exigency of a crisis so momentous may require.

Resolved, That the Hon. George Cabot, the Hon. Chauncey Goodrich, and the Hon. Daniel Lyman, or any two of them, be authorized to call another meeting of this convention, to be holden in Boston, at any time before new delegates shall be chosen, as recommended in the above resolution, if in their judgment the situation of the country shall urgently require it.

Massachusetts

GEORGE CABOT,	SAMUEL SUMNER WILDE,
NATHAN DANE,	JOSEPH LYMAN,
WILLIAM PRESCOTT,	STEPHEN LONGFELLOW, JUN.
HARRISON GRAY OTIS,	DANIEL WALDO,
TIMOTHY BIGELOW,	HODIJAH BAYLIES,
JOSHUA THOMAS,	GEORGE BLISS.

Connecticut

CHAUNCEY GOODRICH,	NATHANIEL SMITH,
JOHN TREADWELL,	CALVIN GODDARD,
JAMES HILLHOUSE,	ROGER MINOT SHERMAN.
ZEPHANIAH SWIFT,	

Rhode-Island

DANIEL LYMAN,   EDWARD MANTON,

SAMUEL WARD,   BENJAMIN HAZARD.

N. Hampshire

BENJAMIN WEST,   MILLS OLCOTT.

Vermont

WILLIAM HALL, JUN.

16

Life in the Early Republic

Excerpts from Travelers' Accounts*

Europeans for long had been fascinated with the new world across the Atlantic Ocean and the number of accounts by travelers of their experiences and observations published since the days of Columbus would fill a small library. The flow of books instead of diminishing after the establishment of a new government grew by leaps and bounds. To the general curiosity concerning North America was added an intense interest in the possible outcome of what most observers thought was an experiment in self-government. No society familiar to Europeans had ever embarked upon such a trial as the Americans—government without kings, aristocracy, and an established church. The Americans, for their part, once the new government under Washington was successfully launched, became self-conscious about their achievements and gradually a sense of nationalism emerged, which was further stimulated by the constant urging of publicists and others that Americans should declare their cultural as well as political independence from England and Europe. Boasting and bragging soon became habitual among many which was not always appreciated by the foreign visitor. On the other hand, having put forward claims of superiority in all things, Americans displayed extreme sensitivity to criticism by foreigners. What particularly rankled Americans were the travel books written by British visitors who, subjected to the interminable bragging about the excellences of their constitution and their invincibility in war, vented their resentment in what Americans called "effusions of splenetic hostility." "They begin with a sneer," exclaimed an outraged American, "and end with a calumny." Some refused to believe that these travelers had ever visited the United States and were therefore no more worthy of credit than was Baron Münchhausen.

Isaac Weld, an Englishman who traveled extensively in the United States during 1797–1799, obviously does not fall within the category of a splenetic,

* Bibliographical data appear with each of the selections.

caustic, and implacably hostile critic of all things American. Although Weld was exposed to American bragging, and, as a true-born Englishman, resented being told that he was "a slave" because he admitted to being "subject," his criticisms of the United States were remarkably temperate. The roads were a trial; the curiosity of the people insufferable; the tavern accommodations primitive, yet Weld conceded that American justice was the fairest and most expeditious in the world. Although Weld condemned slavery, as did nost of the travelers to the United States, he stressed the patriarchal quality of the institution as it existed in Virginia as contrasted with slavery in South Carolina. Henry Fearon, another English traveler, remarked upon the slowness with which slavery was abolished in New York, Pennsylvania, and New Jersey. Although the abolitionists demanded immediate emancipation in the Southern States, the Nothern States, outside of New England, adopted schemes of gradual liberation. Moreover, the lot of the free Negroes in Northern cities was so intolerable that some proponents of slavery used it as an argument against giving slaves their freedom. Fearon also observed the peculiarly American insistence upon equality and some of the means employed to demonstrate, at least outwardly, that all Americans were, indeed, equal. As a matter of fact, most European observers of the United States showed exceptional interest in the American doctrine and practice of equality, some out of fear lest their own societies should become infected, and others out of sympathy and hope that their own lands might adopt more equalitarian ways than then prevalent in Europe. The classic study of the impact of equality on all phases of American life was made in the 1830s by the astute French political scientist Alexis de Tocqueville (1805–1859) in his *Democratie en Amérique* (1835). Most of the travelers before de Tocqueville paid attention to the phenomenon of equality although few were as careful and thorough in their examination as he. Henry Wansey, an Englishman who was in the United States in the mid-1790s, sought some explanation of the practice of equality while the French nobleman, the Duc de la Rochefoucault-Liancourt who came to this country in 1795 seeking sanctuary from the revolutionary upheavals in his own country, found equality to be the dominant theme in American society.

Humanitarianism constituted one aspect of the eighteenth-century Enlightenment; for the first time in the history of western civilization a major segment of the intellectual community concerned itself with the poor and dispossessed and sought to ameliorate their lot in this world rather than in the next. The United States was peculiarly suited to serve as a proving ground for Enlightenment ideas. In this new country, where everything was in a state of flux, far fewer barriers blocked efforts to give concrete form to the dreams of reformers than in Europe. Respecting changes in the criminal code and the treatment of prisoners, for example, the United States clearly assumed leadership. The ideas came from Europe —in this instance, from an Italian, Cesare Beccaria, whose *Essay on Crimes and Punishments* (1767) is a landmark in the history of penology. Beccaria advocated abolishing the death penalty because it failed to deter crime and asserted that the principal purpose of imprisonment ought to be the rehabilitation rather than the punishment of criminals. The most far-reaching application of Beccaria's ideas occurred in Pennsylvania. In 1785–1787, Dr. Benjamin Rush (1745–1813), a Philadelphia physician and one of the forerunners of psychiatry (he diagnosed crime as a disease of the mind), popularized in two pamphlets his own and Beccaria's views. Rush urged that all public punishment be abolished; that prisoners be set to work at productive labor; that they be given a low diet, clean rooms, and religious instruction; and that solitary confinement be substituted for corporal and capital punishment. Rush's reformist zeal bore fruit in 1794 when Pennsylvania abolished the death penalty except for first degree murder. Meanwhile, the Walnut Street prison in Philadelphia witnessed a unique experiment in penology; Lieutenant Francis Hall, a British visitor, pronounced it "a more interesting object to humanity than the most gorgeous palaces." The letters of Henry Franklin printed in Priscilla Wakefield's *Excursions in North America* (1806) describe some of the conditions in the Philadelphia prison.

Europeans, too, were enchanted (as were some Americans) with the wilderness, what it might portend, and how it might be tamed. The *wilderness*, as the word itself implies, was where savagery and barbarism held sway. Equally fearful to some Enlightened minds were the great cities of Europe and America where civilization seemed to threaten decay and dissolution. The American west offered the ideal compromise especially in those regions between the farthest outposts of settlement and the Eastern seaboard cities. Hector St. John de Crèvecoeur (1735–1813) in his *Letters from an American Farmer* (1782) provided an idyllic picture of the life in that half-way region. Needless to say, European travelers found the frontier an exciting change from London, Paris, and Rome. The frontier experience, too, left its impress upon generations of westward-moving American pioneers. Although this experience evoked qualities of self-reliance and what came to be called "rugged individualism," it did not create an atomized society. As William Priest observed in his *Travels in the United States* (1802), the survival of frontier communities also required collective effort.

Despite the great range of quality and reliability among them, the accounts of travelers to the United States provide us with one of our better sources of information concerning the social life and customs of our earlier history. For a midnineteenth century treatment of the subject see H. T. Tuckerman, *America and Her Commentators With a Critical Sketch of Travel in America* (New York: Charles Scribner, 1864). The best study of

the English tourists to America during the early period is to be found in
Jane Louise Mesick's *The English Traveller in America, 1785–1835* (New
York: The Columbia University Press, 1922).

In reading the selection from Isaac Weld's *Travels* note (1) his description
of the Maryland countryside and his generalization respecting Americans'
disregard for their natural endowment of trees; (2) what he observed
concerning political and judicial processes in America; (3) his observations
concerning geographical mobility and its probable causes; (4) his description of social changes in Virginia and what he saw of the operation of the
slave system; and (5) what he reported on the subject of violence. In
reading the excerpts from Henry Fearon's *Sketches* note (1) the extent to
which slavery and racial prejudice existed in the free state of New York;
(2) evidences of American parochialism; and (3) some of the exceptional
ways in which the Americans expressed their equalitarianism. In reading
the selection from Henry Wansey's *Excursion* note (1) the contrasts he made
between the United States and Great Britain; and (2) to what causes he
attributed the well-being of the Americans. In reading the selection from
the Duc de la Rochefoucault's *Travels* note (1) aspects of the operation of
the equality principle that impressed him most; (2) the food and drink
habits he observed; (3) how he accounted for the differences in appearance
of the workers of Europe and America; and (4) to what extent he thought
America was a classless society. In reading the letter from Henry Franklin
note (1) what he learned about the economy of Philadelphia; (2) how he
accounted for the scarcity of poverty in Pennsylvania; (3) his description
of Philadelphia's practice of "social security"; (4) the kind of prison he
found there and how the inmates were treated; (5) how he judged the
efficacy of Philadelphia's penal program and to whom he attributed the
innovations in prison reform; and (6) his observations concerning Negro
slavery. In reading the material from William Priest's *Travels* note (1) what
Priest learned about liberty and equality while in Philadelphia; (2) his
observations respecting the eating habits of Americans; (3) how he accounted
for the price of labor in America; (4) information he gained concerning
the process and problems of pioneering in the American backcountry;
and (5) what he observed about the nature of the American girl.

T HE TRAVELERS' REPORT.

Wilmington is the capital of the state of Delaware,
and contains about six hundred houses, which are chiefly of brick.
The streets are laid out on a plan somewhat similar to that of

Isaac Weld, *Travels Through the States of North America . . . During the Years 1795,
    1796, and 1797 . . .* 2 vols. (London: J. Stockdale, 1799), I, pp. 36–39; 46–47;
    124–33; 146–51; 190–93.

Philadelphia. There is nothing very interesting in this town, and the country round about it is flat and insipid. Elkton, twenty-one miles distant from Wilmington, and the first town in Maryland, contains about ninety indifferent houses, which are built without any regularity; it is a dirty disagreeable place. In this neighbourhood I first took notice of log-houses; those which I had hitherto seen having been built either of brick or stone, or else constructed with wooden frames, sheathed on the outside with boards. The log-houses are cheaper than any others in a country where there is abundance of wood, and generally are the first that are erected on a new settlement in America. The sides consist of trees just squared, and placed horizontally one upon the other; the ends of the logs of one side resting alternately on the ends of those of the adjoining sides, in notches; the interstices between the logs are stopped with clay; and the roof is covered with boards or with shingles, which are small pieces of wood in the shape of slates or tiles, and which are used for that purpose, with a few exceptions, throughout America. These habitations are not very sightly, but when well built they are warm and comfortable, and last for a long time.

A considerable quantity of wheat and Indian corn is raised in this neighbourhood, to the production of which the soil is favourable; but the best cultivated parts of the country are not seen from the road, which passes chiefly over barren and hilly tracts, called "ridges." The reason for carrying the road over these is, because it is found to last longer than if carried over the flat part of the country, where the soil is deep, a circumstance which the people of Maryland always take into consideration; for after a road is once cut, they never take pains to keep it in good repair. The roads in this state are worse than in any one in the Union; indeed so very bad are they, that on going from Elkton to the Susquehannah ferry, the driver frequently had to call to the passengers in the stage, to lean out of the carriage first at one side, then at the other, to prevent it from oversetting in the deep ruts with which the road abounds: "Now, gentlemen, to the right;" upon which the passengers all stretched their bodies half way out of the carriage to balance it on that side: "Now, gentlemen, to the left," and so on. This was found absolutely necessary at least a dozen times in half the number of miles. Whenever they attempt to mend these roads, it is always by filling the ruts with saplings or bushes, and covering them over with earth. This, however, is done only when there are fields on each side of the road. If the road runs contiguous to a wood, then, instead of mending it where it is bad, they open a new passage through the trees, which they call making a road. It is very common in Maryland to see six or seven different roads branching out from one, which all lead to the same place. A stranger, before he is acquainted with this circumstance, is frequently puzzled to know which he ought to take. The dexterity with which the drivers of the stages guide their horses along these new roads, which are full of stumps of trees, is astonishing, yet to appearance they are the most awkward drivers possible; it is more by the different noises which they make, than by their reins, that they manage their horses.

Charleston stands at a few miles distance from Elkton; there are about twenty houses only in it, which are inhabited chiefly by people who carry on a herring fishery. Beyond it the country is much diversified with hill and dale, and the soil being but of an indifferent quality, the lands are so little cleared, that in many parts the road winds through uninterrupted woods for four or five miles together. The scenery in this neighbourhood is extremely interesting. From the top of the hills you meet with numberless bold and extensive prospects of the Chesapeak Bay and of the river Susquehannah; and scarcely do you cross a valley without beholding in the depths of the wood the waters of some little creek or rivulet rushing over ledges of rock in a beautiful cascade. The generality of Americans stare with astonishment at a person who can feel any delight at passing through such a country as this. To them the sight of a wheat field or a cabbage garden would convey pleasure far greater than that of the most romantic woodland views. They have an unconquerable aversion to trees; and whenever a settlement is made, they cut away all before them without mercy; not one is spared; all share the same fate, and are involved in the general havoc. . . . There are two theatres here [Baltimore], in which there are performances occasionally. The oldest of them, which stands in the road to Fell's Point, is most wretched, and appears little better than a heap of loose boards; for a long time it lay quite neglected, but has lately been fitted up for a company of French actors, the only one I ever heard of in the country. Baltimore, like Philadelphia, has suffered from the ravages of the yellow fever. During the autumn it is generally unhealthy, and those who can afford it retire to country seats in the neighbourhood, of which some are most delightfully situated.

From Baltimore to Washington, which is forty miles distant, the country wears but a poor appearance. The soil in some parts consists of a yellow clay mixed with gravel; in other parts it is very sandy. In the neighbourhood of the creeks and between the hills are patches of rich black earth, called Bottoms, the trees upon which grow to a large size; but where there is gravel they are very small. The roads passing over these bottoms are worse than any I ever met with elsewhere. In driving over one of them, near the head waters of a branch of Patuxent river, a few days after a heavy fall of rain, the wheel of a sulky which I was in sunk up to the very boxes. For a moment I despaired of being able to get out without assistance, when my horse, which was very powerful, finding himself impeded, threw himself upon his haunches, and disengaging his fore-feet, made a vigorous plunge forwards, which luckily disengaged both himself and the sulky, and freed me from my embarrassment. I was afterwards informed that General Washington, as he was going to meet congress a short time before, was stopped in the very same place, his carriage sinking so deep in the mud that it was found necessary to send to a neighbouring house for ropes and poles to extricate it. Over some of the bottoms, which were absolutely impassable in their natural state, causeways have been thrown, which are made with large trees laid side by side across the road. For a time these causeways afford a commodious passage; but they do not last long, as many of the trees sink into the soft soil, and others, exposed to the continual attrition of waggon wheels in a particular part, breaking asunder. In this state, full of unseen obstacles, it is absolutely a matter of danger for a person unacquainted with the road to attempt to drive a carriage along it. The bridges over the creeks, covered with loose boards, are as bad as the causeways, and totter as a carriage passes over. . . .

[In a tavern,] a stranger must tell where he came from, where he is going, what his name is, what his business is; and until he gratifies their curosity on these points, and many others of equal importance, he is never suffered to remain quiet for a moment. In a tavern, he must satisfy every fresh set that comes in, in the same manner, or involve himself in a quarrel, especially if it is found out that he is not a native, which it does not require much sagacity to discover.

The Germans give themselves but little trouble about politics; they elect their representatives to serve in congress and the state assemblies; and satisfied that deserving men have been chosen by the people at large, they trust that these men do what is best for the public good, and therefore abide patiently by their decisions: they revere the constitution, conscious that they live happily under it, and express no wishes to have it altered. The Americans, however, are for ever cavilling at some of the public measures; something or other is always wrong, and they never appear perfectly satisfied. If any great measure is before congress for discussion, seemingly distrustful of the abilities or the integrity of the men they have elected, they meet together in their towns or districts, canvass the matter themselves, and then send forward instructions to their representatives how to act. They never consider that any important question is more likely to meet with a fair discussion in an assembly, where able men are collected together from all parts of the states, than in an obscure corner, where a few individuals are assembled, who have no opportunity of getting general information on the subject. Party spirit is for ever creating dissentions amongst them, and one man is continually endeavouring to obtrude his political creed upon another. If it is found out that a stranger is from Great Britain or Ireland, they immediately begin to boast of their own constitution and freedom, and give him to understand, that they think every Englishman a slave, because he submits to be called a subject. Their opinions are for the most part crude and dogmatical, and principally borrowed from newspapers, which are wretchedly compiled from the pamphlets of the day; having read a few of which, they think themselves arrived at the summit of intellectual excellence, and qualified for making the deepest political researches.

The Germans, as I have said, are fond of settling near each other: when the young men of a family are grown up, they generally endeavour to get a piece of land in the neighbourhood of their relations, and by their industry soon make it valuable; the American, on the contrary, is of a roving disposition, and wholly regardless of the ties of consanguinity; he takes his wife with him, goes to a distant part of the country, and buries himself in the woods, hundreds of miles distant from the rest of his family, never perhaps to see them again. In the back parts of the country, you always meet numbers of men prowling about to try and buy cheap land; having found what they like, they immediately remove: nor having once removed, are these people satisfied; restless and discontented with what they possess, they are for ever changing. It is scarcely possible in any part of the continent to find a man, amongst the middling and lower classes of Americans, who has not changed his farm and his residence many different times. Thus it is, that though there are not more than four millions of people in the United States, yet they are scattered from the confines of Canada to the farthest extremity of Georgia, and from the Atlantic to the banks of the Mississippi. Thousands of acres of waste land are annually taken up in unhealthy and unfruitful parts of the country, notwithstanding that the best settled and healthy parts of the middle states would maintain five times the number of inhabitants that they do at present. The American, however, does not change about from place to place in this manner merely to gratify a wandering disposition; in every change he hopes to make money. By the desire of making money, both the Germans and Americans of every class and description, are actuated in all their movements; self-interest is always uppermost in their thoughts; it is the idol which they worship, and at its shrine thousands and thousands would be found, in all parts of the country, ready to make a sacrifice of every noble and generous sentiment that can adorn the human mind.

In coming to this place from Lancaster, I crossed the Susquehannah River, which runs nearly midway between the two towns, at the small village of Columbia, as better boats are kept there than at either of the ferries higher up or lower down the river. The Susquehannah is here somewhat more than a quarter of a mile wide; and for a considerable distance, both above and below the ferry, it abounds with islands and large rocks, over which last the water runs with prodigious velocity: the roaring noise that it makes is heard a great way off. The banks rise very boldly on each side, and are thickly wooded; the islands also are covered with small trees, which, interspersed with the rocks, produce a very fine effect. The scenery in every point of view is wild and romantic. . . .

On entering into the courts, a stranger is apt to smile at the grotesque appearance of the judges who preside in them, at their manners on the bench; but this smile must be suppressed when it is recollected, that there is no country, perhaps in the world, where justice is more impartially administered, or more easily obtained by those who have been injured. The judges in the country parts of Pennsylvania are no more than plain farmers, who from their infancy have been accustomed to little else than following the plough. The laws expressly declare that there must be, at least, three judges resident in every county; now as the salary allowed is but a mere trifle, no lawyer would accept of the office, which of course must be filled from amongst the inhabitants,* who are all in a happy state of mediocrity, and on a perfect equality with each other. The district judge, however, who presides in the district or circuit, has a larger salary, and is a man of a different cast. The district or circuit consists of at least three, but not more than six counties. The county judges, which I have mentioned, are "judges of the court of common pleas, and by virtue of their offices also justices of oyer and terminer, and general gaol delivery, for the trial of capital and other offenders therein." Any two judges compose the court of quarter sessions. Under certain regulations, established by law, the accused party has the power of removing the proceedings into the supreme court, which has jurisdiction over every part of the state. This short account of the courts relates only to Pennsylvania: every state in the union has a separate code of laws for itself, and a district judicature. . . .

STRATFORD, MARCH

In the neighbourhood of York and Lancaster, the soil consists of a rich, brown, loamy earth; and if you proceed in a south-westerly course, parallel to the Blue Mountains, you meet with the same kind of soil as far as Frederic in Maryland. Here it changes gradually to a deep reddish colour, and continues much the same along the eastern side of the mountains, all the way down to North Carolina. On crossing over the mountains, however, directly from Frederic, the same fertile brown soil, which is common in the neighbourhood of York and Lancaster, is again met with, and it is found throughout the Shenandoah Valley, and as far down as the Carolinas, on the west side of the mountains.

* This is also the case in Philadelphia, where we find practising physicians and surgeons sitting on the bench as judges in a court of justice.

Between York and Frederic in Maryland there are two or three small towns; viz. Hanover, Petersburgh, and Woodsburgh, but there is nothing worthy of mention in any of them. Frederic contains about seven hundred houses and five churches, two of which are for German Lutherans, one for Presbyterians, one for Calvinists, and one for Baptists. It is a flourishing town, and carries on a brisk inland trade. The arsenal of the state of Maryland is placed here, the situation being secure and central.

From Frederic I proceeded in a southerly course through Montgomery county in Maryland. In this direction the soil changes to a yellowish sort of clay mixed with gravel, and continues much the same until you come to the federal city, beyond which, as I have before mentioned, it becomes more and more sandy as you approach the sea coast. The change in the face of the country after leaving Frederic is gradual, but at the end of a day's journey a striking difference is perceptible. Instead of well cultivated fields, green with wheat, such as are met with along that rich track which runs contiguous to the mountains, large pieces of land, which have been worn out with the culture of tobacco, are here seen lying waste, with scarcely an herb to cover them. Instead of the furrows of the plough, the marks of the hoe appear on the ground; the fields are overspread with little hillocks for the reception of tobacco plants, and the eye is assailed in every direction with the unpleasant sight of gangs of male and female slaves toiling under the harsh commands of the overseer. . . . It was here [Virginia] that numbers of English gentlemen, who migrated when Virginia was a young colony, fixed their residence; and several of the houses which they built, exactly similar to the old manor houses in England, are still remaining, particularly in the counties of Richmond and Westmoreland. Some of these, like the houses in Maryland, are quite in ruins; others are kept in good repair by the present occupiers, who live in a style, which approaches nearer to that of English country gentlemen, than what is to be met with any where else on the continent, some other parts of Virginia alone excepted.

Amongst the inhabitants here, and in the lower parts of Virginia, there is a disparity unknown elsewhere in America, excepting in the large towns. Instead of the lands being equally divided, immense estates are held by a few individuals, who derive large incomes from them, whilst the generality of the people are but in a state of mediocrity. Most of the men also, who possess these large estates, having received liberal educations, which the others have not, the distinction between them is still more observable. I met with several in this neighbourhood, who had been brought up at the public schools and universities in England, where, until the unfortunate war which separated the colonies from her, the young men were very generally educated; and even still a few are sent there, as the veneration for that country from whence their ancestors came, and with which they were themselves for a long time afterwards connected, is by no means yet extinguished.

There is by no means so great a disparity now, however, amongst the inhabitants of the Northern Neck, as was formerly, and it is becoming less and less perceptible every year, many of the large estates having been divided in consequence of the removal of the proprietors to other parts of the country that were more healthy, and many more on account of the present laws of Virginia, which do not permit any one son to inherit the landed estates of the father to the exclusion of his brothers.

The principal planters in Virginia have nearly every thing they can want on their own estates. Amongst their slaves are found taylors, shoemakers, carpenters, smiths, turners, wheelwrights, weavers, tanners, &c. I have seen patterns of excellent coarse woollen cloth, made in the country by slaves, and a variety of cotton manufactures, amongst the rest good nankeen. Cotton grows here extremely well; the plants are often killed by frost in winter, but they always produce abundantly the first year in which they are sown. The cotton from which nankeen is made is of a particular kind, naturally of a yellowish colour.

The large estates are managed by stewards and overseers, the proprietors just amusing themselves with seeing what is going forward. The work is done wholly by slaves, whose numbers are in this part of the country more than double that of white persons. The slaves on the large plantations are in general very well provided for, and treated with mildness. During three months, nearly, that I was in Virginia, but two or three instances of ill treatment towards them came under my observation. Their quarters, the name whereby their habitations are called, are usually situated one or two hundred yards from the dwelling house, which gives the appearance of a village to the residence of every planter in Virginia; when the estate, however, is so large as to be divided into several farms, then separate quarters are attached to the house of the overseer on each farm. Adjoining their little habitations, the slaves commonly have small gardens and yards for poultry, which are all their own property; they have ample time to attend to their own concerns, and their gardens are generally found well stocked, and their flocks of poultry numerous. Besides the food they raise for themselves, they are allowed liberal rations of salted pork and Indian corn. Many of their little huts are comfortably furnished, and they are themselves, in general, extremely well clothed. In short, their condition is by no means so wretched as might be imagined. They are forced to work certain hours in the day; but in return they are clothed, dieted, and lodged comfortably, and saved all anxiety about provision for their offspring. Still, however, let the condition of a slave be made ever so comfortable, as long as he is conscious of being the property of another man, who has it in his power to dispose of him according to the dictates of caprice; as long as he hears people around him talking of the blessings of liberty, and considers that he is in a state of bondage, it is not to be supposed that he can feel equally happy with the free-man. It is immaterial under what form slavery presents itself, whenever it appears, there is ample cause for humanity to weep at the fight, and to lament that men can be found so forgetful of their own situations, as to live regardless of the feelings of their fellow creatures.

With respect to the policy of holding slaves in any country, on account of the depravity of morals which it necessarily occasions, besides the many other evil consequences attendant upon it, so much has already been said by others, that it is needless here to make any comments on the subject.

The number of the slaves increases most rapidly, so that there is scarcely any estate but what is overstocked. This is a circumstance complained of by every planter, as the maintenance of more than are requisite for the culture of the estate is attended with great expense. Motives of humanity deter them from selling the poor creatures, or turning them adrift from the spot where they have been born and brought up, in the midst of friends and relations.

What I have here said respecting the condition and treatment of slaves, appertains, it must be remembered, to those only who are upon the large plantations in Virginia; the lot of such as are unfortunate enough to fall into the hands of the lower class of white people, and of hard task-masters in the towns, is very different. In the Carolinas and Georgia again, slavery presents itself in very different colours, from what it does even in its worst form in Virginia. I am told, that it is no uncommon thing there, to see gangs of negroes staked at a horse race, and to see these unfortunate beings bandied about from one set of drunken gamblers to another, for days together. How much to be deprecated are the laws which suffer such abuses to exist! yet these are the laws enacted by people, who boast of their love of liberty and independence, and who presume to say, that it is in the breasts of Americans alone that the blessings of freedom are held in just estimation!

The Northern Neck, with the exception of some few spots only, is flat and sandy, and abounds with pine and cedar trees. Some parts of it are well cultivated, and afford good crops; but these are so intermixed with extensive tracts of waste land, worn out by the culture of tobacco, and which are almost destitute of verdure, that on the whole the country has the appearance of barrenness.

This is the case wherever tobacco has been made the principal object of cultivation. It is not, however, so much owing to the great share of nutriment which the tobacco plant requires, that the land is impoverished, as to the particular mode of cultivating it, which renders it necessary for people to be continually walking between the plants, from the moment they are set out, so that the ground about each plant is left exposed to the burning rays of the sun all the summer, and becomes at the end of the season a hard beaten pathway. A ruinous system has prevailed also of working the same piece of land year after year, till it was totally exhausted; after this it was left neglected, and a fresh piece of land was cleared, that always produced good crops for one or two seasons; but this in its turn was worn out. . . .

The Falls in the river, or the Rapids, as they should be called, extend six miles above the city, in the course of which there is a descent of about eighty feet. The river is here full of large rocks, and the water rushes over them in some places with great impetuosity. A canal is completed at the north side of these Falls, which renders the navigation complete from Richmond to the Blue Mountains, and at particular times of the year, boats with light burthens can proceed still higher up. In the river, opposite the town, are no more than seven feet water, but ten miles lower down about twelve feet. Most of the vessels trading to Richmond unlade the greater part of their cargoes at this place into river craft, and then proceed up to the town. Trade is carried on here chiefly by foreigners, as the Virginians have but little inclination for it, and are too fond of amusement to pursue it with much success.

Richmond contains about four thousand inhabitants, one half of whom are slaves. Amongst the freemen are numbers of lawyers, who, with the officers of the state government, and several that live retired on their fortunes, reside in the upper town; the other part is inhabited principally by the traders.

Perhaps in no place of the same size in the world is there more gambling going forward than in Richmond. I had scarcely alighted from my horse at the tavern, when the landlord came to ask what game I was most partial to, as in such a room there was a faro table, in another a hazard table, in a third a billiard table, to any one of which he was ready to conduct me. Not the smallest secrecy is employed in keeping these tables; they are always crowded with people, and the doors of the apartment are only shut to prevent the rabble from coming in. Indeed, throughout the lower parts of the country in Virginia, and also in that part of Maryland next to it, there is scarcely a petty tavern without a billiard room, and this is always full of a set of idle low-lived fellows, drinking spirits or playing cards, if not engaged at the table. Cock-fighting is also another favourite diversion. It is chiefly, however, the lower class of people that partake of these amusements at the taverns; in private there is, perhaps, as little gambling in Virginia as in any other part of America. The circumstance of having the taverns thus infested by such a set of people, renders travelling extremely unpleasant. Many times I have been forced to proceed much farther in a day than I have wished, in order to avoid the scenes of rioting and quarrelling that I have met with at the taverns, which it is impossible to escape as long as you remain in the same house where they are carried on, for every apartment is considered as common, and that room in which a stranger sits down is sure to be the most frequented.

Whenever these people come to blows, they fight just like wild beasts, biting, kicking, and endeavouring to tear each other's eyes out with their nails. It is by no means uncommon to meet with those who have lost an eye in a combat, and there are men who pride themselves upon the dexterity with which they can scoop one out. This is called *gouging*. To perform the horrid operation, the combatant twists his forefingers in the side locks of his adversary's hair, and then applies his thumbs to the bottom of the eye, to force it out of the socket. If ever there is a battle, in which neither of those engaged loses an eye, their faces are however generally cut in a shocking manner with the thumb nails, in the many attempts which are made at gouging. But what is worse than all, these wretches in their combat endeavour to their utmost to tear out each other's testicles. Four or five instances came within my own observation, as I passed through Maryland and Virginia, of men being confined in their beds from the injuries which they had received of this nature in a fight. In the Carolinas and Georgia, I have been credibly assured, that the people are still more depraved in this respect than in Virginia, and that in some particular parts of these states, every third or fourth man appears with one eye.

The existence of *slavery* in the United States has, I know, long been to you all a subject both of regret and astonishment. New York is called a "free state:" that it may be so *theoretically*, or when compared with its southern neighbours, I am not prepared to dispute; but if, in England, we saw in the Times newspaper such advertisements as the following, we should conclude that freedom from slavery existed only in words. The first is from the New York Daily Advertiser. I have not made a memorandum of the paper from which I extracted the second; but no American will deny their originality; and, what is worse, I fear there are few who would acknowledge their iniquity:

To Be Sold

A Servant woman acquainted with both city and country business, about 30 years of age, and sold because she wishes to change her place. Enquire at this office, or at 91 Cherry-street.

For Sale Or Hire

A likely young Man Servant, sober, honest and well behaved. He would suit very well for a house servant or gentleman's waiter, being accustomed to both. Enquire at this office.

Henry B. Fearon, *Sketches of America: A Narrative of a Journey of Five Thousand Miles Through the Eastern and Western States of America* ... (London: Longman, Hurst, Reese, Orme, and Brown, 1818), pp. 56–61; 80–81.

The number of blacks in this city is very great: they have instituted a "Wilberforce Society;" and look upon the Englishman whose name they have taken as the great saviour of their race. At Mrs. Bradish's boarding-house I saw but one white servant, and I should suppose there were of her own, and of her boarders', at least sixteen blacks. A negro child, about six years of age, often waited upon us at tea: the strength and dexterity of the little thing frequently excited my attention and sympathy. Female blacks often obstructed my passage up and down stairs. They lie about, clinging to the boards as though that had been the spot on which they had vegetated: several belonged to families from the south, and were, as a matter of course, *held in unconditional slavery*. The men, whether regular servants of the house or not, equally attended upon all at table. There was one waiter on an average to four gentlemen; yet such was the want of system observed, that few could obtain what they desired. Soon after landing I called at a hair-dresser's in Broadway, nearly opposite the city-hall: the man in the shop was a negro. He had nearly finished with me, when a black man, very respectably dressed, came into the shop and sat down. The barber enquired if he wanted the proprietor or his *boss*, as he termed him, who was also a black: the answer was in the negative; but that he wished to have his hair cut. My man turned upon his heel, and with the greatest contempt, muttered in a tone of proud importance, "We do not cut coloured men here, Sir." The poor fellow walked out without replying, exhibiting in his countenance confusion, humiliation, and mortification. I immediately requested, that if the refusal was on account of my being present, he might be called back. The hair-dresser was astonished: "You cannot be in earnest, Sir," he said. I assured him that I was so, and that I was much concerned in witnessing the refusal from no other cause than that his skin was of a darker tinge than my own. He stopped the motion of his scissars; and after a pause of some seconds, in which his eyes were fixed upon my face, he said, "Why, I guess as how, Sir, what you say is mighty elegant, and you're an elegant man; but I guess you are not of these parts."—'I am from England,' said I, 'where we have neither so cheap nor so enlightened a government as yours, but we have no slaves.'—"Ay, I guessed you were not raised here; you salt-water people are mighty grand to coloured people; you are not so proud, and I guess you have more to be proud of; now I reckon you do not know that my boss would not have a single ugly or clever gentleman come to his store, if he cut coloured men; now my boss, I guess, ordered me to turn out every coloured man from the store right away, and if I did not, he would send me off slick; for the slimmest gentleman in York would not come to his store if coloured men were let in; but you know all that Sir, I guess, without my telling you; you are an elegant gentleman too, Sir." I assured him that I was ignorant of the fact which he stated; but which, from the earnestness of his manner, I concluded must be true. "And you come all the way right away from England. Well! I would not have supposed, I guess, that you come from there from your tongue; you have no hardness like, I guess, in your speaking; you talk almost as well as we do, and that is what I never see, I guess, in a gentleman so lately from England. I guess your talk is within a grade as good as ours. You are a mighty elegant gentleman, and if you will tell me where you keep, I will bring some of my coloured friends to visit you. Well, you must be a smart man to come from England, and talk English as well as we do that were raised in this country." At the dinner-table I commenced a relation of this occurrence to three American gentlemen, one of whom was a doctor, the others were in the law: they were men of education and of liberal opinions. When I arrived at the point of the black being turned out, they exclaimed, "Ay right, perfectly right, I would never go to a barber's where a coloured man was cut!" Observe, these gentlemen were not from the south; they are residents of New York, and I believe were born there. I was upon the point of expressing my opinion, but withheld it, thinking it wise to look at every thing as it stood, and form a deliberate judgment when every feature was finally before me. They were amused with the barber's conceit about the English language, which I understand is by no means a singular view of the subject.

The exclusion of blacks from the places of public worship where whites attend, I stated at the commencement. In perfect conformity with this spirit is the fact, that the most degraded white will not walk or eat with a negro; so that, although New York is a free state, it is such only on parchment: the black Americans are in it *practically* and politically slaves; the laws of the mind being, after all, infinitely more strong and more effective than those of the statute book; and it is these *mental* legislative enactments, operating in too many cases besides this of the poor negroes, which excite but little respect for the American character. . . .

Mr. De Wint's residence is within half a mile: I had the pleasure of dining with him in company with several ladies and gentlemen of a very superior class. The following day Judge Vanpelt, a neighbouring gentleman and farmer, had the politeness to take me to his house. My reception at both, as well as the style of living, the substantial elegance of the furniture, and the mental talents of the company, was *essentially English*. I felt, indeed, for the first time, that I was once more in your little island. That *peculiarly* British word *comfort* was well understood in these hospitable mansions. Another thing, too, was here an evident favourite, though, I lament to say, scarcely known on this side the Atlantic—*cleanliness:* the servants also were in their dress neat, and in their manners attentive, forming a striking contrast to what I have too often seen on other occasions.

Servants, let me here observe, are called "helps:" if you call them servants they leave you without notice. Englishmen often incur their displeasure by negligence in continuing to use this prohibited word. The difference, however, would appear merely verbal; for indeed I should misrepresent the impressions I have received on the subject, if I stated that the Americans *really* shewed more feeling, or were more considerate in their conduct towards this class of society than the English: every one who knows them will, I think, pronounce the direct contrary to be the case. A friend of mine, the other day, met with a rebuff at his hotel, which taught him the necessity of altering—not his ideas indeed, but his words. Addressing the female "help" he said, "Be kind enough to tell your mistress that I should be glad to see her."—"My *mistress*, Sir! I tell you I have no mistress, nor master either. I will not tell her, Sir, I guess; if you want Mrs. M—— you may go to her yourself, I guess. I have no mistress, Sir. In this country there is no mistresses nor masters; I guess I am a woman citizen."—The term "boss," as I have before observed, is substituted for that of master: but these, I would remark, are not the only instances in this country of the alteration of *names*, while *things* remain the same: indeed some very absurd, and even indelicate changes have been made which cannot well be communicated on paper.

Servants are usually engaged by the week: enquiry as to character is not practised: blacks and whites are seldom kept in the same house. . . .

It is remarked, that the United States have flourished more during the last three or four years, than thrice that time during any former period. This, I observe, is since the federal constitution has come into full exercise.

In England, the degree of liberty, we have enjoyed, is considered as the grand cause of our greatness, and superiority over other nations; yet here [in England], genius is often cramped by poverty and misfortune, and the exertions of a vast body of people lost to the community, by partial laws, chartered rights, appropriations, &c.

It is not so in the United States; every man feels himself equal in the estimation of his country, according to his virtue and usefulness, and the state provides for his education. The civil rights of no one are abridged on account of religious belief or worship; and every one is at liberty to follow the bent of his genius, uncontrouled in its exertions by any of these impediments. Three fourths of the people are actively employed in either agriculture, trade or commerce. There are but few idle drones in the hive, and, with all these advantages, their rapid progress to wealth and improvement is certain, and must be great beyond conception.

We overtook the stage-coach again at the White Horse, where the passengers breakfasted. It appears somewhat strange to Europeans, to see the coachman eat at the same table with the passengers; but it would seem equally strange to Americans, to see the coachman eating by himself. It is futile to argue against the customs of a country; we must submit. Equality, pretended equality, which widely differs from true freedom, is the foundation of this custom, which, in fact, injures nobody; it is for the same reason, that the servants, who wait at dinner or breakfast, are seated, except while they are serving you, and that the landlord attends you with his hat on his head. A man may be allowed to dislike this custom,

Henry Wansey, *The Journal of an Excursion to the United States of North America in the Summer of 1794* (Salisbury, England, [1796] 2nd ed., with additions, 1798), p. 236.

François Alexandre Frederic Duc de la Rochefoucauld-Liancourt, *Travels through the United States of America . . . in the Years 1795, 1796, and 1797 . . .* translated from the original French edition of 1799 by H. Neuman, 2 vols. (London: T. Davison, 1799), I, pp. 23–24, 68; II, pp. 215, 671–72.

without possessing any extravagant share of weak pride. An inn-keeper, a shoe-maker, a taylor, are naturally at liberty to wait on people, or to let it alone; but if they choose to wait on others, they should keep at a proper distance, and observe the respect, which becomes their situation. It must be observed, however, that many an inn-keeper in America is a captain or a major; nay, I have seen drivers of stagecoaches, who were colonels: such things are very common in America. There is much greater propriety in the custom that prevails in England, where the tradesman is treated with politeness and respect by his employers, whilst he, in return, observes the due decorum of his situation, without meanly sacrificing that noble principle of liberty, which every Englishman cherishes with conscious pride: it will soon be the same in France. . . .

A spirit, or rather habit of equality, is diffused among this people, as far as it possibly can go. In several inns, especially such as are situate on less frequented roads, the circumstance of our servant not dining with us at the same table excited general astonishment, without its bespeaking any bad intention on the part of those who manifested it. The inhabitants exhibit to strangers striking instances both of the utmost cleanliness and excessive nastiness. They are much surprised at a refusal, to sleep with one or two other men in the same bed, or between dirty sheets, or to drink after ten other persons out of the same dirty glass; and they wonder no less, when they see strangers neglect to wash their hands and face every morning. Whisky mixed with water is the common drink in the country. There is no settler, however poor, whose family do not drink coffee and chocolate, and eat salt meat at breakfast. At dinner comes salt meat again, or salt fish and eggs; and at supper, once more salt meat and coffee. This is also the general rule in inns. An American sits down at the table of his landlord, and lies down in the bed, which he finds empty, or occupied but by one person, without in the least enquiring, in the latter of these cases, who that person may be. . . .

The spirit of equality is carried as far as is consistent with order in a great society. The man who is possessed of the greatest wealth, and the most happily circumstanced in every respect, shakes hands with the workman whom he met on his way, converses with him, not under the idea of doing him an honour, as is often the notion elsewhere—but from a consciousness, in the first instance, that he may at some future time stand in need of his assistance—afterward, without any such interested consideration, but merely through habit, and the force of education, and because he sees in him his fellow-man, only placed in a different situation, to whom he is the less tempted to think himself superior, as it often happens that the now rich man has himself once been in a less enviable situation. This natural homage paid to the character of man possesses a certain charm which is truly pleasing to an independent soul, especially when experience proves that the different functions of society are not the less scrupulously respected in consequence of it, and that no individual is thereby subject to any greater restriction in the exercise of his own liberty. . . .

The inferior classes of workmen, down to those who labour in the ports, do not appear to me to be so rustic in America as they generally do in the old world. The reason of this is, without doubt, that they are treated with more civility, and considered by those who employ them as free men with whom they have contracted, rather than as workmen, whom they compel to labour. They are like the workmen of every class, both in town and country, much better paid than in Europe, by which they are enabled to live well. There is not a family, even in the most miserable hut in the midst of the woods, who does not eat meat twice a day at least, and drink tea and coffee; and there is not one who drinks pure water; the proverbial wish of *having a chicken in the pot*, is more than accomplished in America. The shopkeeper and the artisan live much better here than in Europe; and the table of a family, in easy circumstances, living upon their income, is not better served in England and France, than a great many of those of tailors, hair-dressers, &c. of Philadelphia, of New York, or of all other large towns in America.

Though there be no distinctions acknowledged by law in the United States, fortune, and the nature of professions form different classes. The merchants, the lawyers, the landowners, who do not cultivate their land themselves (and the number, which is small from the state of Delaware to the north, is great in the states of the south), the physicians, and the clergy, form the first class. The inferior merchants, the farmers, and the artisans, may be included in the second; and the third class is composed of workmen, who let themselves by the day, by the month, &c.

In balls, concerts, and public amusements, these classes do not mix; and yet, except the labourer in ports, and the common sailor, every one calls himself, and is called by others, a *gentleman*; a small fortune is sufficient for the assumption of this title, as it carries men from one class to another. They deceive themselves very much who think that pure republican manners prevail in America. . . .

Dear Brother: A vessel being ready to sail for England, I gladly embrace the opportunity of making a few remarks on some subjects that have excited my attention.

Commerce is the universal occupation of the inhabitants of this city, though many of the monied men employ their capitals in buying and selling land, which is here as much an article of traffic as any other commodity. Philadelphia is the grand emporium of the whole province and adjoining states, collecting from them the following articles for exportation: charcoal, pot-ash, beer, cyder, salt meat and fish, butter, cheese, corn, flour, tallow candles, linseed, soap, timber staves, hides, deer and beaver skins, bark, and pigs of iron. The accommodations for commerce are excellent, the quay being large, and so conveniently constructed, that merchantmen of considerable size can unload their cargoes without difficulty. There are also several wet and dry docks for building and repairing ships, besides numerous magazines and stores; (the American name for warehouses;) to which may be added, the advantage, both to utility and beauty, by the introduction of canals, and the situation of the city between two rivers, the Delaware and the Schuylkill, which nearly enclose it. It was founded by the celebrated William Penn, in 1682. He received a grant of lands, on the western side of the Delaware, from the crown, since erected into a province, called Pennsylvania. The wisdom, moderation, justice, and humanity of this great man's character, were eminently displayed in the plan of his city, the code of laws for the government of his province, and his upright and generous treatment of the Indians from whom he made the purchase. Their veneration for his memory is so deeply rooted, and their confidence in his veracity so unshaken, that, to this day, they are never perfectly satisfied with any treaty, unless some Quakers are present at the conference; for, say they, the descendants of William Penn will never suffer us to be deceived. A

Henry Franklin to his brother, Philadelphia in Priscilla Wakefield, *Excursions in North America: Described in Letters from a Gentleman and His Young Companion to Their Friends in England* (London: Daton and Harvey, 1806), pp. 14–19.

more noble testimony to his integrity, than the sculptured bust, or marble monument.

There are but few poor, as may be expected in a country, where every man who enjoys health and strength, may earn a comfortable subsistence: but great attention is paid to those few who want it. The hospital is built in the form of a Roman H, and is under excellent regulations; supplying the sick and infirm with every necessary comfort, besides affording an asylum for lunatics, lying-in women, and children who are deserted by their parents.

The Bettering House is a kind of workhouse, where employment and support are provided for the aged, the destitute, and the friendless.

Philadelphia has the honour of giving to mankind, an example of the advantages to be derived from the wise, humane treatment of criminals. By the new penal laws adopted in this city, solitary confinement (on some few occasions, for twenty-one years, but generally for a much shorter period, proportioned to the nature of the crime, and the behaviour of the offender) is the severest punishment inflicted on any delinquent except a malicious murderer, who atones for his crime by his death. Nothing can be better contrived for the design than the gaol, which is a spacious building, of common stone. It is fitted up with solitary cells, each apartment being arched, to prevent the communication of fire. Behind the building are extensive yards, which are secured by lofty walls. The awful silence of the place (for not a word is suffered to be spoken; not a laugh, or the voice of mirth is to be heard; but a melancholy solemnity pervades the whole) affected the sensible mind of Arthur deeply; he squeezed my hand in his, which I felt was in a cold damp, as we passed through the long ranges of cells, and shuddered at the sound of our footsteps, which echoed through the passages. What must these poor wretches feel, said he, shut up from all converse, some even deprived of light, with no other object to occupy their thoughts or attention, than the reproaches of their own conscience. The punishment, I replied, is terrible to endure, but the good of society requires that offenders should be made an example, to deter others from injuring their fellow-citizens; and if their sufferings tend to their reformation, it has not been inflicted in vain. Upon this the conductor assured us of the good effects of the regulations observed in this gaol; and told us, that as soon as a prisoner is admitted, he is washed, and furnished with clean cloaths: he is then led to one of the solitary cells, where he remains secluded from the sight of every living creature but the gaoler, who is forbidden to speak to him without absolute occasion. If he is refractory, or committed for an atrocious crime, he is confined in a dark cell.

The first improvement in the condition of a prisoner, is the permission to do some kind of work; an indulgence, prized even by the idle, after they have endured the wearisomeness of solitude and privation of employment. On further amendment, they are allowed to labour in company, but still without partaking of the pleasures of conversation. Our countenances assumed a more cheerful appearance, when we saw the variety of arts carried on by those who have attained ... the liberty of working with others. One room is set apart for taylors, another for shoemakers, a third for carpenters, &c. and in the yards are stone-cutters, smiths, nailers, and other trades that require room. This part of the gaol is more like a manufactory than a prison, and from the decent behaviour of the prisoners, as well as the many instances related of their return to virtue and comfort, I am led to believe, that this mode of punishment is superior in efficacy, to any other ever yet adopted. The honour of the establishment, protection, and success of this wise and humane system, is due to the Quakers. A member of their body, named Caleb Lownes, proposed the experiment; and such was his perseverance, that he was neither to be deterred by scoffs or opposition, till he had effected it. At length his arguments prevailed with William Bradford, one of the judges, to assist him in this great undertaking; and by their joint endeavours, and the Divine blessing, it has attained its present state of perfection. What trophies are too great to perpetuate the memory of such citizens!

That sociable hospitality that makes a stranger feel at home, is not very common here, though we have received successive invitations to splendid dinners, where the table was covered with dainties, and the sideboard plentifully supplied with the finest Madeira.

After one of these handsome entertainments, where we had been attended by negro slaves, I observed a cloud upon the brow of my young friend, for which I could not account, till he confessed, that the sight of men, who were the property of their fellow creatures, and subject to every indignity, excited such painful reflections, that he could not banish them from his mind. I endeavoured to soothe him, by representing that their treatment here is gentle, compared with that exercised in the southern states, and in the West Indies; though the efforts that have been made for the abolition of slavery, have improved their condition everywhere. . . .

Philadelphia, March 7th, 1794

Dear Sir: It is a general observation with respect to the English, that they eat more animal food than the people of any other nation. The following statement of the manner of living of the Americans* will convince you of the falsity of this opinion.

About eight or nine in the morning they breakfast on tea and coffee, attended always with what they call *relishes*, such as salt fish, beef-steaks, sausages, broiled fowls, ham, bacon, &c. At two they dine on what is usual in England, with a variety of american dishes, such as bear, opossum, racoon, &c. At six or seven in the evening they have their supper, which is exactly the same as their breakfast, with the addition of what cold meat is left at dinner. I have often wondered how they acquired this method of living, which is by no means calculated for the climate; such stimulating food at breakfast and supper naturally causes thirst, and there being no other beverage at these meals than tea, or coffee, they are apt to drink too freely of them, particularly the female part of the family; which, during the excessive heats in summer, is relaxing and debilitating; and in winter, by opening the pores, exposes them to colds of the most dangerous kind.

The manner of living I have been describing is that of people in moderate circumstances; but this taste for *relishes* with coffee and tea extends to all ranks of people in these states.

Soon after my arrival at this city, I went on a party of pleasure to a sort of tea-garden and *tavern*†, romantically situate on the bank of the Scuylkill. At six in the evening we ordered coffee, which I was informed they were here famous for serving *in style*. I took a memorandum of what was on the table; viz. *coffee, cheese, sweet*

William Priest, *Travels in the United States, 1793–97, With His Journals of Two Voyages Across the Atlantic* (London, 1802), pp. 24; 32–38; 46.

* By the term *American* you must understand a white man descending from a native of the Old Continent; and by the term *Indian*, or *Savage*, one of the aborigines of the New World.

† By the word *tavern*, in America, is meant an inn or public house of any description.

cakes, hung beef, sugar, pickled salmon, butter, crackers, ham, cream, and *bread.* The ladies all declared, it was a most *charming relish!*

> *Yours sincerely, &c.*

> *Philadelphia, March 12th, 1794*

Dear Friend: The price of labour in this country is very great, owing to the prospect an industrious man has of procuring an independance by cultivating a tract of the waste lands; many millions of acres of which are now on sale by government; to say nothing of those held by individuals. The money arising from the sale of the former is appropriated to the discharge of the national debt.

During my residence in Jersey, I was at no little pains to inform myself of the difficulties attending a back settler. We will suppose a person making such an attempt to possess one hundred pounds, though many have been successful with a much less sum: his first care is to purchase about three hundred acres of land, which, if it is in a remote western settlement, he will procure for about nineteen pounds sterling: he may know the quality of the land by the trees, with which it is entirely covered. The hickory and the walnut are an infallible sign of a rich, and every species of fir, of a barren, sandy, and unprofitable soil. When his land is properly registered, his next care is to provide himself with a horse, a plough, and other implements of agriculture; a rifle, a fowling piece, some ammunition, and a large dog of the blood-hound breed, to hunt deer. We will suppose him arrived at the place of his destination in spring, as soon as the ground is clear of frost. No sooner is the arrival of a new settler circulated, than, for many miles round, his neighbours flock to him: they all assist in erecting his hut; this is done with logs; a bricklayer is only wanting to make his chimney and oven. He then clears a few acres by cutting down the large trees about four feet from the *ground**, grubs up the underwood, splits some of the large timber for railing fences, and sets fire to the rest upon the spot; ploughs round the stumps of the large timber, and in May plants maize, or indian corn. In October he has a harvest of eight hundred or a thousand fold. This is every thing to him and his family. Indian corn, ground and made into cakes, answers the end

---

* These stumps are many years rotting, and, when completely rotted, afford an excellent manure.

of bread, and when boiled with meat, and a small proportion of a sort of kidney-bean (which it is usual to sow with this grain), it makes an excellent dish, which they call *hominy*. They also coarsely pound the indian corn, and boil it for five hours; this is by the Indians called *mush*; and, when a proportion of milk is added, forms their breakfast. Indian corn is also the best food for horses employed in agriculture in this climate: black cattle, deer, and hogs are very fond of it, and fatten better than on any other grain. It is also excellent food for turkies, and other poultry.

When this harvest is in, he provides himself with a cow, and a few sheep and hogs; the latter run wild in the woods. But for a few years he depends chiefly on his *rifle*, and *faithful dog*; with these he provides his family with deer, bear, racoon, &c.; but what he values most are the black and gray squirrels; these animals are large and numerous, are excellent roasted, and make a soup exceedingly rich and nourishing.

He gradually clears his land, a few acres every year, and begins to plant wheat, tobacco, &c. These, together with what hogs, and other increase of his stock he can spare, as also the skins of deer, bear, and other animals he shoot in the woods, he exchanges with the nearest storekeeper, for clothing, sugar, coffee, &c.

In this state he suffers much for want of the comforts and even *necessaries* of life. Suppose him afflicted with a flux or fever, attacked by a panther, bitten by a rattlesnake, or any other of the dreadful circumstances peculiar to his situation: but, above all, suppose a war to break out between the Indians, and him and his whole family scalped, and their plantations burnt! . . .

The daughters are brought up in habits of virtue and industry; the strict notions of female delicacy, instilled into their minds from their earliest infancy, never entirely forsake them. Even when one of these girls is decoyed from the peaceful dwelling of her parents, and left by her infamous seducer a prey to poverty and prostitution in a *brothel* at Philadelphia, her whole appearance is neat, and breathes an air of modesty: you see nothing in her dress, language, or behaviour, that could give you any reason to guess at her unfortunate situation; (how unlike her unhappy sisters so circumstanced in England!) she by no means gives over the idea of a husband, she is seldom disappointed: and, I am informed, often makes an excellent wife.

I have often heard it asserted, that a servant should be born under an absolute monarchy: whether this observation is just or or not, I cannot tell, but I know, that a republic is *not* the place to find good servants. If you want to hire a maid servant in this city (Philadelphia) she will not allow you the title of *master*, or herself to be called a *servant*; and you may think yourself favoured if she condescends to inform you when she means to spend an evening abroad; if you grumble at all at this, she will leave you at a moment's warning; after which you will find it very difficult to procure another on any terms. This is one of the natural consequences of liberty and equality. . . .

17

American Democracy in the Early Republic

Hugh Henry Brackenridge's Modern Chivalry

Much of the literature produced during this period consisted of paeans of self-congratulation by American writers upon the superiority of the republic's political institutions and the manners and morals of the American people. A notable exception to this kind of literary activity was Hugh Henry Brackenridge's best seller, *Modern Chivalry*, the first part of which was published in 1792 and finally completed in 1815. Brackenridge, a contemporary of Philip Freneau at Princeton and co-author with him of *The Rising Glory of America*, became a lawyer in western Pennsylvania. During the Whiskey Rebellion (1794), while supporting the farmers' grievances, he was careful to dissociate himself from all acts of violence. The follies, prejudices, and ignorance which he observed everywhere in the United States, and especially on the Pennsylvania frontier, provided him with a copious store of material for satire. *Modern Chivalry*, in form a picaresque novel of adventure, is essentially a criticism of what most of Brackenridge's fellow citizens were glorifying as "The American Way."

Captain Farrago, an upright man who cherishes the republican institutions of the United States, is engaged in making a tour of the United States in company with his servant, Teague O'Regan. The people, disposed as always to adopt "what is new and ignoble," insist upon electing Teague, an ignorant and illiterate "bog-trotter," to Congress. When Captain Farrago attempts to point out Teague's lack of qualifications for the office, the captain draws upon himself the resentment of the people for interfering with the free exercise of their sovereign will. It is only after Captain Farrago

H. H. Brackenridge, *Adventures of Captain Farrago* (Philadelphia: T. B. Peterson and Brothers, 1856), pp. 19–48; 102–06; 145–64. Titles of books in successive editions often underwent considerable change. Although the title, *Modern Chivalry*, is now generally used, the 1856 edition from which our selection was taken bears the title as given in this footnote.

warns Teague that by becoming a member of Congress he will be exposed to so much vilification in the newspapers that the name O'Regan would be no better than that of a sheep-stealer that Teague is finally persuaded to decline the proferred office. Whereupon the people, deprived of their first choice, elect an ignorant weaver to Congress.

But Brackenridge's satire was not directed merely at frontiersmen; the pervasive influence of ignorance and folly, he implied, had infected the ministry, legal and teaching professions, journalism, and even the American Philosophical Society. All careers are open to Teague because in America a total absence of qualifications is the highest recommendation. When he finds a dead owl he is immediately invited to become a member of the American Philosophical Society. Finally, being a handsome man with a plausible demeanor, he is taken up by the world of fashion—there is, in fact, "a kind of Teague-o-mania among the females'—and he becomes Major O'Regan, a satirical thrust at the American's fondness for military titles (these episodes are omitted from the selection).

For a general introduction to the American novel see Alexander Cowie's *The Rise of the American Novel* (New York: The American Book Company, 1948). Vernon Louis Parrington, writing in the spirit of the Progressive tradition of historiography, makes much of the relationship of economic interest and literature. The first two volumes of his Pulitzer prize-winning *Main Currents in American Thought* (New York: Harcourt, Brace and Company, 1927–1930) are full of perceptive observations and judgments concerning the development of ideas in America. Parrington's discussion of Brackenridge is to be found in volume I, *The Colonial Mind, 1620–1800*. For a biography of Brackenridge the student might consult Claude M. Newlin, *The Life and Writings of Hugh Henry Brackenridge* (Princeton: The Princeton University Press, 1932). In reading this selection note (1) the captain's observations concerning the stability of genius or the lack of it in families; (2) moral instruction the captain received from his confrontation with the jockeys and the surgeon; (3) the captain's views of the qualifications of candidates for the legislature and how they were received by the candidates and the electors; (4) the grounds the captain advanced for arguing that in a democracy, although all men enjoyed equal rights, those rights should not be equally exercised; (5) evidences of the author's concern with the state of philosophy in his country; (6) how the author described the deliberations of Congress; (7) what he thought of the administration of the American college; (8) how the captain defended slavery and what views the author held regarding the institution; (9) what Brackenridge sensed were the fundamental defects of American democracy; (10) the author's message to his fellow countrymen; (11) the form used by Brackenridge in this piece; and (12) the literary devices he used to achieve his purposes.

Chapter I

*The Hero Is Introduced to the Reader—Resolves To
See the World—His Character, and That of Teague
O'Regan—Sallying Forth, and an Adventure—
Query Whether Merit, or Talents Are Hereditary*

CAPTAIN JOHN FARRAGO WAS A MAN ABOUT FORTY-FIVE
years of age, of good natural sense and considerable
reading; but in some things whimsical, owing perhaps to his greater
knowledge of books, than of the world; but in some degree, also, to
his having never married, being what we call an old bachelor; a
characteristic of which is, usually, singularity and whim. He had
the advantage of having had in early life an academic education;
but having never applied himself to any of the learned professions,
he had lived the greater part of his life near a village of western
Pennsylvania, on a small farm, which he cultivated with servants,[1]
or hired hands, as he could conveniently supply himself with either.
He was himself no idler, for he often held his own plough, or swung
his flail, while his hands were embrowned by exposure to the sun,
and hardened by the use of the axe. In person he was tall, and what
is called raw-boned; his features were strongly marked, and rather
coarse but not disagreeable, although his nose somewhat exceeded
the usual length. The servant he had at this time was an Irishman,
whose name was Teague O'Regan. I shall say nothing at present of the
character of this man, because the very name imports what he was.

A strange idea came into the head of the captain about this
time; for, by the by, I had forgot to mention that having been a
captain of a company of militia, he had gone by the name of captain
ever since; for the rule is, once a captain, always a captain; but, as
I was observing, the idea had come into his head, to saddle an old
horse that he had, and ride about the world a little, with his man
Teague at his heels, to see how things were going on here and there,
and to observe human nature. For it is a mistake to suppose, that
a man cannot learn man by reading him in a corner, as well as on
the widest space of transaction. At any rate, it may yield amuse-

---

[1] Redemptioners or those bound for a term, to pay for their passage, were called
servants.

ment. He accordingly sold off his personal effects, pocketed some cash, and leased out his small farm near the village, retaining only the old saddle-horse, which had been for some time relieved from the ordinary services in the plough or wagon.

Equipped in the manner we have described, in about a score of miles from his own house, he fell in with what we call Races. The jockeys seeing him advance, with Teague by his side, whom they took for his groom, conceived him to be some person who had brought his horse to enter for the purse. "You seem to be for the races, sir," said one of them, "and have a horse to enter." "Not at all," replied the captain; "this is but a common hack, and by no means remarkable for speed or bottom [endurance]; he is a plough horse which I have used on my farm for several years, and can scarce go beyond a trot; much less match himself with your blooded horses."

The jockeys suspected from this speech, that the horse was what they call a *bite*, and that under the appearance of leanness and stiffness, there was concealed some hidden quality of swiftness uncommon. For they had heard of instances, where the most knowing had been taken in by mean-looking horses: so that having laid two, or more, to one, they were nevertheless bitten by the bet; and the mean-looking nags proved to be horses of more than common speed and bottom. They could have no idea, that a man could come there in so singular a manner, with a groom at his foot, unless he had some great object of making money by the adventure. Under this idea, they began to interrogate him with respect to the blood and pedigree of his horse: whether he was of the Dove, or the Bay mare that took the purse; and was imported by such a one at such a time? whether his sire was Tamerlane or Bajazet?

The captain, somewhat out of humour, said "Gentlemen, it is a strange thing that you should suppose that it is of any consequence what may be the pedigree of a horse. For even in men it is of no avail. Do we not find that sages have had blockheads for their sons; and that blockheads have had sages? It is remarkable, that as estates have seldom lasted three generations, at least in this country, where there is no artificial entailment, so understanding and ability have seldom been transmitted to the second. There never was a greater man, take him as an orator and philosopher, than Cicero: and never was there a person who had greater opportunities than his son Marcus; and yet he proved of no account or reputation.

This is an old instance, but there are a thousand others. Chesterfield and his son are mentioned. It is true, Philip and Alexander may be said to be exceptions; Philip of the strongest possible mind; capable of almost everything we can conceive; the deepest policy and the most determined valour; his son Alexander not deficient in the first, and before him in the last; if it is possible to be before a man than whom you can suppose nothing greater. It is possible, in modern times, that Tippo Saib may be equal to his father Hyder Ali. Some talk of the two Pitts. I have no idea that the son is, in any respect, equal to old Sir William. The one is a laboured artificial minister; the other spoke with the thunder, and acted with the lightning of the gods. I will venture to say, that when the present John Adams,[1] and Lee, and Jefferson, and Jay, and Henry, and other great men, who appear upon the stage at this time, have gone to sleep with their fathers, it is a hundred to one if there is any of their descendants who can fill their places. Were I to lay a bet for a great man, I would sooner pick up the brat of a tinker, than go into the great houses to choose a piece of stuff for a man of genius. Even with respect to personal appearance, which is more in the power of natural production, we do not see that beauty always produces beauty; but on the contrary, the homeliest persons have oftentimes the best favoured offspring; so that there is no rule or reason in these things. With respect to this horse, therefore, it can be of no moment whether he is blooded or studded, or what he is. He is a good horse, used to the plough, and carries my weight very well; and I have never yet made inquiry with respect to his ancestor, or affronted him so much as to cast up to him the defect of parentage. I bought him some years ago from Neil Thomas, who had him from a colt. As far as I can understand, he was of a brown mare that John M'Neis had; but of what horse I know no more than the horse himself. His gaits are good enough, as to riding a short journey of seven or eight miles, but he is rather a pacer than a trotter; and though his bottom may be good enough in carrying a bag to the mill, or going in the plough, or the sled, or the harrow, etc., yet his wind is not so good, nor his speed, as to be fit for the heats."

The jockeys, to whom all this was jargon, thought the man a fool, and gave themselves no more trouble about him.

The horses were now entered, and about to start for the purse.

[1] This was written before John Quincy Adams had risen to distinction.

There was Black and All-Black, and Snip, John Duncan's Barbary Slim, and several others. The riders had been weighed, and when mounted, the word was given. It is needless to describe a race; everybody knows the circumstances of it. It is sufficient to say, that from the bets that were laid, there was much interest, and some passion in the minds of those concerned: So, that as two of the horses, Black and All-Black, and Slim, came out near together, such disputing, confusion, and anger, was manifested that it came to kicking and cuffing in some places.

Captain Farrago, who, as a spectator, had witnessed this behaviour among those whom he took to be gentlemen, felt so much hurt at the violation of all propriety, that, coming forward, he addressed them in the following manner: "Gentlemen, this behaviour is unbecoming modern manners, or even the ancient. For at the Olympic games of Greece, where were celebrated horse and chariot races, there was no such hurry scurry as this; and in times of chivalry itself, where men ate, drank, and slept on horseback, though there was a great deal of pell-melling, yet no such disorderly work. If men had a difference, they couched their lances, and ran full tilt at one another; but no such indecent expressions, as villain, scoundrel, liar, ever came out of their mouths. There was the most perfect courtesy in those days of heroism and honour; and this your horse-racing, which is a germ of the amusements of those times, ought to be conducted on the same principles of decorum and good breeding."

As he was speaking, a rush of horsemen, as often happens at such places, threw him from his nag; and had it not been for Teague, who was at hand, he would have suffered a serious injury. As it was, he received a contusion in his head, of which he complained much; and having remounted, left the race-ground, and coming to a log-cabin, stopped a little, to alight and dress the wound. An old woman who was there, thought they ought to take a little of his water, and send it to the doctor; but the captain, having no faith in telling disorders by the urine, thought proper to send for a surgeon who was hard by, to examine the bruise, and apply bandages, if necessary.

The surgeon, after examining the part, pronounced it "A contusion of the cerebrum. But as there appeared but little laceration, and no fracture, simple or compound, the pia mater could not be injured;

nor even could there be more than a slight impression on the dura mater; so that trepanning did not at all appear necessary—a most fortunate circumstance; for a wound in the head, is of all places the most dangerous; because there can be no amputation to save life. There being but one head to a man, and that being the residence of the five senses, it is impossible to live without it. Nevertheless, as the present case was highly dangerous, as it might lead to a subsultus tendinum or lockjaw, it was necessary to apply cataplasms in order to reduce inflammation, and bring about a sanative disposition of the parts. Perhaps it might not be amiss, to take an anodyne as a refrigerant. Many patients had been lost by the ignorance of empirics prescribing tonics; whereas, in the first stage of a contusion, relaxing and antifebrile medicines are proper. A little phlebotomy was no doubt necessary to prevent the rupture of the smaller blood vessels."

The captain hearing so many hard words and bad accounts of his case, was somewhat alarmed. Nevertheless he did not think it could be absolutely so dangerous. For it seemed to him that he was not sick at heart, or under any mortal pain. The surgeon observed, that "in this case he could not himself be a judge. For the very part was affected by which he was to judge, viz. the head; that it was no uncommon thing for men in the extremest cases to imagine themselves out of danger; whereas in reality, they were in greatest possible; that notwithstanding the symptoms were mild, yet from the contusion, a mortification might ensue. Hypocrates, who might be styled an elementary physician, and has a treatise on this very subject, is of opinion, that the most dangerous symptom is a topical insensibility; but among the moderns, Sydenham considers it in another point of view, and thinks that where there is no pain, there is as great reason to suppose that there is no hurt, as that there is a mortal one. Be this as it may, antispetic medicines might be very proper."

Captain Farrago, conscious to himself that he was by no means in so bad a state as this son of Esculapius would represent, in some measure lost command over his temper. "It is," said he, "the craft of your profession to make the case worse than it is, in order to increase the perquisites. But if there is any faith in you, make the same demand, and let me know your real judgment."

The surgeon was offended in turn, and took it into his head to fix some apprehensions in the mind of his patient, if possible, that his case was not without danger. Looking steadfastly at him for some time, and feeling his pulse; "there is," said he, "an evident delirium approaching. This argues an affection of the brain; but it will be necessary, after some soporiferous draughts, to put the patient to sleep."

Said the patient, "If you will give me about a pint of whiskey and water, I will try to go to sleep myself."

"A deleterious mixture, in this case, especially a distillation of that quality," said the surgeon.

He would hear no more; but requesting the man of the cabin to let him have the spirits proposed, drank a pint or two of grog, and having bound up his head with a handkerchief, went to bed, and after a profound sleep, awoke the next morning, perfectly well.

Chapter II

*Containing Some Reflections Which Will Enable the
Reader To Find the Moral of the Preceding*

THE FIRST REFLECTION THAT ARISES, IS THE GOOD sense of our hero, (and why may we not give him that title,) who was unwilling to impose his horse for a racer, not being qualified for the course. Because, as an old lean beast, attempting a trot, he was respectable enough; but going out of his nature and affecting speed, he would have been contemptible. The great secret of preserving respect, is the cultivating and showing to the best advantage the powers that we possess, and the not going beyond them. Everything in its element is good, and in their proper sphere all natures and capacities are excellent. This thought might be turned into a thousand different shapes, and clothed with various expressions; but, after all, it comes to the old proverb at last, *Ne sutor ultra crepidam*—let the cobbler stick to last; a sentiment we are about to illustrate in the sequel to this work.

The second reflection that arises, is, the simplicity of the captain, who was so unacquainted with the world, as to imagine that jockeys and men of the turf could be managed by reason and good sense; whereas there are no people who are by education of a less philo-

sophic turn of mind. The company of horses is by no means favourable to good taste and genius. The rubbing and currying them but
little enlarges the faculties, or improves the mind; and even riding,
by which a man is carried swiftly through the air, though it contributes to health, yet stores the mind with few or no ideas; and as
men naturally consimilate with their company, so it is observable
that your jockeys are a class of people not far removed from the
sagacity of a good horse. Hence most probably the fable of the
centaur, among the ancients; by which they held out the moral of
the jockey and the horse being one beast.

A third reflection is, that which he expressed, viz., the professional
art of the surgeon to make the most of the case, and the technical
terms used by him. I have to declare, that it is with no attempt at
wit, that the terms are set down, or the art of the surgeon hinted
at; because it is a thing so commonplace to ridicule the peculiarities
of a profession, or its phraseologies, that it savours of mean parts
to indulge it. For a man of real genius will never walk in the beaten
path, because his object is what is new and uncommon. This
surgeon does not appear to have been a man of very great ability;
but, the captain was certainly wrong in declining his prescriptions;
for the maxim is, *unicuique, in arte sua, perito, credendum est*; every one
is to be trusted in his profession.

Chapter III

*The Election—The Captain Dissuades a Weaver
from Being a Candidate, but Is Near Losing Teague,
Whom the Voters Wish to Take up in His Place*

At an early hour, our knight-errant and his
squire set out on their way, and soon arrived at a
place of cross-roads, at a public house and store, where a number
of people were convened, for the purpose of electing persons to
represent them in the legislature of the state. This was not the
annual election, but to fill an occasional vacancy. There was a
weaver who was a candidate, and seemed to have a good deal of
interest among the people. But another, who was a man of education,
was his competitor. Relying on some talent of speaking which he

thought he possessed, and getting on the stump of a large oak tree for the convenience of a more elevated position, he thus addressed the people.

"Fellow citizens," said he, "I pretend not to any great abilities; but am conscious to myself that I have the best good will to serve you. But it is very astonishing to me, that this man should conceive himself qualified for the trust. For though my acquirements are not great, yet his are still less. The business which he pursues, must necessarily take up so much of his time, that he cannot apply himself to political studies. I should therefore think it would be more answerable to your dignity, and conducive to your interest, to be represented by a man at least of some letters, than by an illiterate man like this. It will be more honourable for himself, to remain at his loom and knot threads, than to come forward in a legislative capacity; because in the one case, he is in the sphere suited to his education; in the other, he is like a fish out of water, and must struggle for breath in a new element. It is not because he is a weaver that I object to him, but because he is nothing but a weaver, and entirely destitute of the qualifications necessary to fill the office to which he aspires. The occupation a man pursues for a livelihood is but a secondary consideration, if any consideration at all. Warriors and statesmen, and sages, may be found at the plough, and the work bench, but this man has not the slightest pretensions beyond the mysteries of his trade.

"Is it possible that he can understand the affairs of government, whose mind has been entirely concentered to the small object of weaving webs; to the price by the yard, the grist of the thread, and such like matters as concern the manufacturer of clothes? The feet of him who weaves, are more occupied than the head, or at least as much; and therefore he must be, at least, but in half, accustomed to exercise his mental powers. For these reasons, all other things set aside, the chance is in my favour, with respect to information. However, you will decide, and give your suffrages to him or to me, as you shall judge expedient."

The captain hearing these observations, and looking at the weaver, made free to subjoin something in support of what had been just said. Said he, "I have no prejudice against a weaver more than another man. Nor do I know any harm in the trade; save that from the sedentary life in a damp place, there is usually a paleness of the countenance: but this is a physical, not a moral evil. Such usually occupy subterranean apartments; not for the purpose, like Demosthenes, of shaving their heads and writing over eight times the history of Thucydides, and perfecting a style of oratory; but rather to keep the thread moist; or because this is considered but as an inglorious sort of trade, and is frequently thrust away into cellars, and damp out-houses, which are not occupied for a better use.

"But to rise from the cellar to the senate house, would be an unnatural hoist for one whose mind had not been prepared for it by a previous course of study or training, either self-instructed, and gifted with superior intellect, or having the good fortune to have received an education, with also the advantage of actual experience in public affairs. To come from counting threads, and adjusting them to the splits of a reed, to regulate the finances of a government, would be preposterous; there being no congruity in the case. There is no analogy between knotting threads and framing laws. It would be a reversion of the order of things. Not that a manufacturer of linen or woolen, or other stuffs, is an inferior character, but a different one, from that which ought to be employed in affairs of state. It is unnecessary to enlarge on this subject; for you must all be convinced of the truth and propriety of what I say. But if you will give me leave to take the manufacturer aside a little, I think I can explain to him my ideas on the subject; and very probably prevail with him to withdraw his pretensions." The people seeming to acquiesce, and beckoning to the weaver, they withdrew aside, and the captain addressed him in the following words:

"Mr. Traddle," said he, "I have not the smallest idea of wounding your feelings, but it would seem to me, it would be more your interest to pursue your occupation, than to lanch out into that of which you have no knowledge. When you go to the senate house, the application to you will not be to warp a web; but to make laws for the commonwealth. Now, suppose that the making these laws requires a knowledge of commerce, of finance, and of the infinite variety of subjects embraced by the laws, civil or criminal, what service could you render? It is possible you might think justly; but could you speak? You are not in the habit of public speaking. You are not furnished with those commonplace ideas, with which even very ignorant men can pass for knowing something. There is nothing makes a man so ridiculous, as to attempt what is beyond his capacity. You are no tumbler for instance; yet should you give out that you could vault upon a man's back; or turn heels over head like the wheels of a cart; the stiffness of your joints would encumber you; and you would fall to the ground. Such a squash as that, would do you damage. The getting up to ride on the state is an unsafe thing to those who are not accustomed to such horsemanship. It is a disagreeable thing for a man to be laughed at, and there is no way of keeping one's self from it but by avoiding all affectation." These observations did not seem to make much impression on the weaver, who argued that common sense was often better than learning.

While they were thus discoursing, a bustle had taken place among the crowd. Teague hearing so much about elections, and serving the government, took it into his head, that he could be a legislator himself. The thing was not displeasing to the people, who seemed to favour his pretensions; owing, in some degree, to there being several of his countrymen among the crowd; but more especially to the fluctuation of the popular mind, and a disposition to what is new and ignoble. For though the weaver was not the most elevated object of choice, yet he was still preferable to this tatter-demalion.

The captain coming up, and finding what was on the carpet, was chagrined at not having been able to give the voters a better idea of the importance of a legislative trust; alarmed also, from an apprehension of the loss of his servant. Under these impressions he resumed his address to the people. Said he, "This is making the matter still worse, gentlemen: this servant of mine is but a bog-trotter, who can scarcely speak the dialect in which your laws ought to be written; but certainly has never read a single treatise on any political subject; for the truth is, he cannot read at all. The young people of the lower class, in Ireland, have seldom the advantage of a good education; especially the descendants of the ancient Irish, who have most of them a great assurance of countenance, but little information or literature. This young man, whose family name is O'Regan, has been my servant for several years; and, except a too great fondness for whiskey, which now and then brings him into scrapes, he has demeaned himself in a manner tolerable enough. But he is totally ignorant of the great principles of legislation; and more especially the particular interests of the government. A free government is a noble acquisition to a people: and this freedom consists in an equal right to make laws, and to have the benefit of the laws when made. Though doubtless, in such a government, the lowest citizen may become chief magistrate; yet it is sufficient to possess the right, not absolutely necessary to exercise it. Or even if you should think proper, now and then, to show your privilege, and exert, in a signal manner, the democratic prerogative, yet is it not descending too low to filch away from me a servant whom I cannot well spare, and for whom I have paid my money? You are surely carrying the matter too far, in thinking to make a senator of this hostler; to take him away from an employment to which he has been bred, and put him to another, to which he has served no apprenticeship: to set those hands, which have lately been employed in currying my horse, to the draughting bills, and preparing business for the house."

The people were tenacious of their choice, and insisted on giving Teague their suffrages; and by the frown upon their brows, seemed to indicate resentment at what had been said; as indirectly charging them with want of judgment; or calling in question their privilege to do what they thought proper. "It is a very strange thing," said one of them, who was a speaker for the rest, "that after having conquered Burgoyne and Cornwallis, and got a government of our own, we cannot put in whom we please. This young man may be your servant, or another man's servant; but if we choose to make him a delegate, what is that to you? He may not be yet skilled in the matter, but there is a good day coming. We will empower him; and it is better to trust a plain man like him, than one of your high-flyers, that will make laws to suit their own purposes."

"I had much rather," said the captain, "you would send the weaver, though I thought that improper, than to invade my household, and thus take from me the person who is employed to curry my horse, and black my boots."

The prolocutor of the people gave him to understand that his objections were useless, for the people had determined on the choice, and Teague they would have, for a representative.

Finding it answered no end to expostulate, he requested to speak a word with Teague by himself. Stepping aside, he said to him, composing his voice, and addressing him in a soft manner: "Teague, you are quite wrong in this matter they have put into your head.

Do you know what it is to be a member of a deliberative body? What qualifications are necessary? Do you understand anything of geography? If a question should be put to make a law to dig a canal in some part of the state, can you describe the bearing of the mountains, and the course of the rivers? Or, if commerce is to be pushed to some new quarter, by the force of regulations, are you competent to decide in such a case? There will be questions of law, and astronomy, on the carpet. How you must gape and stare like a fool, when you come to be asked your opinion on these subjects! Are you acquainted with the principles of finance; with the funding public securities; the ways and means of raising the revenue; providing for the discharge of the public debts, and all other things which respect the economy of the government? Even if you had knowledge, have you a facility of speaking? I would suppose you would have too much pride to go to the house just to say, ay or no. This is not the fault of your nature, but of your education; having been accustomed to dig turf in your early years, rather than instructing yourself in the classics, or common school books.

"When a man becomes a member of a public body, he is like a raccoon, or other beast that climbs up the fork of a tree; the boys pushing at him with pitchforks, or throwing stones, or shooting at him with arrows; the dogs barking in the meantime. One will find fault with your not speaking; another with your speaking, if you speak at all. They will put you in the newspapers, and ridicule you as a perfect beast. There is what they call the *caricatura*; that is, representing you with a dog's head, or a cat's claw. It is the devil to be exposed to the squibs and crackers of the gazette wits and publications. You know no more about these matters than a goose; and yet you would undertake rashly, without advice, to enter on the office; nay, contrary to advice. For I would not for a hundred guineas, though I have not the half to spare, that the breed of the O'Regans should come to this; bringing on them a worse stain than stealing sheep. You have nothing but your character, Teague, in a new country to depend upon. Let it never be said, that you quitted an honest livelihood, the taking care of my horse, to follow the new fangled whims of the times, and be a statesman. And, besides, have I not promised to do something clever towards settling you in life hereafter, provided you will serve me faithfully in my travels? Something better than you have thought of may turn up in the course of our rambles."

Teague was moved chiefly with the last part of the address, and consented to relinquish his pretensions.

The captain, glad of this, took him back to the people, and announced his disposition to decline the honour which they had intended him.

Teague acknowledged that he had changed his mind, and was willing to remain in a private station.

The people did not seem well pleased; but as nothing more could be said about the matter, they turned their attention to the weaver, and gave him their suffrages.

Chapter IV

The Captain Goes to the Abode of a Conjurer, to Ask Why the People Are So Prone to Elect Low Persons to High Stations

CAPTAIN FARRAGO AND TEAGUE, HAVING LEFT THE election ground without any further incident, proceeded on their way, and at the distance of a mile or two, met a man with a bridle in his hand, who had lost a horse, and had been at a conjurer's to make inquiry, and recover his property. Hearing this, the captain suddenly bethought him of going to the same conjuring person, and make a demand of him, "Why it was that the multitude were so disposed to elevate the low to the highest station?" He had rode but about a mile, when the habitation of the conjurer, by the direction and description which the man who had lost the horse had given, began to be in view. Coming up to the door, and inquiring if that was not where conjurer Cobb lived, they were answered, "Yes." Alighting, and entering the domicil, all those things took place which usually happen, or are described in cases of this nature, viz., there was the conjurer's assistant, who gave the captain to understand that the master had withdrawn a little, but would be in shortly.

In the meantime, the assistant endeavoured to draw from him some account of the occasion of his journey; which the other readily communicated; and the conjurer, who was listening through a crack in the partition, overheard. Finding it was not a horse or a cow or a piece of linen that was lost, but an abstract question of political philosophy which was to be put, he came from his lurking-place, and entered, as if not knowing that any person had been waiting for him.

After mutual salutations, the captain gave him to understand the object which he had in view by calling on him.

Said the conjurer, "This lies not at all in my way. If it had been a dozen of spoons, or a stolen watch, that you had to look for, I could very readily, by the assistance of my art, have assisted you in the recovery; but as to this matter of men's imaginations and attachments in political affairs, I have no more understanding than another man."

"It is very strange," said the captain, "that you who can tell by what means a thing is stolen, and the place where it is deposited, though at a thousand miles distance, should know so little of what is going on in the breast of man, as not to be able to develop his secret thoughts, and the motives of his actions."

"It is not our business," said the other; "but should we undertake it, I do not see that it would be very difficult to explain all that puzzles you at present. There is no need of a conjurer to tell why it is that the common people are more disposed to trust one of their own class, than those who may affect to be superior. Besides, there is a certain pride in man, which leads him to elevate the low, and pull down the high. There is a kind of creating power exerted in making a senator of an unqualified person; which when the author has done, he exults over the work, and like the Creator himself, when he made the world, sees that 'it is very good.' Moreover, there is in every government a patrician class against whom the spirit of the multitude naturally militates: and hence a perpetual war: the aristocrats endeavouring to detrude the people, and the people contending to obtrude themselves. And it is right it should be so; for, by this fermentation, the spirit of democracy is kept alive."

The captain, thanking him for his information, asked him "what was to pay;" at the same time pulling out half a crown from a green silk purse which he had in his breeches pocket. The conjurer gave him to understand, that as the solution of these difficulties was not within his province, he took nothing for it. The captain expressing his sense of his disinterested service, bade him adieu.

Chapter V

*Containing Reflections on the Nature, and Advantages
of a Democracy. The Author Shows Himself a
Democrat in the Genuine Sense*

A DEMOCRACY IS BEYOND ALL QUESTION THE FREEST
government; because, under this, every man is equally
protected by the laws, and has equally a voice in making them. But
I do not say an equal voice; because some men have stronger lungs
than others, and can express more forcibly their opinions of public
affairs. Others, though they may not speak very loud, yet have a
faculty of saying more in a short time; and even in the case of others,
who speak little or none at all, yet what they do say, containing
good sense, comes with greater weight; so that, all things considered,
every citizen has not, in this sense of the word, an equal voice. But
the right being equal, what great harm if it is unequally exercised?
Is it necessary that every man should become a statesman? No
more than that every man should become a poet or a painter. The
sciences are open to all; but let him only who has taste and genius
pursue them. "If any man covets the office of a bishop," says St.
Paul, "he covets a good work." But again, he adds this caution,
"Ordain not a novice, lest being lifted up with pride, he falls into
the condemnation of the devil." It is indeed making a devil of a
man to lift him up to a state to which he is not suited. A ditcher is a
respectable character, with his over-alls on, and a spade in his hand,
but put the same man to those offices which require the head,
whereas he has been accustomed to impress with his foot, and there
appears a contrast between the individual and the occupation.

There are individuals in society, who prefer honour to wealth; or
cultivate political studies as a branch of literary pursuits; and offer
themselves to serve public bodies in order to have an opportunity of
discovering their knowledge, and exercising their judgment. It must
be matter of chagrin to these, and hurtful to the public, to see those
who have no talent this way, and ought to have no taste, preposter-
ously obtrude themselves upon the government. It is the same as if
a bricklayer should usurp the office of a tailor, and come with his
square and perpendicular, to take the measure of a pair of breeches.

It is proper that those who cultivate oratory, should go to the house of orators. But for mere ay and no men, who can neither speak nor think, to be ambitious of that place, is to sacrifice their credit to their vanity.

I would not mean to insinuate that legislators are to be selected from the more wealthy of the citizens, or from any particular calling; yet a man ought to have the habits of study and reflection, whatever may be his situation; and it is no objection if his circumstances have afforded him leisure for such pursuits. But there is often wealth without taste or talent. I have no idea, that because a man lives in a great house, and has a cluster of bricks or stones about him, that he is therefore fit for a legislator. There is so much pride and arrogance with those who consider themselves the first in a government, that it deserves to be checked by the populace, and the evil most usually commences on this side. Men associate with their own persons, the adventitious circumstances of birth and fortune: so that a fellow, blowing with fat and repletion, conceives himself superior to the poor lean man, that lodges in an humble dwelling. But as in all cases, so in this, there is a medium. Genius and virtue are independent of rank and fortune; and it is neither the opulent, nor the indigent, but the man of ability and integrity that ought to be called forth to serve his country;[1] and while, on the one hand, the aristocratic part of the government arrogates a right to represent; on the other hand, the democratic contests the point; and from this conjunction and opposition of forces, there is produced a compound resolution, which carries the object to an intermediate direction. When we see, therefore, a Teague O'Regan lifted up, the philosopher will reflect that it is to balance some purse-proud Fellow, equally as ignorant, that comes down from the sphere of aristocratic interest. Still, it would undoubtedly be better if both were suffered to remain in their original stations. Every man ought to consider for himself, whether it is to his use to be this drawback, on either side. As when good liquor is distilled, you throw in some material useless in itself to correct the effervescence of the spirit, so it may be his part to act as a sedative. For though we commend the effect, yet still the material retains but its original value.

But as the nature of things is such, let no man who means well to the commonwealth, and offers to serve it, be hurt in his mind when

[1] The Chinese policy in this matter is worthy of imitation.

some one of inferior talents is preferred. The people are a sovereign, and greatly despotic; but in the main, just.

It might be advisable, in order to elevate the composition, to make quotations from the Greek and Roman history. And I am conscious to myself, that I have read the writers on the government of Italy and Greece, in ancient, as well as in modern times. But I have drawn a great deal more from reflection on the nature of things, than from all the writings I have ever read. Nay, the history of the election, which I have just given, will afford a better lesson to the American mind, than all that is to be found in other examples. We have seen here, a weaver a favored candidate, and in the next instance, a bog-trotter superseding him. Now it may be said, that this is fiction; but fiction or no fiction, the nature of the thing will make it a reality. But I return to the adventures of the captain, whom I have upon my hands; and who, as far as I can yet discover, is a good honest man; and means what is benevolent and useful; though his ideas may not comport with the ordinary manner of thinking, in every particular.

Chapter VI

*The Society of Philosophers—When the Useful Is
Lost Sight of, Philosophy Is Apt to Become Frivolity*

THERE WAS, IN A CERTAIN GREAT CITY, A SOCIETY who called themselves Philosophers. They had published books, under the title of Transactions. These contained dissertations on the nature and causes of things, from the stars of heaven to the fire flies of the earth; and from the sea crab, to the woodland buffalo. Such disquisitions, are doubtless useful and entertaining to an inquisitive mind.

There is no question, but there were in this body some very great men; whose investigations of the arcana of nature deserve attention. But so it was, there had been introduced, by some means, many individuals, who were no philosophers at all. This is no unusual thing with institutions of this nature; though, by the bye, it is a very great fault. For it lessens the incentives of honour, to have the access made so easy, that every one may obtain admission. It has been a reproach to some colleges, that a diploma could be purchased for half a crown. This society were still more moderate; for the bare scratching the back of a member has been known to procure a membership. At least, there have been those admitted, who appeared capable of nothing else.

Nevertheless, it was necessary, even in these cases, for the candidates to procure some token of a philosophic turn of mind; such as the skin of a dead cat, or some odd kind of a mouse trap; or have praises in their mouths about minerals and petrifactions; so as just to support some idea of natural knowledge, and pass muster. There was one who got in, by finding accidentally, the tail of a rabbit, which had been taken off in a boy's trap. The beard of an old fox, taken off and dried in the sun, was the means of introducing another: or rather, as I have already hinted, it was beforehand intended he should be introduced; and these spoils of the animal kingdom were but the tokens and apologies for admission.

It happened as the captain was riding this day, and Teague trotting after him, he saw a large owl, that had been shot by somebody, and was placed in the crotch of a tree, about the height of a man's head from the ground, for those that passed by to look at. Being struck with it, as somewhat larger than such birds usually are, he desired Teague to reach it to him, and tying it to the hinder part of his saddle, rode along.

He had not rode more than two or three miles, before he was met, and accosted by a respectable looking traveller, well mounted, and attended by a servant following him on another horse with the portmanteau. This traveller, who proved to be a member of the Philosophical Society, seeing the bird at the saddle skirts, stopped to make inquiry with regard to the genus and nature of the fowl.

"Sir," said the captain, "I know nothing more about it, than that it is nearly as large as a turkey buzzard."

"It is doubtless," said the other, "the great Canada owl, that comes from the lakes; and if you will give me leave, squire, I will take it and submit it to the society, and have yourself made a member."

Consent was readily given to the first, but as to the second, the being a member, he chose rather to decline it; conceiving himself unqualified for a place in such a body. The other assured him that he was under a very great mistake; for there were members who scarcely knew a B from a bull's foot. "That may be," said the captain:

"but if others choose to degrade themselves, by suffering their names to be used in so preposterous a way as that, it was no reason he should."

The other gave him to understand, that the society would certainly wish to express their sense of his merit, and show themselves not inattentive to a virtuoso; that as he declined the honour himself, he probably might not be averse to let his attendant take a seat among them.

"He is but a simple Irishman," said the captain, "and of a low education; his language being that spoken by the aborigines of his country. And if he speaks a little English, it is with the brogue on his tongue, which would be unbecoming in a member of your body. It would seem to me that a philosopher ought to know how to write, or at least to read; but Teague can neither write not read. He can sing a song or whistle an Irish tune; but is totally illiterate in all things else. I question much if he could tell you how many new moons there are in the year; or any the most common things you could ask him. He is a long-legged fellow, it is true, and might be of service clambering over rocks, or going to the shores of rivers to gather curiosities. But could you not get persons to do this, without making them members? I have more respect for science, than to suffer this bog-trotter to be so advanced at its expense. In these American states, there is a wide field for philosophical research; and these researches may be of great use in agriculture, manufactures, and architecture. There is but little immediate profit attending these pursuits; but if there can be inducements of honour, these may supply the place. What more alluring to a young man, than the prospect of being one day received into the society of men truly learned, the admission being a test and a proof of distinguished knowledge? But the fountain of honour, thus contaminated by a sediment foreign from its nature, who would wish to drink of it?"

"As to that," said the philosopher, "at the first institution of the society by Dr. Franklin and others, it was put upon a narrow basis, and only men of science were considered proper to compose it; and this might be a necessary policy at that time, when the institution was in its infancy, and could not bear much drawback of ignorance. But it has not been judged so necessary of late years. The matter stands now on a broad and catholic bottom; and like the gospel itself, it is our orders 'to go out into the highways and hedges, and compel them to come in.' There are hundreds, whose names you may see on our list, who are not more instructed than your man Teague."

"They must be a sad set indeed then," said the captain.

"Sad or no sad," said the other, "it is the case; and if you will let Teague go, I will engage him a membership."

"I take it very ill of you, Mr. Philosopher," said the captain, "to put this nonsense in his head. If you knew what trouble I have lately had with a parcel of people that were for sending him to Congress, you would be unwilling to draw him from me for the purpose of making him a philosopher. It is not an easy matter to get servants nowadays; and when you do get one, it is a mere chance whether he will suit your purpose. It would be a very great loss to me to have him taken off at this time, when I have equipped myself for a journey."

Teague who had been attentive to what had been passing, but without comprehending it, supposed that he was about to be prevented from the possession of something to his advantage, declared that he would accept of his honour's offer, and be a philosopher in spite of his master.

"You are an ignoramus," said the captain. "It is not the being among philosophers will make you one."

He insisted that he had a right to make the best of his fortune: and as there was a door open to his advancement he did not see why he might not make use of it.

The captain finding that it answered no end to dispute the matter with him by words of sense and reason, took a contrary way to manage him.

"Teague," said he, "I have a regard for you, and would wish to see you do well. I have not forgotten my promise; but if you will be a philosopher, which you erroneously suppose will lead to fortune, let me speak a word or two in private on the subject. If you will go, I may suggest some things that may be of service to you, for your conduct in this new line of life."

Teague consenting, they stepped aside, and his master addressed him in the following manner:

"Teague," said he, "do you know what you are about? It is a fine thing at first sight, to be a philosopher, and get into this society, as they call it. And, indeed, if you were a real philosopher, it might be some honour, and also safe, to take that leap. But do you think it is to make a philosopher of you that they want you? Far from it. It is their great study to find curiosities; and they will have you away through the bogs and marshes, catching fire flies; or oblige you to descend into draw-wells for fogs, and phlogistic air. You must go into wolves' dens, run over mountains like a catamount, and dig the earth like a ground hog. You will have to climb over trees, and be bit by flying squirrels. There will be no end to the mosquitoes you will have to dissect. What is all this, to diving into milldams and rivers, to catch craw-fish? Or if you go to the ocean, there are sharks to devour you. Will they give wages, think you? No, certainly—you must work for the honour of the thing, and find your own food and clothing. Who knows but it may come your turn, in a windy night, to go aloft to the heavens, to rub down the stars, and give fodder to the goats and ram? The keeping the stars clean and bright is a laborious work. There is a bull there, would think no more of tossing you on his horns than he would a puppy dog. If the crab should get you into his claws, he would squeeze you like a lobster. But what is all that to your having no place to stand on? How would you like to be up at the moon, and to fall down when you had missed your hold, like a boy from the topmast of a ship, and have your brains beat out upon the top of some great mountain, where your skeleton would be picked by the turkey buzzards?

"Or if they should, in the meantime, excuse you from such out-of-door services, they will rack and torture you with hard questions. You must tell them how long the rays of light are coming from the sun; how many drops of rain fall in a thundergust; what makes the grasshopper chirp when the sun is hot; how muscle shells get up to the top of the mountains; how the Indians got over to America. You will have to prove that the negroes were once white, and that their flat noses came by some one giving a slap in the face when the clay was soft. Take my advice, and stay where you are. Many men have ruined themselves by their ambition, and made bad worse. There is another kind of philosophy, which lies more within your sphere; that is moral philosophy. Every hostler or hireling can study this, and you have the most excellent opportunity of acquiring this knowledge in our traverses through the country, or communications at the different taverns or villages, where we may happen to sojourn."

Teague had long ago, in his own mind, given up all thoughts of the society, and would not for the world have any more to do with it; especially as there was nothing to be got; therefore, without bidding the philosopher adieu, they pursued their route as usual.

Chapter VII

Containing Some Reflections and Explanations, Partly Apologetic

THE INSTITUTION OF THE AMERICAN PHILOSOPHICAL Society does great honour to the founders, and what has been published by that body, comes not behind what has appeared from societies of the same nature elsewhere. But of late years, it has ceased to be presumptive evidence, at least what the lawyers call violent presumption, or philosophical attainments, to be a member; owing to the spurious brood of illiterate persons that have been admitted indiscriminately with the informed; this again, owing to a political dispute in the government where this society exists. For where there are parties in the commonwealth, they naturally subdivide themselves, and are found even in the retreats of the muses. It has become the question with this society, not, whether a man is a philosopher or not, but what part he has taken in some question on the carpet. The body conceived itself to pay a compliment to the person admitted, as if it could be any honour to a man to be announced what he is not. The contrary is the case here. As honour is the acknowledgment which the world makes of a man's respectability, there can be no honour here; for it has become a mere matter of moonshine to be a member. To be, or not to be, that is the question; but so trifling, that it is scarcely ever made. The way to remedy this, would be, to have an overhauling of the house, and derange at least three parts in four. As in the case of Tarquin, and the three remaining books of the Sybils, you would receive as much for the fourth part of that body, should you set them up at market, as for the whole at present.

I have often reflected with myself, what an honour it must be, to be one of the society of the French academy; forty, of twenty-four millions of people, are selected in consequence of literary characters already established.

I recollect the time when I had high ideas of philosophical membership in America. But it does not appear to me now to be the highest thing that a man could wish, since even a common Teague O'Regan trotting on the highway, has been solicited to take a seat. It may be said, that this is an exaggeration of the facts; and can be considered only as burlesque. I profess it is not intended as such, but as a fair picture of what has taken place. Should it be considered in the light of burlesque, it must be a very lame one; because where there is no excess there can be no caricature. But omitting all apologies and explanations, let the matter rest where it is. . . .

Chapter XXI

The Captain Leaves the Inn—The Grave Adventure with the Man of the Two Kegs—Of the Power of Whiskey, and Other Strong Drinks at Elections

RISING EARLY NEXT MORNING, THE CAPTAIN WITH HIS man Teague, took leave of the inn, and breakfasted at another about a half a score of miles further; but as nothing material happened, we shall come as far down in the day as eleven o'clock; though, by the by, it might have been more correct to have said up in the day, because the sun rises until twelve o'clock, and then descends: but waiving this nicety, we shall go on to relate what actually took place. A man was seen before them, driving leisurely, a horse with two kegs upon his back. The captain took him for what is called a pack-horse man, carrying salt or sugar to some place of market. A man of philosophic turn of mind never hesitates to enter into conversation with any character; because human nature is the field whence he gathers thoughts and expressions. The captain therefore accosting this man, said, "Is it salt or molasses you have in you kegs, countryman? You are going home from some country-store, I suppose, where you have been dealing; or going to set up a small shop of your own, and vend goods."—"No," said the man, with a Scotch-Irish pronunciation, "this is the general-election day, and the election is to be held for this district a little way before us. I am setting up for the legislature, and have these two kegs of whiskey to give a dram to the voters." The captain was thrown into a reverie of thought, and began to reflect with himself on the nature of a republican government, where canvassing by such means as this, can work so great an evil to elevate the most unqualified persons to the highest stations. But, in the meantime, roused a little from his thought, he had presence of mind to recollect the danger in which he was about to be involved afresh with his man Teague; whom, now looking round he saw to be about forty yards behind him. It would have been advisable to have diverted him from the road, and taken a circuitous route, to avoid the election ground. But, as the devil, or some worse being, would have it, it was a lane in which they were, with a fence on each side; so that he could not divert without leaping like a fox-hunter, or one of your light-horse men, to which the sober nag on which he rode was not competent. Besides, if Teague did not leap after him, he would be left exposed in the lane to the populace, who might solicit him to be their representative. To turn directly back would appear indecorous, and unless he could urge Teague on before him, which was not customary, and to which he might not all at once submit, his station would of course be in the rear, where he might be picked up as a straggler, and sent to some public body.

In this quandary of thought, looking up, he saw the breakers just ahead; that is, the people met for the purpose of electing, and that it was now impossible to avoid them. Depending therefore, on his own address to make the best of circumstances, he suffered himself to be carried along towards them, keeping, in the meantime, an eye upon Teague, who was the cause of his concern.

Meeting accidentally with a Scotch gentleman on the ground, whom he knew, he communicated to him the delicacy of his situation, and the apprehensions he had on the part of Teague. Said the Scotch gentleman, "Ye need na gie yoursel any trouble on that head, man; for I sal warrant the man wi the twa kegs will carry the election; there is na resisting guid liquor; it has an unco effec on the judgment in the choice of a representative. The man that has a distillery or twa, canna want suffrages. He has his votaries about him like ane o' the Heathen gods, and because the fluid exhilarates the brain, they might think he maun be a deity that makes it; and they fa' down, especially whan they have drank ower muckle, and worship him, just as at the shrine of Apollo or Bacchus, among the ancients."

The candidate that opposed the man of the two kegs, was a person of gravity and years, and said to be of good sense and experience. The judgment of the people was in his favor, but their appetite leaned against him.

There is a story of one Manlius, a Roman, who had saved the capitol from the Gauls, by putting his breast to the ramparts, and throwing them down as they ascended. When this man afterwards, elated with the honours paid him, forgot the duties of a citizen, wishing to subvert the republic, by usurping power; the people, jealous of liberty, were incensed; and being convicted of the crime, he was dragged to punishment. It was not the way at that time, to hang, as you would a dog; or behead, as you would a wild beast; but to throw from a high rock, which they called the Tarpeian. The capitol was just in view, and while they were dragging him along to the place, he would stretch his hand towards it, as much as to say, "There, O Romans, I saved you:" The populace at this would stop a while, irresolute whether to desist or drag him on. While they recollected his offence, they marched a step; but when they cast their eye on the capitol, they stood still; and not until some principal men directed the route out of the view of the capitol, could he be bought to justice.

So it was with the multitude convened on this occasion, between the man with the two kegs and the gravelooking person. When they looked on the one, they felt an inclination to promote him. But when, again, on the other hand, they saw two kegs which they knew to be replenished with a very cheering liquor, they seemed to be inclined in favour of the other. The candidates were called upon to address the people, and the grave person mounted the stump of a tree, many of them standing round, as the place was a new clearing. His harangue was listened to by some of the older and more sedate, and one man, hard of hearing, seemed to make great effort to catch the sounds. As soon as the man of the two kegs took a stump, he was surrounded by an eager crowd.—"Friends," said he, in the native Scotch-Irish, "I'm a good dimicrat, and hates the Bratish—I'm an elder of the meetin', forby, and has been overseer of the roads for three years.—An' ye all know, that my mammy was kilt o' the Ingens—now all ye that's in my favour, come forit an' drenk."—Appetite, or rather thirst, prevailed, and the voters gave their votes to the man with the two kegs.

Teague, in the meantime, thinking he had another chance of being a great man, had been busy, but to no purpose; for the people gave their votes as already mentioned. The captain thought himself fortunate to be thus relieved, and proceeded on his journey.

The perplexity of the captain, in the late transaction, on account of his servant, may serve to put those in mind who travel with a waiter, not to go much about at the election seasons, but avoid them as you would the equinoxes. It might not be amiss, if for this reason the times of electing members for the several bodies were put down in the almanac, that a man might be safe in his excursions, and not have an understrapper picked up when he could not well spare him.

I mean this as no burlesque on the present generation; for mankind in all ages have had the same propensity to magnify what was small, and elevate the low. We do not find that the Egyptians, though there were lions in the kingdom of Libya, not far distant, ever made a god of one of them. They rather chose the cow kind, the stork, and the crocodile, or the muskrat, or mire-snipe, or other inferior animal, for an object of deification. The Romans and the Greeks also, often worshipped small matters. As

> Cannons shoot the higher pitches,
> The lower you put down their breeches.—

The smaller the objects we take up, and make great, the act is greater; for it requires an equal art in the formation of the glass to magnify, as to diminish, and if the object is not of itself, there is no magnifying. Caligula is celebrated for making his horse a senator. It would have been nothing to have made a Roman Knight one; but to endow a mere quadruped with the qualities of a legislator, bespeaks great strength of parts and judgment. . . .

Chapter XXX

Captain Farrago Visits the Hall of Congress, in Search of Teague, But Without Success, Although Some He Saw There Resembled Him—The Debates— Goes to the University and Makes a Ludicrous Discovery, But Not of Teague

THE NEXT DAY, REVOLVING EVERY THING IN HIS MIND, it occurred to the captain that the Irishman [Teague O'Regan, who had become separated from the captain] might have gone out of town, hearing of an election at a district, and have been elected to Congress. As that body was then sitting, he thought it could be no great trouble to go to the house, and cast an eye from the gallery, and see if the ragamuffin had got there. There was one that had a little of the brogue of Teague upon his tongue, but nothing of his physiognomy; others had a great deal of his manner, but there was none that came absolutely up to the physic of his person.

However, being here, the captain thought it not amiss to listen awhile to the debates upon the carpet. A certain bill was depending, and made, it seems, the order of the day. Mr. Cogan being on the floor, spoke:—"Sir," said he, addressing himself to the chair, "the bill in contemplation is, in my opinion, of a dangerous tendency. I will venture to foretell, that, if it goes into a law, the cows will have fewer calves, and the sheep less wool; hens will lay fewer eggs, and the cocks forget to crow day-light. The horses will be worse shod, and stumble more; our watches go too slow; corns grow upon our toes; young women have the stomach-ache; old men the gout; and middle-aged persons, fainting fits. The larks will fall dead in the field; the frogs croak till they burst their bags; and the leaves of the trees fall before the autumn. Snow will be found in the heat of harvest, and the dog-days in winter. The rivers will revert—and the shadows fall to the east in the morning. The moon will be eclipsed, and the equinoxes happen at a wrong season of the year. Was it not such a bill as this that changed the old style; that made the eclipse in the time of Julius Cæsar; that produced an earthquake at Jamaica, and sunk Port Royal? All history, both ancient and modern, is full of the mischiefs of such a bill. I shall therefore vote against it."

Mr. Bogan was now on the floor, and advocated the good effects of the bill.

"Sir," said he, addressing himself to the chair, "I appear in support of the bill. I say, it will have a good effect on the physical world especially. The ducks will be fatter, the geese heavier, and the swans whiter. The red-birds sing better, and partridges come more easily into traps. It will kill rats, muzzle calves, and cut colts; and multiply the breed of oysters, and pickle codfish. It will moderate the sun's heat, and the winter's cold; prevent fogs, and cure the ague. It will help the natural brain, brace the nerves, cure sore eyes and the colic, and remove rheumatisms. Consult experience, and it will be found that provisions of the nature proposed by this bill, have an astonishing influence in this respect, where they have been tried. I must take the liberty to say, the gentleman's allegations are totally *unfounded;* and he has *committed* himself in the matter of his history; the earthquakes in Jamaica not happening in the time of Julius Cæsar; and therefore could have nothing to do with the eclipse of the sun. I shall, therefore, vote in favour of the bill."

Mr. Cogan rose to explain, and said, "that he did not say that the earthquake at Jamaica was at the same time with the eclipse of the sun, which happened at the birth of Julius Cæsar."

Mr. Bogan rose to correct the gentleman: "It was not at the birth of Julius Cæsar, but at his death, that the earthquake happened."

Mr. Hogan was on the floor: said, "he thought he could reconcile the gentlemen on that head. It was well known, Julius Cæsar lived about the time of the rebellion in Scotland, a little after Nebuchadnezzar, king of the Jews. As to the earthquake, he did not remember what year it happened, and therefore could say nothing about it."

At this period, the question being called, it was put and carried by a majority of fifteen.

The captain, satisfied with this sample of congressional debates, retired, and came to his lodgings.

It was about three o'clock in the afternoon, that some one, who read the advertisement respecting Teague, came to the captain, and informed him that a person, answering to the description, had been lately employed to teach Greek in the University. Struck with the idea, that the bog-trotter might have passed himself for a Greek scholar, whereas he understood only Irish, he set out to the University to make inquiry. Knocking at the door of the principal, he was admitted; and, being seated, addressed him, as follows: said he, "Sir, a pedeseque of mine, (for talking to a rector of a college, he did not choose to use the vulgar terms—waiter, or bog-trotter,) a pedeseque of mine, whom I have found useful, save that he is somewhat troublesome in pretending to places of appointment, for which he is not qualified: a thing, by the by, too common in this country: where men, without the aid of academic knowledge, thrust themselves into places requiring great learning and ability: [This he said to flatter the man of letters; as if a man could know but little that had not been furbished at his school.]* I say, this pedeseque of mine has absconded for some days, and I have been able to collect no account of him until last evening, that a person, having read an

* Editor's Note: Brackets in the original.

advertisement of mine in the Gazette, came to me, and informed, that one answering the description I had given, both as to appearance and accomplishments, had been lately employed as Professor of the Greek Language in this University. Now, though I well know this Paddy, as I may call him, to understand no Greek, yet as he speaks Irish, and has much assurance, and little honesty in matters where his ambition is concerned, I did not know but he might have imposed himself upon you for a Greek scholar, and obtained a professorship."

The principal made answer, that it was true that a person from Ireland had been lately employed in that capacity, and that should he be discovered to be an imposter, it would be using the University very ill. The captain thought so too; and taking it for granted that it was Teague, expressed his surprise that they had not examined him before he was admitted; or at least had such proof by letters, as would have ascertained his being qualified. The principal observed, that as to examination, they had no one at hand to examine, as there were none of the trustees or professors of other branches in the University, who understood Greek; as for himself he did not, having not studied it in early life, and for a series of years having given himself to politics and mathematics; so that, unless they could send out for a Roman Catholic priest, or a Scotch clergyman, there was none to examine. The improbability of any person passing himself, above all things, for a master of the Greek language, on the score of understanding Irish, was such, that it never came into their heads to suspect it, so as to demand letters.

"Had you known," said the captain, "this bog-trotter of mine, (here he forgot the word pedeseque) as well as I do, you would not be surprised at his attempting anything: and that he should be now in your academy giving Greek lectures, understanding nothing but the vernacular tongue of his own country." Here he gave an account of his setting up for Congress, etc., as explained in the preceding part of this narrative.

However, wishing to see the ragamuffin, that he might unkennel him, he was accompanied by the principal to the chamber of the pseudo professor, considering, as he went along, in what manner he should accost him; whether he should break out upon him with a direct invective, or with ironical words; such as, "Mr. Professor, you must be a very learned man, not only to understand Irish, but

Greek: but perhaps the Greek and Irish languages are much the same. It must be so, for I know that a few days ago you did not understand a word of this, and to acquire a dead language in such a short time would be impossible, unless the living tongue was a good deal a-kin to it. But I had never understood that Irish had any more affinity to the language of Athens and Sparta, than the Erse, or the German, or the Welsh: however, we must live and learn, as the saying is; you have shown us what we never knew before."

Conning a speech of this sort in his own mind, with a view to divert the principal, and amuse himself with Teague, he entered the chamber of the professor, who sat in an elbow chair, with Thucydides before him.

What was the surprise of the captain, to find that it was not Teague?

In fact, it was a person not wholly unlike him, especially in a tinge of the brogue which he betrayed in his discourse: for, though the professor was really a man of education, having been early sent to St. Omer's, where he had studied, being intended for a priest, and understood not only the Greek and Latin, but spoke French: yet, in the pronunciation of the English tongue, he had that prolongation of the sound of a word, and articulation of the vowel o, which constitutes what is vulgarly called the brogue, as being the pronunciation of the native Irish, who being an oppressed people, are most of them poor—and wear a kind of mean shoe, which they call a brogue.

After an apology to the professor for mistaking him for a certain Teague O'Regan, whom he had in his employment; at the request of the professor, the principal and the captain took seats.

The professor said, his name was not O'Regan, being O'Dougherty; but he knew the O'Regans very well in Ireland. There was a Paddy O'Regan in the same class with him at St. Omer's, when he read Craike. That he was a good scholar, and understood Craike very well; and he would be glad if he was over in this country to teach Craike here; it appeared to be a very scarce language; but he had become a praste, and was now a missionary at Paraguay, in South America.

The captain, punning on his pronunciation of the word Greek, and willing to amuse himself a little with the professor, could not help observing, that he was under a mistake as to the scarceness of the Craike language in these states. That there were whole tribes who spoke the Craike language: there was that of the heron, and the raven, and several other fowls.—A German professor, who was present, apprehending the captain to be under a mistake, and willing to correct him, observed: "It is," said he, "the Creek language that the professor means."—"As to that," said the captain, "it is also spoken plentifully in America. There is a whole nation of Indians on the borders of South Carolina and Georgia, that speak the Creek language, men, women, and children."

The professor, knowing more of the classics than of the geography of these United States; and of the heathen gods more than of the aborigines of this country, expressed astonishment. "If what you tell me be a trut," said he, "it is a crate discovery:—perhaps dese may have de fragments o' de books o' de philosophers and poets dat are lost, and de professors cannot come across in deir own countries: but I have tought dat de Craike language was spoke only in de Morea, and a little in Russia and Constantinople."

The captain assured him, the principal favouring the mistake by a grave face, and bowing as the captain spoke, that it was absolutely the vernacular language of these people.

"Why den," said the other, "do dey not get professors from amongst dese to tache Craike in deir colleges?"

"Because," said the captain, "we have been heretofore on hostile terms with these Indians, and it is but of late that we have made a peace. But now, it is presumed, we will have it in our power to procure from them able teachers."

The professor was alarmed at this, as supposing it would supersede the necessity of his services; or, at least, much reduce the price of his tuition. He could have wished he had not come to this quarter of the world: and was almost ready, in his own mind, to bind up what he had, and go back to Clogher.

So ended the visits to the University, and the captain withdrew.

Chapter XXXI

*The Captain Visits the Secretary at War to Inquire for
Teague, Thinking He Might Have Been Passed for
an Indian Chief, and of What Occurred Thereon*

Oᴜʀ ᴄʜᴇᴠᴀʟɪᴇʀ ᴡᴀs ɴᴏᴡ ᴀᴛ ʜɪs ᴡɪᴛ's ᴇɴᴅ, ɴᴏᴛ being able to conceive of any other place in which Teague might be found; when all at once it came into his head (led to it, perhaps, from the reference, in his late conversation, to the Indian tribes,) that probably he might have fallen in with the Indian treaty man, and have been prevailed on to personate a chief. It appeared to him, therefore, advisable, to go directly to the secretary at war, to know if any party of Indians had been there lately to negotiate a treaty.

Being introduced, and after some ceremony accosting the secretary, he gave him to understand why it was that he had the honour to wait upon him, viz., that he had a servant by the name of Teague O'Regan, who had been absent some days, and that from a circumstance which happened in the way to the city, he had reason to suspect, he might have been picked up by a certain Indian treaty man, to supply the place of a Welsh blacksmith, who had died, and had passed for a chief of the Kickapoos.

The secretary stared at his visitor for some moments with surprise, mingled with displeasure, believing him to be some wag, that had come to make this inquiry by way of burlesque on the Indian treaties; and with some irritation of mind, gave him to understand, that there had been no Indian treaty man, or Kickapoo chief there; that on treaty had been held with the Indians for above a month past, since the king of the Togamogans had drawn goods; but treaty or no treaty, it ill became him, in the appearance of a gentleman, to throw a burlesque on government, by insinuating that his Irishman could be imposed upon them for a chief.

"I mean no burlesque," said the captain, a little irritated in his turn; "I have had too much trouble to keep him from the Indian treaty man that was coming here, to be disposed to jest with so serious an affair. The hair-breadth escape of going to Congress, or being licensed as a preacher, or being chosen as a member of the philosophical society, was nothing to this, as it was so difficult to guard against it, the Indian recruiters imitating savages, not only in their dress and painting, but in the dexterity to way-lay and surprise."

"I wish you to know, Sir," said the secretary, "that I comprehend your burlesque very well. But though you and others may misrepresent our policy in the Indian treaties, it is base irony and ridicule to insinuate that the Indians we treat with are not chiefs."

"Chiefs, or no Chiefs," said the captain, "I am not saying, nor care; but only wish to know if you have been instituting any treaty with my Teague who has been absent some days."

"I will be much obliged to you to withdraw from my office," said the secretary.

"I shall withdraw," said the captain, "and not with that respect for your understanding and politeness which I could have wished to entertain. I have addressed you with civility; and I was entitled to a civil answer; but I see the 'insolence of office,' is well enumerated by the poet, amongst the evils that make us sick of life. Your humble servant, Monsieur Secretary, I shall trouble you no further."

Returning to the Indian Queen, a play bill for the evening had announced the performance of the tragedy of Macbeth, and a farce called the Poor Soldier. A party of the gentlemen from the public house, had taken a box, and the captain agreed to go with them to the play. Having delivered their tickets, and being admitted to the box, the captain almost involuntarily cast his eyes upon the pit and galleries, to observe if he could anywhere descry the physiognomy of Teague. As before, when with the same view he surveyed the members of Congress, he could discover several that resembled him; but yet not the identical person. The curtain being now drawn, the play began. Nothing material occurred during the performance of the tragedy, save that when the witches came in, there was one in her cap and broomstick, whose features strongly resembled the Irishman's, and who, had she not been an old woman and a witch, might have passed for Teague. The captain's attention was forcibly arrested by the similarity of features, and stout frame of the bog-trotter, covered with a short gown and petticoat; and borrowing a glass from one that sat in the box with him, endeavoured to reconnoitre more perfectly, and could have sworn that it was the mother or sister of Teague, that had just come from Ireland and joined the company.

The tragedy being ended, the farce began to be acted, and who should come forward in the character of Darby, but the long sought for Teague. The fact was, he had before appeared in the tragedy, in the character of an overgrown witch. It was more natural for him to appear in the character of Darby, his own countryman; for he spoke with the brogue naturally, and not by imitation. The managers had had him all the while of his absence, under tuition, teaching him his part, which was not difficult to do—the manner and pronunciation being already his own.

It was this that induced the managers to take him up as a sub-stitute; the person who actually played the part of Darby, having

in a drunken frolick enlisted as a soldier. As the natural squeal of a
pig is superior to the imitation of it; so it was allowed by the audience,
that Teague exceeded the pseudo Irishman that usually performed
this part. All were pleased but his master, whose sense of propriety
could scarcely restrain him from throwing his cane at the bog-trotter.
Thought he with himself, what avails it that I prevented him from
taking a seat in a legislative body, or from preaching, or being a
philosopher; if, after all, he has relinquished my service, and turned
player; a thing, no doubt, fitter for him, than the being a senator, or
clergyman or philosopher: because he can appear in some low
character, in the comedy or farce, and come off tolerably enough.
For though among the dramatis personæ of learned bodies, there
are Tony Lumpkins, and Darby M'Faddins in abundance, yet there
ought to be none; and Teague had better be on the stage than in
such capacities, since he must be somewhere. But to leave me without notice, after all my kindness, and what I intended to do still
farther for him, is ungrateful, and deserves all that I can say bad
concerning him. I shall give myself no farther trouble on this head;
but let him take his course: I must endeavour to find another
servant to supply his place.

Chapter XXXII

*Captain Farrago Thinks of Purchasing a Negro, and
Has a Conversation with a Quaker on the Subject of
Slavery*

THE FOREGOING HAD BEEN THE REFLECTIONS OF THE
captain during the exhibition of the farce. But the
play being ended, and having come home, the next day he began
to put his resolution in practice; and to think how he could supply
himself with another servant. He thought of purchasing a negro;
and mentioning this to the company at breakfast, at the Indian
Queen, one of the people called Quakers, who was present, and
overheard the conversation, made an apology for the liberty he
took in making some objections. "Friend," said he, "thee appears to
be a discreet man from thy behaviour, and conversation; and if
thee will not be offended, I would ask if thee canst reconcile it with
thy principles, to keep a slave?"—"As to that," said the captain,

"I have thought upon the subject, and do not see any great harm in the matter. If we look to inanimate nature, we shall find, that the great law is Force. The Cartesians call it pressure and suction: The Newtonians call it attraction and gravitation. The sun, the largest body in the system, endeavours to draw all towards it; while the lesser globes struggle to fly off at a tangent. The denser, that is, denser air, takes place of the rare; and the heavier particles of water cause the lighter to recede. The tall oak overshades the under-wood. There is a predominancy, and subordination in all things. In the animal creation, the weak is always subject to the strong; who even devour them, when the flesh suits their appetite: and the very teeth and jawbone of carnivorous animals, show the intention of nature, that they should make a prey of living creatures. Do you blame yourselves, when you subjugate elephants, or horses, or oxen of the plough, to your use? What right have you to invade the liberty of a playful young colt, more than of an African inhabitant? Or have you not as good a right to take up a negro, and put him to your work, as you have to cut a calf, and manufacture him for the draft."

"In this case there is a difference," said the Quaker; "a negro is a human creature, and possesses all the natural rights of man."

"That may be," said the captain. "But what are the natural rights of men? Are they not finally resolvable, as in the inanimate world, into power on the one hand, and weakness on the other?

"Who is it, that abstains from dominion, when he has it in his power to assert it? Power is the great law of nature; and nothing but the pacts or conventions of society can contravene it. I should think myself justifiable in making any man a slave to answer my purposes, provided I treated him well while he was such. This I take to be the only condition which the law of reason annexes to the enjoyment of such property. I may be warranted in taking, and managing an animal of the horse kind; but it is my indisputable duty not to abuse him by causing him to suffer famine, or endure too much toil. The same with any other animal that I enslave; there is a tacit condition annexed to the grant which the law of nature gives; that the service be exacted with moderation; and proper nourishment provided. I admit also, that humanity would dictate that the happiness of a slave ought to be consulted as much as is consistent with my own convenience. For instance: if I had the

Grand Turk in my power, as he has been accustomed to a soft and effeminate way of living, it would be hard to put him all at once to maul rails, or clearing our meadow ground; or if it should fall in my way to have Catharine of Russia in that capacity, as she is a woman of an elevated mind, it would be inhuman to put her to the lowest drudgery, such as scrubbing out rooms, and carrying water from the pump: but rather indulge her if I could afford it, with a more easy employment, especially as she is an old woman, of knitting stockings, and carding wool. There is no man would be more disposed to treat a slave with tenderness than myself, but to deny me of my right altogether of making one, or of trafficking for one when made, is carrying the matter too far.

"So much for the right of enslaving. But if we put it on the principle of what will conduce to the aggregate happiness of mankind, we shall find it to be, that there should be master and servant, or in other words owner and slave. The economy of nature illustrates this, in the subserviency of one thing to another. But independent of any illustration, it must be known on reflection, and is felt in experience, that all is not competent to all things; and in the case of temporary servants, much time is taken up in contracting with them for their remanence; and it is a considerable time before they get into the habit of our service; and, having it in their power to retire from us when inclination may direct, there is an insecurity in the attachment. But as the slave has the master always to provide for him; so the master has the slave always to subserve him: and thus by a conjoint interest, the felicity of both is promoted, and the sum of human happiness increased. Hence it is, that most nations have made use of slaves. The patriarch Abraham had threescore-and-ten servants born in his house. What were these but slaves? The Jews, his descendants, had bond-men, and bond-women: Were not these slaves? The Roman slaves were more in number than the citizens; and amongst the Greeks, the most virtuous of them, the Spartans, kept in their service the most depressed of all slaves, the Helots; who, when we consider the black broth, the food, and severe life of the masters, must have lived on poor fare, and in a laborious service indeed.

"But it may be said, That example of wrong never constitutes right. Grant it: but if you examine the capacities, and even inclinations of men, will you not find that some are qualified only to be slaves? They have not understanding to act for themselves. Nor do all love freedom, even when they have it—do not many surrender it, and prefer kissing a great man's posteriors, to being independent? It is not always, even from the views of advantage, that men are sycophants; but from an abstract pleasure in being drawn into the vortex of others. There is a pleasure in slavery, more than unenslaved men know. Why is it, that even after the convulsion of a revolution in a government, in favour of liberty, there is a natural tendency to slavery: and it finally terminates in this point? The fact is, a state of liberty is an unnatural state. Like a bone out of place, the mind, in an individual, or political capacity, seeks the condition of a master or servant; avoiding, as the particular propensity may be, the one or the other. There cannot be a greater proof that this is founded in nature, than the common moral observation, that the greatest tyrants, that is, the worst master, make the most abject slaves, and *vice versa*, that the most subservient of mankind, when you give them power, make the worst use of it. All this because, in these cases, the persons are misplaced, and not in their proper stations. Julius Cæsar made a humane generous master; but he would have made a very intriguing, troublesome valet de chambre. It would have been impossible to have got any good of him. On the other hand, Tiberius would have made an excellent hostler, and taken a beating, with as much resignation as a house beagle, who is used to it. So that it evidently is the provision of nature, that there are materials of slavery; and the fault of those whom she intends for master, if they do not make slaves. But as it is difficult to determine, *a priori*, who are intended for slavery or freedom, so as to make a judicious distribution, things must take their course; and the rule be, catch, who catch can; and every man have a servant when he can get one. It is in vain to be squeamish, and stick at colour. It is true, I would rather have a white person, if such could be got; as I prefer white to black, especially in the summer season, as being a more light and airy colour."

"Thy reasoning," said the Quaker, "is more rhetorical than logical; and thy analogies of nature, and historical proofs, cannot so far oppress the light within, as to make me think, that it is given to thee, or me, to make slaves of our species."

"As to that," said the captain, "I am not clear that a negro is

270] THE YOUNG REPUBLIC

of our species. You may claim kindred with him if you please; but I shall not."

"I shall not dispute that with thee," said the Quaker, "for I perceive thee does not give credit to what the book says of the first man, and his descendants. But will thee not grant me, that the African, though not of the same stock, is, at least a man; that is, of the human genus, though the species of the white and the black may not be the same; if so, hast thou more right to enslave him, than he thee?"

"Grant it," said the captain; "for my reasoning tends to that, and resolves the right into the power."

"If so," said the Quaker, "thee may be the slave in thy turn."

"Doubtless," said the captain; "and it is not of so much consequence who is the slave as that there be one. It is better that the foot be foot, and the head be head; but if there is a conversion, nevertheless, let there be head and foot. It is necessary that there be domination and subjection, in order to produce a compound improvement and advantage."

You could see by the Quaker's countenance, that he thought the reasoning sophistical; but as he did not know very well what he could say more, he was silent.

Chapter XXXIII

Containing Some Grave Remarks on the Subject of the Preceding Chapter

IT IS THOUGHT BY SOME THE CAPTAIN WAS NOT SERIOUS in thus advocating the cause of slavery. Be that as it may, he omitted some serious arguments, that naturally present themselves on that side on which he reasoned. For instance, it strikes me at first blush, that there can be no moral wrong in catching a young African, and bringing him away from his own happiness to pursue ours. For if there were, is it to be supposed, that humane and just persons would promote and support the evil, by purchasing such negro, and retaining him, and his offspring, when purchased? For, on the principle that the receiver is the thief, or to speak more strictly, a thief, the purchaser of the African takes the guilt along with the possession; and in the language of the law, every act of retainer is a new trespass. For the evil of the original act, if there be evil in it, cannot be rendered pure by the filtration of purchase, and retaining. So that the holder of the negro, in the tenth transmission, is an aider, or abettor, of the original act of taking; if I may use the word aider, or abettor, in a case of trespass, where, by the definition of the law, all who any way concur in the act, and further it, are *principals*. The holder of a negro must, therefore, look back to that act which first made him, or an ancestor, a slave; and if he cannot justify the retaining him in servitude:— What a consequence must this be! There is no man that pretends to humanity, much less to religion, would be safe in being the possessor of a slave. The only way therefore to get rid of the difficulty is to justify, *ab origine*, traffic in all such property.

That it is justifiable I have no doubt. Is there any religious denomination, except the fanatical people called Quakers, that have made it a term of communion not to hold a slave? In admitting to church privileges, I have never heard of the question asked, Have you any negroes, and do you keep slaves? If it was a matter of conscience, would not conscientious persons themselves make it?

The assemblies of synods of the Presbyterian church, or conventions of the Episcopal, in America, have said nothing on this subject. Is an omission of this kind reconcilable with the idea, that it is a natural evil, or a moral wrong?

In the phrenzy of the day, some weak-minded powers in Europe begin to consider what is called the African trade as a moral wrong, and to provide for a *gradual* abolition of it. If they will abolish it, I approve of its being done gradually; because, numbers being embarked in this trade, it must ruin them all at once, to desist from it. On this principle, I have always thought it a defect in the criminal codes of most nations, not giving license to the perpetrators of offences, to proceed, for a limited time, in larcenies, burglaries, etc., until they get their hands out of use to these pursuits, and in use to others. For it must be greatly inconvenient to thieves and cut-throats, who have engaged in this way of life, and run great risks in acquiring skill in their employment, to be obliged all at once to withdraw their hands, and lay aside picking locks, and apply themselves to industry in other ways for a livelihood.

The law of Pennsylvania on this principle, has provided for the *gradual abolition* of the slavery of negroes; for those who have got

them could not do without them, no more than one can do without
the money he has obtained by unlawful means, being compelled
by necessity to resort to this mode of recruiting his purse. All those
therefore who have been originally taken from the coast of Africa,
and deprived of liberty, or descended from such, and inheriting
slavery, when recorded agreeably to the act in question, continue
slaves, and for life, and their offspring to a certain period. But were
we to entrammel the case with *political* or *moral* doubts respecting
the original right of caption, and subjugation, the difficulty would
exist of reconciling it with *natural right to hold a slave for a moment
even whether the law sanctioned it or not*; in which case we should find
it necessary to go as far as the fanatics in religion, and set our
slaves *free altogether.*

It is from duly attending to this circumstance, that abstract
reasoners talk of abolition; a doctrine which, however absurd, is
becoming the whim of the day; and the phrenzy seems to gain
such ground, that I would not wonder if they would next assert
that it is unlawful to use the servitude of horses, or other beasts of
burden, as having a natural right to live in the fields, and be as
free as mankind. The best way to avoid the extremes, is to check
the principle; I hold the right of absolute subjugation of whites,
blacks, and browns of all nations, against gradual abolition, or
any abolition whatsoever. This being the only consistent principle,
short of an absolute emancipation, made instantly; for in no *mean*
is there reason, or a rest for conscience.

That it is of importance to settle the consciences of sober-minded
persons in Pennsylvania, clergymen, and members of the Presbyterian church especially, who have negroes, must be well known
from that tenderness of conscience, for which such are remarkable.[1]
Some, indeed, carry their ideas of the extent of duties so far, as not
to omit grace at meals, or the formal worship of prayer, reading
chapters, and singing psalms on the set occasions, on any consideration whatsoever; what is more, would not shave a beard on the
Sabbath day for a vow. Now, should they, by any means, come
once to think of the wickedness of enslaving men, there would be
no getting them to keep a negro. For those of this denomination,
and, indeed, most, or all others of the Christian, hold that the

---

[1] The law for the *gradual* abolition of slavery in Pennsylvania had been passed a
few years before, but its effects had not yet become visible.

African, though of a sable race, is of their own species; being descended from Adam.—This being the case, a slight matter, the bare directing their attention to the subject, would alarm pious people, and lead them to the favourite maxim of the gospel—"Do to others, as you would have others to do to you."

As opposed to the enfranchisement of negroes, generally, and in Pennsylvania in particular, I have been under apprehensions, that some of our young lawyers in the courts, might plead the constitution of the state, by which it is established that "all *men* are born equally free and independent." Now admitting that a negro is a man, how shall any master retain him as a slave? On a habeas corpus, he must be set at liberty. At least I cannot conceive how the judge could remand him to his drudgery. The constitution is the law paramount, and framed by a convention of the people, recognising the original right of freedom in a negro, allowing him to be a man; and carries us above the act of the legislature for the gradual abolition, etc., which by implication seems to suppose that the negroes may be slaves:—An implication inconsistent with the power exercised by the law. For if negroes were slaves, and so the *property* of those who claimed them, could the legislature affect that property without indemnification to the masters?

I shall say no more on this head, lest I should furnish hints to pettifoggers, who may make an ill use of their information.

In truth this chapter, in the first edition of this book, or something else, gave rise to a habeas corpus in the case of a negro: and which came to trial in the Supreme Court of the state. The argument occupied a whole week; but it was determined that slavery by law did exist in Pennsylvania, maugre the constitution; which did not respect those in a state of slavery at the time of forming the constitution, and who were not parties to the *compact;* that it is a claim of property founded in wrong; but tolerated, until it can be consentient with general safety, and the happiness of the slave and master to abolish it altogether. . . .

18

The Romantic Novel Comes to America

A Selection from Charles Brockden Brown's
Ormond (1799)

The novel, a new form of literary expression, appeared coincidently with the emergence of the new American nation. American men, and women, of letters became attracted to the modern novel (as did their colleagues in Europe) as a vehicle because it seemed so well suited to the new forces and currents associated with Romanticism that were flowing through Western culture. Romanticism—a complex cultural phenomenon —partly expressed a reaction against the rationalism of the Enlightenment and partly an affirmation of faith in emotion and sentiment as proper guides to thought and action. *The Power of Sympathy* (1789) by William Hill Brown (1765–1793) is generally regarded as the first American novel. Charles Brockden Brown (1771–1810), a Philadelphia lawyer turned novelist, was not long in emulating the elder Brown in exploiting the new literary form. Charles Brockden Brown in the 1790s abandoned the law and attempted to live by his pen—the first creative writer in the United States to join what Adam Smith described as "that unprosperous race of men commonly called men of letters." Although he survived the ordeal— he lived in a "dismal room in a dismal street," wore threadbare clothing and down-at-the-heel shoes—he could not bear to inflict these hardships upon his family. In 1801, after a frenzied stint of writing in which he produced six novels in three years, he turned to magazine editing for a living. One after another of his magazines failed until, at the age of thirty-nine,

Charles Brockden Brown, *Ormond: or The Secret Witness* (Port Washington, N.Y.: Kennikat Press, Inc., reprinted from the David McKay edition of 1887, 1963), pp. 61–69.

Brown himself passed out of circulation. As a disciple of William Godwin (1756–1836), a contemporary English philosophical anarchist, Brown was one of the most advanced thinkers of his day. He prided himself upon being a novelist of ideas; calling himself a "moral painter," he used the novel and essays to agitate for freer divorce laws, political rights for women, humanitarian reform, the rule of reason, and the "truths" of Deism. His women characters are paragons of virtue and courage in adversity; they talk learnedly about philosophy, literature, and science. But Brown could not bring himself to eliminate the "vapors," those fainting fits and other evidences of extreme sensibility dear to writers of the Romantic school.

In his fondness for the "cult of horror," Brown derived from the Gothic novelists of the late eighteenth century; in his fascination with psychology and the macabre he foreshadowed Edgar Allen Poe (1809–1849). One of his heroines is given to self-analysis: when she hears a shriek in her closet at midnight she devotes five minutes to analyzing her emotions. In *Wieland*, Brown dealt with a case of religious melancholia aggravated by ventriloquism: by means of his skill as a ventriloquist, the enemy of the central character urges him to put his wife and children to death. *Edgar Huntley* (1799) is a detective novel—another link with Poe—whereas the scene of *Ormond* is the yellow fever epidemic in Philadelphia in 1793. *Ormond*, in fact, provides a good example of Brown's consistent effort to domesticate the novel by giving it an American setting. He explicitly renounced Gothic castles, clanking chains, and the other paraphernalia used by Horace Walpole, Anne Radcliffe, and Matthew "Monk" Lewis. Instead, Brown said, "The incidents of Indian hostility, and the perils of the Western wilderness, are far more suitable; and for a native of America to overlook these could admit of no apology."

One might begin his study of the new forces in American literature becoming apparent after 1800 with Vernon Louis Parrington's second volume in his *Main Currents in American Thought, The Romantic Revolution in America, 1800–1860* (New York: Harcourt, Brace and Company, 1927). Also of considerable value is George Snell, *The Shapers of American Fiction, 1798–1947* (New York: E. P. Dutton and Company, 1947). More specialized is William B. Blake's "Brockden Brown and the Novel," in *Sewanee Review*, XVIII (1910), pp. 431–43. An excellent biography is Henry R. Warfel's *Charles Brockden Brown, American Gothic Novelist* (Gainesville, Fla.: The University of Florida Press, 1942).

In reading this selection from *Ormond* note (1) the techniques Brown used to intensify the sense of horror in the reader's mind; (2) evidences of antiforeignism; and (3) suggestions of the author's attempt to portray emotion and sentiment as acceptable features of human responses to crises.

An Incident of the Yellow Fever Panic in Philadelphia

ADJACENT TO THE HOUSE OCCUPIED BY BAXTER WAS an antique brick tenement. It was one of the first erections made by the followers of William Penn. It had the honour to be used as the temporary residence of that venerable person. Its moss-grown pent-house, crumbling walls, and ruinous *porch*, made it an interesting and picturesque object. Notwithstanding its age, it was still tenable.

This house was occupied, during the preceding months, by a Frenchman. His dress and demeanour were respectable. His mode of life was frugal almost to penuriousness, and his only companion was a daughter. The lady seemed not much less than thirty years of age, but was of a small and delicate frame. It was she that performed every household office. She brought water from the pump and provisions from the market. Their house had no visitants, and was almost always closed. Duly, as the morning returned, a venerable figure was seen issuing from his door, dressed in the same style of tarnished splendour and old-fashioned preciseness. At the dinner-hour [noon] he as regularly returned. For the rest of the day he was invisible.

The habitations in this quarter are few and scattered. The pestilence soon showed itself here, and the flight of most of the inhabitants augmented its desolateness and dreariness. For some time, Monrose (that was his name) made his usual appearance in the morning. At length the neighbours remarked that he no longer came forth as usual. Baxter had a notion that Frenchmen were exempt from this disease. He was, besides, deeply and rancorously prejudiced against that nation. There will be no difficulty in accounting for this, when it is known that he had been an English grenadier at Dettingen and Minden. It must likewise be added, that he was considerably timid, and had sickness in his own family. Hence it was that the disappearance of Monrose excited in him no inquisitiveness as to the cause. He did not even mention this circumstance to others.

The lady was occasionally seen as usual in the street. There were always remarkable peculiarities in her behaviour. In the midst of grave and disconsolate looks, she never laid aside an air of solemn dignity. She seemed to shrink from the observation of others, and her eyes were always fixed upon the ground. One evening Baxter was passing the pump while she was drawing water. The sadness which her looks betokened, and a suspicion that her father might be sick, had a momentary effect upon his feelings. He stopped and asked how her father was. She paid a polite attention to his question, and said something in French. This, and the embarrassment of her air, convinced him that his words were not understood. He said no more, (what, indeed, could he say?) but passed on.

Two or three days after this, on returning in the evening to his family, his wife expressed her surprise in not having seen Miss Monrose in the street that day. She had not been at the pump, nor had gone, as usual, to market. This information gave him some disquiet; yet he could form no resolution. As to entering the house and offering his aid, if aid were needed, he had too much regard for his own safety, and too little for that of a frog-eating Frenchman, to think seriously of that expedient. His attention was speedily diverted by other objects, and Monrose was, for the present, forgotten.

Baxter's profession was that of a porter. He was thrown out of employment by the present state of things. The solicitude of the guardians of the city was exerted on this occasion, not only in opposing the progress of disease and furnishing provisions to the destitute, but in the preservation of property. For this end the number of nightly watchmen was increased. Baxter entered himself in this service. From nine till twelve o'clock at night it was his province to occupy a certain post.

On this night he attended his post as usual. Twelve o'clock arrived, and he bent his steps homeward. It was necessary to pass by Monrose's door. On approaching this house, the circumstance mentioned by his wife occurred to him. Something like compassion was conjured up in his heart by the figure of the lady, as he recollected to have lately seen it. It was obvious to conclude that sickness was the cause of her seclusion. The same, it might be, had confined her father. If this were true, how deplorable might be their present condition! Without food, without physician or friends, ignorant of the language of the country, and thence unable to communicate their wants or solicit succour, fugitives from their native land, neglected, solitary, and poor.

His heart was softened by these images. He stopped involuntarily when opposite their door. He looked up at the house. The shutters were closed, so that light, if it were within, was invisible. He stepped into the porch, and put his eye to the keyhole. All was darksome and waste. He listened, and imagined that he heard the aspirations of grief. The sound was scarcely articulate, but had an electrical effect upon his feelings. He retired to his home full of mournful reflections.

He was willing to do something for the relief of the sufferers, but nothing could be done that night. Yet succour, if delayed till the morning, might be ineffectual. But how, when the morning came, should he proceed to effectuate his kind intentions? The guardians of the public welfare, at this crisis, were distributed into those who counselled and those who executed. A set of men, self-appointed to the generous office, employed themselves in seeking out the destitute or sick, and imparting relief. With this arrangement Baxter was acquainted. He was resolved to carry tidings of what he had heard and seen to one of those persons early the next day.

Baxter, after taking some refreshment, retired to rest. In no long time, however, he was awakened by his wife, who desired him to notice a certain glimmering on the ceiling. It seemed the feeble and flitting ray of a distant and moving light, coming through the window. It did not proceed from the street, for the chamber was lighted from the side and not from the front of the house. A lamp borne by a passenger, or the attendants of a hearse, could not be discovered in this situation. Besides, in the latter case it would be accompanied by the sound of the vehicle, and, probably, by weeping and exlamations of despair. His employment, as the guardian of property, naturally suggested to him the idea of robbery. He started from his bed, and went to the window.

His house stood at the distance of about fifty paces from that of Monrose. There was annexed to the latter a small garden or yard, bounded by a high wooden fence. Baxter's window overlooked this space. Before he reached the window, the relative situation of the two habitations occurred to him. A conjecture was instantly formed that the glimmering proceeded from this quarter. His eye, therefore, was immediately fixed upon Monrose's back-door. It caught a glimpse of a human figure passing into the house through this door. The person had a candle in his hand. This appeared by the light which streamed after him, and which was perceived, though faintly, through a small window of the dwelling, after the back-door was closed.

The person disappeared too quickly to allow him to say whether it was male or female. This scrutiny confirmed rather than weakened the apprehensions that first occurred. He reflected on the desolate and helpless condition of this family. The father might be sick; and what opposition could be made by the daughter to the stratagems or violence of midnight plunderers? This was an evil which it was his duty, in an extraordinary sense, to obviate. It is true, the hour of watching was past, and this was not the district assigned to him; but Baxter was, on the whole, of a generous and intrepid spirit. In the present case, therefore, he did not hesitate long in forming his resolution. He seized a hanger that hung at his bedside, and which had hewn many a Hungarian and French hussar to pieces. With this he descended to the street. He cautiously approached Monrose's house. He listened at the door, but heard nothing. The lower apartment, as he discovered through the keyhole, was deserted and dark. These appearances could not be accounted for. He was, as yet, unwilling to call or to knock. He was solicitous to obtain some information by silent means, and without alarming the persons within, who, if they were robbers, might thus be put upon their guard and enabled to escape. If none but the family were there, they would not understand his signals, and might impute the disturbance to the cause which he was desirous to obviate. What could he do? Must he patiently wait till some incident should happen to regulate his motions?

In this uncertainty, he bethought himself of going round to the back part of the dwelling and watching the door which had been closed. An open space, filled with rubbish and weeds, adjoined the house and garden on one side. Hither he repaired, and, raising his head above the fence, at a point directly opposite the door, waited with considerable impatience for some token or signal by which he might be directed in his choice of measures.

Human life abounds with mysterious appearances. A man perched on a fence at midnight, mute and motionless, and gazing at a dark and dreary dwelling, was an object calculated to rouse curiosity. When the muscular form and rugged visage, scarred and furrowed into something like ferocity, were added,—when the nature of the calamity by which the city was dispeopled was considered,—the motives to plunder, and the insecurity of property, arising from the pressure of new wants on the poor and the flight or disease of the rich, were attended to,—an observer would be apt to admit fearful conjectures.

We know not how long Baxter continued at this post. He remained here, because he could not, as he conceived, change it for a better. Before his patience was exhausted, his attention was called by a noise within the house. It proceeded from the lower room. The sound was that of steps, but this was accompanied with other inexplicable tokens. The kitchen-door at length opened. The figure of Miss Monrose, pale, emaciated, and haggard, presented itself. Within the door stood a candle. It was placed on a chair within sight, and its rays streamed directly against the face of Baxter as it was reared above the top of the fence. This illumination, faint as it was, bestowed a certain air of wildness on features which nature, and the sanguinary habits of a soldier, had previously rendered, in an eminent degree, harsh and stern. He was not aware of the danger of discovery in consequence of this position of the candle. His attention was, for a few seconds, engrossed by the object before him. At length he chanced to notice another object.

At a few yards' distance from the fence, and within it, some one appeared to have been digging. An opening was made in the ground, but it was shallow and irregular. The implement which seemed to have been used was nothing more than a fire-shovel, for one of these he observed lying near the spot. The lady had withdrawn from the door, though without closing it. He had leisure, therefore, to attend to this new circumstance, and to reflect upon the purpose for which this opening might have been designed.

Death is familiar to the apprehensions of a soldier. Baxter had assisted at the hasty interment of thousands, the victims of the sword or of pestilence. Whether it was because this theatre of human calamity was new to him, and death, in order to be viewed with his ancient unconcern, must be accompanied in the ancient manner, with halberds and tents, certain it is that Baxter was irresolute and timid in every thing that respected the yellow fever. The circumstances of the time suggested that this was a grave, to which some victim of this disease was to be consigned. His teeth chattered when he reflected how near he might now be to the source of infection; yet his curiosity retained him at his post.

He fixed his eyes once more upon the door. In a short time the lady again appeared at it. She was in a stooping posture, and appeared to be dragging something along the floor. His blood ran cold at this spectacle. His fear instantly figured to itself a corpse, livid and contagious. Still, he had no power to move. The lady's strength, enfeebled as it was by grief, and perhaps by the absence of nourishment, seemed scarcely adequate to the task which she had assigned herself.

Her burden, whatever it was, was closely wrapped in a sheet. She drew it forward a few paces, then desisted, and seated herself on the ground, apparently to recruit her strength and give vent to the agony of her thoughts in sighs. Her tears were either exhausted or refused to flow, for none were shed by her. Presently she resumed her undertaking. Baxter's horror increased in proportion as she drew nearer to the spot where he stood; and yet it seemed as if some fascination had forbidden him to recede.

At length the burden was drawn to the side of the opening in the earth. Here it seemed as if the mournful task was finished. She threw herself once more upon the earth. Her senses seemed for a time to have forsaken her. She sat buried in reverie, her eyes scarcely open, and fixed upon the ground, and every feature set to the genuine expression of sorrow. Some disorder, occasioned by the circumstance of dragging, now took place in the vestment of what he had rightly predicted to be a dead body. The veil by accident was drawn aside, and exhibited to the startled eye of Baxter the pale and ghastly visage of the unhappy Monrose.

This incident determined him. Every joint in his frame trembled, and he hastily withdrew from the fence. His first motion in doing this produced a noise by which the lady was alarmed; she suddenly threw her eyes upward, and gained a full view of Baxter's extraordinary countenance, just before it disappeared. She manifested her terror by a piercing shriek. Baxter did not stay to mark her subsequent conduct, to confirm or to dissipate her fears, but retired, in confusion, to his own house.

Hitherto his caution had availed him. He had carefully avoided all employments and places from which he imagined imminent danger was to be dreaded. Now, through his own inadvertency, he had rushed, as he believed, into the jaws of the pest. His senses had not been assailed by any noisome effluvia. This was no unplausible ground for imagining that his death had some other cause than the yellow fever. This circumstance did not occur to Baxter. He had been told that Frenchmen were not susceptible of this contagion. He had hitherto believed this assertion, but now regarded it as having been fully confuted. He forgot that Frenchmen were undoubtedly mortal, and that there was no impossibility in Monrose's dying, even at this time, of a malady different from that which prevailed.

Before morning he began to feel very unpleasant symptons. He related his late adventure to his wife. She endeavoured, by what arguments her slender ingenuity suggested, to quiet his apprehensions, but in vain. He hourly grew worse, and, as soon as it was light, despatched his wife for a physician. On interrogating this messenger, the physician obtained information of last night's occurrences; and, this being communicated to one of the dispensers of the public charity, they proceeded, early in the morning, to Monrose's house. It was closed, as usual. They knocked and called, but no one answered. They examined every avenue to the dwelling, but none of them were accessible. They passed into the garden, and observed, on the spot marked out by Baxter, a heap of earth. A very slight exertion was sufficient to remove it and discover the body of the unfortunate exile beneath.

After unsuccessfully trying various expedients for entering the house, they deemed themselves authorized to break the door. They entered, ascended the staircase, and searched every apartment in the house, but no human being was discoverable. The furniture was wretched and scanty, but there was no proof that Monrose had fallen a victim to the reigning disease. It was certain that the lady had disappeared. It was inconceivable whither she had gone.

Baxter suffered a long period of sickness. The prevailing malady appeared upon him in its severest form. His strength of constitution, and the careful attendance of his wife, were insufficient to rescue him from the grave. His case may be quoted as an example of the force of imagination. He had probably already received, through the medium of the air, or by contact of which he was not conscious, the seeds of this disease. They might perhaps have lain dormant, had not this panic occurred to endow them with activity.

19

Political Satire

Washington Irving's *History of New York*

Washington Irving (1783–1859) of New York, the first American professional writer to win a reputation abroad, began his literary career as an essayist. In January, 1807, Irving and a group of friends began the publication in New York of *Salmagundi: or the Whim-Whams and Opinions of Launcelot Langstaff, Esq. and Others*—a magazine modelled upon Addison and Steele's *The Spectator* of London and *The Citizen of the World*. It satirized the foibles of the bon ton of Gotham (*Salmagundi* was the first to call New York Gotham), the beaux, belles, and coxcombs; poked fun at the "whims, eccentricities, and unseemly deceits" of the ladies of New York; reviewed plays and purveyed the gossip of the streets, taverns, and drawing rooms. *Salmagundi* served as an apprenticeship for the publication in 1809 of Diedrich Knickerbocker's (Washington Irving's) *History of New York from the Beginning of the World to the End of the Dutch Dynasty*, a mock history, with political overtones, of the history of New Netherlands. Governor William Kieft of New Netherlands figures as a Dutch Thomas Jefferson. Like Jefferson, Kieft has an eccentric taste in dress, encyclopedic learning, and a passion for ingenious but futile inventions—Kieft invented "carts that went before the horse, Dutch ovens for roasting meat without fire and weather-cocks that turned against the wind." During his term of office, Kieft tried so many political experiments that he ended by entangling the government in more knots "than half a dozen successors could have untied." Among these experiments was an embargo directed against the Yankees of New England, but this "new and cheap method of fighting" recoiled disastrously upon its projectors. Irving's contemporaries who read

Washington Irving, *A History of New York from the Beginning of the World to the End of the Dutch Dynasty ... by Diedrich Knickerbocker* (1809) in *The Works of Washington Irving* (New York: Worthington Co., 1887), I, pp. 138–41; 155–73.

his best-selling *History* doubtless smiled knowingly when they read that Kieft was a pacifist, an opponent of adequate national defense, an advocate of farcical military preparations (gunboats), and a lover of pompous manifestoes. In addition to the studies of American literature previously cited, the student might consult two biographies of Irving: George S. Hellman's *Washington Irving, Esquire: Ambassador at Large from the New World to the Old* (New York: Alfred A. Knopf, 1925) and Stanley T. Williams's *The Life of Washington Irving*, 2 vols. (New York: The Oxford University Press, 1935).

In reading this selection note (1) how the author characterized William the Testy's plan for defeating the Yankees and how the latter responded to it; (2) Kieft's next move and the response both of the Yankees and the New Netherlanders to it; (3) the benefits to the Nederlanders the author attributed to Kieft's measures; (4) the author's characterization of the military forces available to Kieft; (5) Irving's description of the emergence of political parties and his characterization of the practice of politics in America; (6) his description of the manner in which Kieft administered the affairs of government; (7) his observations concerning the role of historians in society; (8) his summary of Kieft's achievements; (9) his description of the people's response to Kieft's death and his observations concerning the way in which the public usually treats such events; and (10) the elements of form and style Irving employed in his history.

Chapter II

In Which Are Recorded the Sage Projects of a Ruler of Universal Genius—The Art of Fighting by Proclamation—And How That the Valiant Jacobus Van Curlet Came To Be Foully Dishonoured at Fort Goed Hoop

Never was a more comprehensive, a more expeditious, or, what is still better, a more economical measure devised, than this of defeating the Yankees by proclamation —an expedient, likewise, so humane, so gentle and pacific, there were ten chances to one in favour of its succeeding,—but then there was one chance to ten that it would not succeed—as the ill-natured fates would have it, that single chance carried the day! The proclamation was perfect in all its parts, well constructed, well written, well sealed, and well published—all that was wanting to insure its effect was that the Yankees should stand in awe of it;

but, provoking to relate, they treated it with the most absolute contempt, applied it to an unseemly purpose, and thus did the first warlike proclamation come to a shameful end—a fate which I am credibly informed has befallen but too many of its successors.

It was a long time before Wilhelmus Kieft could be persuaded, by the united efforts of all his counsellors, that his war measures had failed in producing any effect. On the contrary, he flew in a passion whenever any one dared to question its efficacy; and swore that, though it was slow in operating, yet when once it began to work, it would soon purge the land of these rapacious intruders. Time, however, that test of all experiments, both in philosophy and politics, at length convinced the great Kieft that his proclamation was abortive; and that notwithstanding he had waited nearly four years in a state of constant irritation, yet he was still farther off than ever from the object of his wishes. His implacable adversaries in the east became more and more troublesome in their encroachments, and founded the thriving colony of Hartford close upon the skirts of Fort Goed Hoop. They, moreover, commenced the fair settlement of New-Haven (otherwise called the Red Hills) within the domains of their High Mightinesses—while the onion-patches of Piquag were a continual eyesore to the garrison of Van Curlet. Upon beholding, therefore, the inefficacy of his measure, the sage Kieft, like many a worthy practitioner of physic, laid the blame not to the medicine, but to the quantity administered, and resolutely resolved to double the dose.

In the year 1638, therefore, that being the fourth year of his reign, he fulminated against them a second proclamation, of heavier metal than the former; written in thundering long sentences, not one word of which was under five syllables. This, in fact, was a kind of non-intercourse bill, forbidding and prohibiting all commerce and connexion between any and every of the said Yankee intruders, and the said fortified post of Fort Goed Hoop, and ordering, commanding, and advising all his trusty, loyal, and well-beloved subjects to furnish them with no supplies of gin, gingerbread, or sourkrout; to buy none of their pacing horses, measly pork, apple-brandy, Yankee rum, cider-water, apple sweetmeats, Weathersfield onions, tinware, or wooden bowls, but to starve and exterminate them from the face of the land.

Another pause of a twelvemonth ensued, during which this

proclamation received the same attention and experienced the same fate as the first. In truth, it was rendered of no avail by the heroic spirit of the Nederlanders themselves. No sooner were they prohibited the use of Yankee merchandise, than it immediately became indispensable to their very existence. The men who all their lives had been content to drink gin and ride Esopus switch-tails, now swore that it was sheer tyranny to deprive them of apple-brandy and Narraghanset pacers; and as to the women, they declared there was no comfort in life without Weathersfied onions, tin kettles, and wooden bowls. So they all set to work, with might and main, to carry on a smuggling trade over the borders; and the province was as full as ever of Yankee wares,—with this difference, that those who used them had to pay double price, for the trouble and risk incurred in breaking the laws.

A signal benefit arose from these measures of William the Testy. The efforts to evade them had a marvellous effect in sharpening the intellects of the people. They were no longer to be governered without laws, as in the time of Oloffe the Dreamer; nor would the jack-knife and tobacco-box of Walter the Doubter have any more served as a judicial process. The old Nederlandt maxim, that "honesty is the best policy," was scouted as the bane of all ingenious enterprise. To use a modern phrase, "a great impulse had been given to the public mind;" and from the time of this first experience in smuggling, we may perceive a vast increase in the number, intricacy, and severity of laws and statutes—a sure proof of the increasing keenness of public intellect.

A twelvemonth having elapsed since the issuing of the proclamation, the gallant Jacobus Van Curlet despatched his annual messenger, with his customary budget of complaints and entreaties. Whether the regular interval of a year, intervening between the arrival of Van Curlet's couriers, was occasioned by the systematic regularity of his movements, or by the immense distance at which he was stationed from the seat of government, is a matter of uncertainty. Some have ascribed it to the slowness of his messengers, who, as I have before noticed, were chosen from the shortest and fattest of his garrison, as least likely to be worn out on the road; and who, being pursy, short-winded little men, generally travelled fifteen miles a day, and then laid by a whole week to rest. All these, however, are matters of conjecture; and I rather think it may be ascribed to the immemorial maxim of this worthy country—and which has ever influenced all its public transactions—not to do things in a hurry.

The gallant Jacobus Van Curlet, in his despatches, respectfully represented that several years had now elapsed since his first application to his late excellency, Wouter Van Twiller; during which interval his garrison had been reduced nearly one-eighth, by the death of two of his most valiant and corpulent soldiers, who had accidentally over-eaten themselves on some fat salmon, caught in the Varsche river. He further stated, that the enemy persisted in their inroads, taking no notice of the fort or its inhabitants: but squatting themselves down, and forming settlements all around it; so that, in a little while, he should find himself inclosed and blockaded by the enemy, and totally at their mercy.

But among the most atrocious of his grievances, I find the following still on record, which may serve to show the bloody-minded outrages of these savage intruders. "In the meantime, they of Hartford have not onely usurped and taken in the lands of Connecticott, although unrighteously and against the lawes of nations, but have hindered our nation in sowing theire own purchased broken up lands, but have also sowed them with corne in the night, which the Netherlanders had broken up and intended to sowe: and have beaten the servants of the high and mighty the honored companie, which were labouring upon theire master's lands, from theire lands, with sticks and plow staves in hostile manner laming, and among the rest, struck Ever Duckings* a hole in his head, with a stick, so that the blood ran downe very strongly downe upon his body."

But what is still more atrocious—

"Those of Hartford sold a hogg, that belonged to the honored companie, under pretence that it had eaten of theire grounde grass, when they had not any foot of inheritance. They proffered the hogg for 5s. if the commissioners would have given 5s. for damage; which the commissioners denied because noe man's own hogg (as men used to say) can trespass upon his owne master's grounde."†

The receipt of his melancholy intelligence incensed the whole

---

* This name is no doubt misspelt. In some old Dutch MSS. of the time, we find the name of Evert Duyckingh, who is unquestionably the unfortunate hero above alluded to.

† Haz. Col. State Papers.

community—there was something in it that spoke to the dull comprehension, and touched the obtuse feelings, even of the puissant vulgar, who generally require a kick in the rear to awaken their slumbering dignity. I have known my profound fellow-citizens bear, without murmur, a thousand essential infringements of their rights, merely because they were not immediately obvious to their senses— but the moment the unlucky Pearce was shot upon our coasts, the whole body politic was in a ferment—so the enlightened Nederlanders, though they had treated the encroachments of their eastern neighbours with but little regard, and left their quill-valiant governor to bear the whole brunt of war with his single pen—yet now every individual felt his head broken in the broken head of Duckings—and the unhappy fate of their fellow-citizen the hog being impressed, carried and sold into captivity, awakened a grunt of sympathy from every bosom.

The governor and council, goaded by the clamours of the multitude, now set themselves earnestly to deliberate upon what was to be done.—Proclamations had at length fallen into temporary disrepute: some were for sending the Yankees a tribute, as we make peace-offering to the petty Barbary powers, or as the Indians sacrifice to the devil; others were for buying them out, but this was opposed, as it would be acknowledging their title to the land they had seized. . . .

Chapter V

How William the Testy Enriched the Province by a Multitude of Laws, and Came to Be the Patron of Lawyers and Bum-bailiffs—And How the People Became Exceedingly Enlightened and Unhappy Under His Instructions

AMONG THE MANY WRECKS AND FRAGMENTS OF exalted wisdom which have floated down the stream of time, from venerable antiquity, and have been carefully picked up by those humble, but industrious wights, who ply along the shores of literature, we find the following sage ordinance of Charondas, the Locrian legislator. Anxious to preserve the ancient laws of the state from the additions and improvements of profound "country members," or officious candidates for popularity, he ordained that whoever proposed a new law, should do it with a halter about his neck; so that in case his proposition was rejected they just hung him up—and there the matter ended.

This salutary institution had such an effect, that for more than two hundred years there was only one trifling alteration in the criminal code—and the whole race of lawyers starved to death for want of employment. The consequence of this was, that the Locrians, being unprotected by an overwhelming load of excellent laws, and undefended by a standing army of pettifoggers and sheriff's officers, lived very lovingly together, and were such a happy people, that they scarce make any figure throughout the whole Grecian history— for it is well known that none but your unlucky, quarrelsome, rantipole nations make any noise in the world.

Well would it have been for William the Testy, had he haply, in the course of his "universal acquirements," stumbled upon this precaution of the good Charondas. On the contrary, he conceived that the true policy of a legislator was to multiply laws, and thus secure the property, the persons, and the morals of the people, by surrounding them in a manner with men-traps and spring-guns, and besetting even the sweet sequestered walks of private life with quickset hedges, so that a man could scarcely turn, without the risk of encountering some of these pestiferous protectors. Thus was he continually coining petty laws for every petty offence that occurred, until in time they became too numerous to be remembered, and remained like those of certain modern legislators, mere dead-letters—revived occasionally for the purpose of individual oppression, or to entrap ignorant offenders.

Petty courts consequently began to appear, where the law was administered with nearly as much wisdom and impartiality as in those august tribunals, the alderman's and justice's courts of the present day. The plaintiff was generally favoured, as being a customer and bringing business to the shop; the offences of the rich were discreetly winked at—for fear of hurting the feelings of their friends;—but it could never be laid to the charge of the vigilant burgomasters, that they suffered vice to skulk unpunished, under the disgraceful rags of poverty.

About this time may we date the first introduction of capital punishments—a goodly gallows being erected on the waterside, about where Whitehall stairs are at present, a little to the east of the Battery. Hard by also was erected another gibbet of a very strange, uncouth, and unmatchable description, but on which the ingenious William Kieft valued himself not a little, being a punishment entirely of his own invention.

It was for loftiness of altitude not a whit inferior to that of Haman, so renowned in Bible history; but the marvel of the contrivance was, that the culprit, instead of being suspended by the neck, according to venerable custom, was hoisted by the waistband, and was kept for an hour together dangling and sprawling between heaven and earth—to the infinite entertainment and doubtless great edification of the multitude of respectable citizens, who usually attend upon exhibitions of the kind.

It is incredible how the little governor chuckled at beholding caitiff vagrants and sturdy beggars thus swinging by the crupper, and cutting antic gambols in the air. He had a thousand pleasantries and mirthful conceits to utter upon these occasions. He called them his dandle-lions—his wild-fowl—his high-flyers—his spread-eagles— his goshawks—his scarecrows, and finally his *gallows-birds*, which ingenious appellation, though originally confined to worthies who had taken the air in this strange manner, has since grown to be a cant name given to all candidates for legal elevation. This punishment, moreover, if we may credit the assertions of certain grave etymologists, gave the first hint for a kind of harnessing, or strapping, by which our forefathers braced up their multifarious breeches, and which has of late years been revived, and continues to be worn at the present day.

Such were the admirable improvements of William Kieft in criminal law—nor was his civil code less a matter of wonderment; and much does it grieve me that the limits of my work will not suffer me to expatiate on both, with the prolixity they deserve. Let it suffice then to say, that in a little while the blessings of innumerable laws became notoriously apparent. It was soon found necessary to have a certain class of men to expound and confound them—divers pettifoggers accordingly made their appearance, under whose protecting care the community was soon set together by the ears.

I would not here be thought to insinuate any thing derogatory to the profession of the law, or to its dignified members. Well am I aware, that we have in this ancient city innumerable worthy gentlemen who have embraced that honourable order, not for the sordid love of filthy lucre, nor the selfish cravings of renown, but through no other motives but a fervent zeal for the correct administration of justice, and a generous and disinterested devotion to the interests of their fellow-citizens!—Sooner would I throw this trusty pen into the flames, and cork up my ink-bottle for ever, than infringe even for a nail's breadth upon the dignity of this truly benevolent class of citizens—on the contrary, I allude solely to that crew of caitiff scouts, who, in these latter days of evil, have become so numerous—who infest the skirts of the profession, as did the recreant Cornish knights the honourable order of chivalry—who, under its auspices, commit their depredations on society—who thrive by quibbles, quirks, and chicanery, and, like vermin, swarm where there is most corruption.

Nothing so soon awakens the malevolent passions, as the facility of gratification. The courts of law would never be so constantly crowded with petty, vexatious, and disgraceful suits, were it not for the herds of pettifogging lawyers that infest them. These tamper with the passions of the lower and more ignorant classes; who, as if poverty were not a sufficient misery in itself, are always ready to heighten it by the bitterness of litigation. They are in law what quacks are in medicine—exciting the malady for the purpose of profiting by the cure, and retarding the cure for the purpose of augmenting the fees. Where one destroys the constitution, the other impoverishes the purse; and it may likewise be observed, that a patient, who has once been under the hands of a quack, is ever after dabbling in drugs, and poisoning himself with infallible remedies; and an ignorant man, who has once meddled with the law under the auspices of one of these empirics, is for ever after embroiling himself with his neighbours, and impoverishing himself with successful law-suits.—My readers will excuse this digression, into which I have been unwarily betrayed; but I could not avoid giving a cool, unprejudiced account of an abomination too prevalent in this excellent city, and with the effects of which I am unluckily acquainted to my cost, having been nearly ruined by a law-suit, which was unjustly decided against me—and my ruin having been completed by another, which was decided in my favour.

It has been remarked by the observant writer of the Stuyvesant manuscript, that under the administration of Wilhelmus Kieft the disposition of the inhabitants of New-Amsterdam experienced an essential change, so that they became very meddlesome and factious. The constant exacerbations of temper into which the little governor was thrown by the maraudings on his frontiers, and his unfortunate propensity to experiment and innovation, occasioned him to keep his council in a continual worry—and the council being, to the people at large, what yest or leaven is to a batch, they threw the whole community into a ferment—and the people at large being to the city what the mind is to the body, the unhappy commotions they underwent operated most disastrously upon New-Amsterdam—insomuch, that in certain of their paroxysms of consternation and perplexity, they begat several of the most crooked, distorted, and abominable streets, lanes, and alleys, with which this metropolis is disfigured.

But the worst of the matter was, that just about this time the mob, since called the sovereign people, like Balaam's ass, began to grow more enlightened than its rider, and exhibited a strange desire of governing itself. This was another effect of the "universal acquirements" of William the Testy. In some of his pestilent researches among the rubbish of antiquity, he was struck with admiration at the institution of public tables among the Lacedæmonians, where they discussed topics of a general and interesting nature—at the schools of the philosophers, where they engaged in profound disputes upon politics and morals—where gray-beards were taught the rudiments of wisdom, and youths learned to become little men before they were boys. "There is nothing," said the ingenious Kieft, shutting up the book, "there is nothing more essential to the well-management of a country, than education among the people: the basis of a good government should be laid in the public mind."—Now this was true enough, but it was ever the wayward fate of William the Testy, that when he thought right, he was sure to go to work wrong. In the present instance, he could scarcely eat or sleep until he had set on foot brawling debating societies among the simple citizens of New-Amsterdam. This was the one thing wanting to complete his confusion. The honest Dutch burghers, though in truth but little given to argument or wordy altercation, yet by dint of meeting often together, fuddling themselves with strong drink, beclouding their brains with tobacco-smoke, and listening to the harangues of some half-a-dozen oracles, soon became exceedingly wise, and—as is always the case where the mob is politically enlightened—exceedingly discontented. They found out, with wonderful quickness of discernment, the fearful error in which they had indulged, in fancying themselves the happiest people in creation—and were fortunately convinced, that, all circumstances to the contrary notwithstanding, they were a very unhappy, deluded, and consequently ruined people.

In a short time, the quidnuncs of New-Amsterdam formed themselves into sage juntos of political croakers, who daily met together to groan over political affairs, and make themselves miserable; thronging to these unhappy assemblages, with the same eagerness that zealots have in all ages abandoned the milder and more peaceful paths of religion, to crowd to the howling convocations of fanaticism. We are naturally prone to discontent, and avaricious after imaginary causes of lamentation—like lubberly monks, we belabour our own shoulders, and seem to take a vast satisfaction in the music of our own groans. Nor is this said for the sake of paradox; daily experience shows the truth of these observations. It is almost impossible to elevate the spirits of a man groaning under ideal calamities; but nothing is more easy than to render him wretched, though on the pinnacle of felicity; as it is a Herculean task to hoist a man to the top of a steeple, though the merest child can topple him off thence.

In the sage assemblages I have noticed, the reader will at once perceive the faint germs of those sapient convocations called popular meetings, prevalent at our day. Thither resorted all those idlers and "squires of low degree," who, like rags, hang loose upon the back of society, and are ready to be blown away by every wind of doctrine. Cobblers abandoned their stalls, and hastened thither to give lessons on political economy—blacksmiths left their handicraft and suffered their own fires to go out, while they blew the bellows and stirred up the fire of faction; and even tailors, though but the shreds and patches, the ninth parts of humanity, neglected their own measures to attend to the measures of government.—Nothing was wanting but half-a-dozen newspapers and patriotic editors, to have completed this public illumination, and to have thrown the whole province in an uproar!

I should not forget to mention, that these popular meetings were held at a noted tavern; for houses of that description have always been found the most fostering nurseries of politics; abounding with those genial streams which give strength and sustenance to faction. We are told that the ancient Germans had an admirable mode of treating any question of importance; they first deliberated upon it when drunk, and afterwards reconsidered it when sober. The shrewder mobs of America, who dislike having two minds upon a subject, both determine and act upon it drunk; by which means a world of cold and tedious speculation is dispensed with—and as it is universally allowed, that when a man is drunk he sees double, it follows most conclusively that he sees twice as well as his sober neighbours.

Chapter VI

Of the Great Pipe Plot—And of the Dolorous Perplexities into Which William the Testy Was Thrown, by Reason of His Having Enlightened the Multitude

WILHELMUS KIEFT, AS HAS ALREADY BEEN MADE manifest, was a great legislator upon a small scale. He was of an active, or rather a busy mind; that is to say, his was one of those small, but brisk minds, which make up by bustle and constant motion for the want of great scope and power. He had, when quite a youngling, been impressed with the advice of Solomon, "Go to the ant, thou sluggard; consider her ways and be wise;" in conformity to which, he had ever been of a restless, ant-like turn, worrying hither and thither, busying himself about little matters, with an air of great importance and anxiety—laying up wisdom by the morsel, and often toiling and puffing at a grain of mustard-seed, under the full conviction that he was moving a mountain.

Thus we are told, that once upon a time, in one of his fits of mental bustle, which he termed deliberation, he framed an unlucky law, to prohibit the universal practice of smoking. This he proved, by mathematical demonstration, to be, not merely a heavy tax on the public pocket, but an incredible consumer of time, a great encourager of idleness, and, of course, a deadly bane to the prosperity and morals of the people. Ill-fated Kieft! had he lived in this enlightened and libel-loving age, and attempted to subvert the inestimable liberty of the press, he could not have struck more closely on the sensibilities of the million.

The populace were in as violent a turmoil as the constitutional gravity of their deportment would permit—a mob of factious citizens had even the hardihood to assemble before the governor's house, where, setting themselves resolutely down, like a besieging army before a fortress, they one and all fell to smoking with a determined perseverance, that seemed as though it were their intention to smoke him into terms. The testy William issued out of his mansion like a wrathful spider, and demanded to know the cause of this seditious assemblage, and this lawless fumigation; to which these sturdy rioters made no other reply, than to loll back phlegmatically in their seats, and puff away with redoubled fury; whereby they raised such a murky cloud, that the governor was fain to take refuge in the interior of his castle.

The governor immediately perceived the object of this unusual tumult, and that it would be impossible to suppress a practice, which, by long indulgence, had become a second nature. And here I would observe, partly to explain why I have so often made mention of this practice in my history, that it was inseparably connected with all the affairs, both public and private, of our revered ancestors. The pipe, in fact, was never from the mouth of the true-born Nederlander. It was his companion in solitude, the relaxation of his gayer hours, his counsellor, his consoler, his joy, his pride; in a word, he seemed to think and breathe through his pipe.

When William the Testy bethought himself of all these matters, which he certainly did, although a little too late, he came to a compromise with the besieging multitude. The result was, that though he continued to permit the custom of smoking, yet did he abolish the fair long pipes which were used in the days of Wouter Van Twiller, denoting ease, tranquillity, and sobriety of deportment; and, in place thereof, did introduce little, captious, short pipes, two inches in length; which, he observed, could be stuck in one corner of the mouth, or twisted in the hat-band, and would not be in the way of business. By this the multitude seemed somewhat appeased, and dispersed to their habitations. Thus ended this alarming insurrection, which was long known by the name of the *pipe plot*, and which, it has been somewhat quaintly observed, did end, like most other plots, seditions, and conspiracies, in mere smoke.

But mark, oh reader! the deplorable consequences that did afterwards result. The smoke of these villainous little pipes, continually ascending in a cloud about the nose, penetrated into, and befogged the cerebellum, dried up all the kindly moisture of the brain, and rendered the people that used them as vapourish and testy as their renowned little governor—nay, what is more, from a goodly, burly race of folk, they became, like our worthy Dutch farmers, who smoke short pipes, a lantern-jawed, smoke-dried, leathern-hided race of men.

Nor was this all, for from hence may we date the rise of parties in this province. Certain of the more wealthy and important burghers adhering to the ancient fashion, formed a kind of aristocracy, which went by the appellation of the *Long Pipes*—while the lower orders, submitting to the innovation, which they found to be more convenient in their handicraft employments, and to leave them more liberty of action, were branded with the plebeian name of *Short Pipes*. A third party likewise sprang up, differing from both the other, headed by the descendants of the famous Robert Chewit, the companion of the great Hudson. These entirely discarded the use of pipes, and took to chewing tobacco, and hence they were called *Quids*. It is worthy of notice, that this last appellation has since come to be invariably applied to those mongrel or third parties, that will sometimes spring up between two great contending parties, as a mule is produced between a horse and an ass.

And here I would remark the great benefit of these party distinctions, by which the people at large are saved the vast trouble of thinking. Hesiod divides mankind into three classes: those who think for themselves, those who let others think for them, and those who will neither do one nor the other. The second class, however, comprises the great mass of society; and hence is the origin of *party*, by which is meant a large body of people, some few of whom think and all the rest talk. The former, who are called the leaders, marshal out and discipline the latter, teaching them what they must approve—what they must hoot at—what they must say—

whom they must support—but, above all, whom they must hate—
for no man can be a right good partisian, unless he be a determined
and thorough-going hater.

But when the sovereign people are thus properly broken to the
harness, yoked, curbed, and reined, it is delectable to see with what
docility and harmony they jog onward, through mud and mire,
at the will of their drivers, dragging the dirt-carts of faction at their
heels. How many a patriotic member of Congress have I seen, who
would never have known how to make up his mind on any question,
and might have run a great risk of voting right, by mere accident,
had he not had others to think for him, and a file-leader to vote
after!

Thus then the enlightened inhabitants of the Manhattoes, being
divided into parties, were enabled to organize dissension, and to
oppose and hate one another more accurately. And now the great
business of politics went bravely on—the parties assembling in
separate beer-houses, and smoking at each other with implacable
animosity, to the great support of the state, and emolument of
the tavern-keepers. Some, indeed, who were more zealous than the
rest, went farther, and began to bespatter one another with numerous very hard names and scandalous little words, to be found in the
Dutch language; every partisan believing religiously that he was
serving his country, when he traduced the character or impoverished
the pocket of a political adversary. But, however they might differ
between themselves, all parties agreed on one point, to cavil at and
condemn every measure of government, whether right or wrong;
for as the governor was by his station independent of their power,
and was not elected by their choice, and as he had not decided in
favour of either faction, neither of them was interested in his success,
or in the prosperity of the country, while under his administration.

"Unhappy William Kieft!" exclaims the sage writer of the
Stuyvesant manuscript—"doomed to contend with enemies too
knowing to be entrapped, and to reign over a people too wise to
be governed!" All his expeditions against his enemies were baffled
and set at nought, and all his measures for the public safety were
cavilled at by the people. Did he propose levying an efficient body
of troops for internal defence—the mob, that is to say those vagabond
members of the community who have nothing to lose, immediately

took the alarm, vociferated that their interests were in danger—
that a standing army was a legion of moths, preying on the pockets
of society; a rod of iron in the hands of government; and that a
government with a military force at its command would inevitably
swell into a despotism. Did he, as was but too commonly the case,
defer preparation until the moment of emergency, and then hastily
collect a handful of undisciplined vagrants—the measure was hooted
at as feeble and inadequate, as trifling with the public dignity and
safety, and as lavishing the public funds on impotent enterprises.
Did he resort to the economic measure of proclamation—he was
laughed at by the Yankees; did he back it by non-intercourse—it
was evaded and counteracted by his own subjects. Whichever way
he turned himself, he was beleaguered and distracted by petitions of
"numerous and respectable meetings," consisting of some half-a-
dozen brawling pot-house politicians—all of which he read, and,
what is worse—all of which he attended to. The consequence was,
that by incessantly changing his measures, he gave none of them a
fair trial; and by listening to the clamours of the mob, and
endeavouring to do every thing, he, in sober truth, did nothing.

I would not have it supposed, however, that he took all these
memorials and interferences good-naturedly, for such an idea
would do injustice to his valiant spirit; on the contrary, he never
received a piece of advice in the whole course of his life, without
first getting into a passion with the giver. But I have ever observed
that your passionate little men, like small boats with large sails, are
the easiest upset or blown out of their course; and this is demonstrated by Governor Kieft, who, though in temperament as hot as an
old radish, and with a mind, the territory of which was subjected
to perpetual whirlwinds and tornadoes, yet never failed to be carried
away by the last piece of advice that was blown into his ear. Lucky
was it for him that his power was not dependent upon the greasy
multitude, and that as yet the populace did not possess the important
privilege of nominating their chief magistrate! They, however, did
their best to help along public affairs; pestering their governor
incessantly, by goading him on with harangues and petitions, and
then thwarting his fiery spirit with reproaches and memorials, like
Sunday jockies managing an unlucky devil of a hack-horse—so that
Wilhelmus Kieft may be said to have been kept either on a worry
or a hand-gallop throughout the whole of his administration.

Chapter VII

Containing Divers Fearful Accounts of Border Wars, and the Flagrant Outrages of the Mosstroopers of Connecticut—With the Rise of the Great Amphyctionic Council of the East, and the Decline of William the Testy

IT WAS ASSERTED BY THE WISE MEN OF ANCIENT TIMES, who were intimately acquainted with these matters, that at the gate of Jupiter's palace lay two huge tuns, the one filled with blessings, the other with misfortunes—and it verily seems as if the latter had been completely overturned and left to deluge the unlucky province of Nieuw-Nederlandts. Among the many internal and external causes or irritation, the incessant irruptions of the Yankees upon his frontiers were continually adding fuel to the inflammable temper of William the Testy. Numerous accounts of these molestations may still be found among the records of the times; for the commanders on the frontiers were especially careful to evince their vigilance and zeal by striving who should send home the most frequent and voluminous budgets of complaints—as your faithful servant is eternally running with complaints to the parlour, of the petty squabbles and misdemeanours of the kitchen.

Far be it from me to insinuate, however, that our worthy ancestors indulged in groundless alarms; on the contrary, they were daily suffering a repetition of cruel wrongs,* not one of

---

* From among a multitude of bitter grievances still on record, I select a few of the most atrocious, and leave my readers to judge if our ancestors were not justifiable in getting into a very valiant passion on the occasion.

"24 June, 1641. Some of Hartford have taken a hogg out of the vlact or common, and shut it up of meer hate or other prejudice, causing it to starve for hunger in the stye!"

"26 July. The forementioned English did drive the Companie's hoggs out of the vlact of Sicojoke into Hartford; contending daily with reproaches, blows, beating the people with all disgrace that they could imagine."

"May 20, 1642. The English of Hartford have violently cut loose a horse of the honoured Companie's, that stood bound upon the common or vlact."

"May 9, 1643. The Companie's horses pastured upon the Companie's ground, were driven away by them of Connecticott or Hartford, and the herdsmen lustily beaten with hatchets and sticks."

"16. Again they sold a young hogg belonging to the Companie, which piggs had pastured on the Companie's land."—*Haz. Col. State Papers.*

which but was a sufficient reason, according to the maxims of national dignity and honour, for throwing the whole universe into hostility and confusion.

Oh, ye powers! into what indignation did every one of these outrages throw the philosophic William! letter after letter, protest after protest, proclamation after proclamation, bad Latin, worse English, and hideous Low Dutch were exhausted in vain upon the inexorable Yankees; and the four-and-twenty letters of the alphabet, which, excepting his champion, the sturdy trumpeter Van Corlear, composed the only standing army he had at his command, were never off duty throughout the whole of his administration. Nor was Antony the trumpeter a whit behind his patron in fiery zeal; but like a faithful champion of the public safety, on the arrival of every fresh article of news, he was sure to sound his trumpet from the ramparts, with most disastrous notes, throwing the people into violent alarms, and disturbing their rest at all times and seasons—which caused him to be held in very great regard, the public pampering and rewarding him, as we do brawling editors for similar services.

I am well aware of the perils that environ me in this part of my history. While raking with curious hands, but pious heart, among the moulding remains of former days, anxious to draw therefrom the honey of wisdom, I may fare somewhat like that valiant worthy, Samson, who, in meddling with the carcass of a dead lion, drew a swarm of bees about his ears. Thus, while narrating the many misdeeds of the Yanokie or Yankee tribe, it is ten chances to one but I offend the morbid sensibilities of certain of their unreasonable descendants, who may fly out and raise such a buzzing about this unlucky head of mine, that I shall need the tough hide of an Achilles or an Orlando Furioso to protect me from their stings.

Should such be the case, I should deeply and sincerely lament— not my misfortune in giving offence—but the wrong-headed perverseness of an ill-natured generation, in taking offence at anything I say. That their ancestors did use my ancestors ill, is true, and I am very sorry for it. I would, with all my heart, the fact were otherwise; but as I am recording the sacred events of history, I'd not bate one nail's breadth of the honest truth, though I were sure the whole edition of my work should be bought up and burnt by the common hangman of Connecticut. And in sooth, now that these testy gentlemen have drawn me out, I will make bold to go farther and observe, that this is one of the grand purposes for which we impartial historians are sent into the world—to redress wrongs and render justice on the heads of the guilty. So that, though a powerful nation may wrong its neighbours with temporary impunity, yet sooner or later a historian springs up who wreaks ample chastisement on it in return.

Thus these mosstroopers of the east little thought, I'll warrant it, while they were harassing the inoffensive province of Nieuw-Nederlandts, and driving its unhappy governor to his wit's end, that a historian should ever arise and give them their own with interest. Since, then, I am but performing my bounden duty as a historian, in avenging the wrongs of our revered ancestors, I shall make no further apology; and indeed, when it is considered that I have all these ancient borderers of the east in my power, and at the mercy of my pen, I trust that it will be admitted I conduct myself with great humanity and moderation.

To resume, then, the course of my history. Appearances to the eastward began now to assume a more formidable aspect than ever—for I would have you note that hitherto the province had been chiefly molested by its immediate neighbours, the people of Connecticut, particularly of Hartford; which, if we may judge from ancient chronicles, was the stronghold of these sturdy moss-troopers, from whence they sallied forth, on their daring incursions, carrying terror and devastation into the barns, the hen-roosts, and pig-styes of our revered ancestors.

Albeit, about the year 1643, the people of the east country, inhabiting the colonies of Massachusetts, Connecticut, New-Plymouth, and New-Haven, gathered together into a mighty conclave, and after buzzing and debating for many days, like a political hive of bees in swarming time, at length settled themselves into a formidable confederation, under the title of the United Colonies of New-England. By this union, they pledged themselves to stand by one another in all perils and assaults, and to co-operate in all measures, offensive and defensive, against the surrounding savages, among which were doubtlessly included our honoured ancestors of the Manhattoes; and to give more strength and system to this confederation, a general assembly or grand council was to be annually held, composed of representatives from each of the provinces.

On receiving accounts of this combination, Wilhelmus Kieft was struck with consternation, and, for the first time in his whole life, forgot to bounce, at hearing an unwelcome piece of intelligence —which a venerable historian of the time observes, was especially noticed among the politicians of New-Amsterdam. The truth was, on turning over in his mind all that he had read at the Hague, about leagues and combinations, he found that this was an exact imitation of the Amphyctionic council, by which the states of Greece were enabled to attain to such power and supremacy, and the very idea made his heart to quake for the safety of his empire at the Manhattoes.

He strenuously insisted that the whole object of this confederation was to drive the Nederlanders out of their fair domains; and always flew into a great rage if any one presumed to doubt the probability of his conjecture. Nor was he wholly unwarranted in such a suspicion; for at the very first annual meeting of the grand council, held at Boston, (which governor Kieft denominated the Delphos of this truly classic league,) strong representations were made against the Nederlanders, forasmuch as that in their dealings with the Indians, they carried on a traffic in "guns, powther, and shott—a trade damnable and injurious to the colonists."* Not but what certain of the Connecticut traders did likewise dabble a little in this "damnable traffic"—but then they always sold the Indians such scurvy guns, that they burst at the first discharge—and consequently hurt no one but these pagan savages.

The rise of this potent confederacy was a deathblow to the glory of William the Testy, for from that day forward, it was remarked by many, he never held up his head, but appeared quite crestfallen. His subsequent reign, therefore, affords but scanty food for the historic pen—we find the grand council continually augmenting in power, and threatening to overwhelm the province of Nieuw-Nederlandts; while Wilhelmus Kieft kept constantly fulminating proclamations and protests, like a shrewd sea-captain firing off carronades and swivels, in order to break and disperse a waterspout —but alas! they had no more effect than if they had been so many blank cartridges.

The last document on record of this learned, philosophic, but unfortunate little man, is a long letter to the council of the Am-

* Haz. Col. State Papers.

phyctions, wherein, in the bitterness of his heart, he rails at the people of New-Haven, or Red Hills, for their uncourteous contempt of his protest, levelled at them for squatting within the province of their High Mightinesses. From this letter, which is a model of epistolary writing, abounding with pithy apophthegms and classic figures, my limits will barely allow me to extract the following recondite passage:—"Certainly when we heare the Inhabitants of New-Hartford complayninge of us, we seem to heare Esop's wolfe complayninge of the lamb, or the admonition of the younge man, who cryed out to his mother, chideing with her neighboures, 'Oh Mother revile her, lest she first take up that practice against you.' But being taught by precedent passages, we received such an answer to our protest from the inhabitants of New-Haven as we expected; *the Eagle always despiseth the Beetle Fly;* yet notwithstanding we do undauntedly continue on our purpose of pursuing our own right, by just arms and righteous means, and doe hope without scruple to execute the express commands of our superiors."* To show that this last sentence was not a mere empty menace, he concluded his letter by intrepidly protesting against the whole council, as a horde of *squatters* and interlopers, inasmuch as they held their meeting at New-Haven, or the Red-Hills, which he claimed as being within the province of the New-Netherlands.

Thus end the authenticated chronicles of the reign of William the Testy—for henceforth, in the troubles, the perplexities, and the confusion of the times, he seems to have been totally overlooked, and to have slipped for ever through the fingers of scrupulous history. Indeed, for some cause or other which I cannot divine, there appears to have been a combination among historians to sink his very name into oblivion, in consequence of which they have one and all forborne even to speak of his exploits. This shows how important it is for great men to cultivate the favour of the learned, if they are ambitious of honour and renown. "Insult not the dervise," said a wise caliph to his son, "lest thou offend thine historian;" and many a mighty man of the olden time, had he observed so obvious a maxim, might have escaped divers cruel wipes of the pen, which have been drawn across his character.

It has been a matter of deep concern to me, that such darkness and obscurity should hang over the latter days of the illustrious

* Vide Haz. Col. State Papers.

Kieft—for he was a mighty and great little man, worthy of being
utterly renowned, seeing that he was the first potentate that introduced into this land the art of fighting by proclamation, and defending a country by trumpeters and windmills—an economic and
humane mode of warfare, since revived with great applause, and
which promises, if it can ever be carried into full effect, to save great
trouble and treasure, and spare infinitely more bloodshed than
either the discovery of gunpowder, or the invention of torpedoes.

It is true, that certain of the early provincial poets, of whom
there were great numbers in the Nieuw-Nederlandts, taking advantage of the mysterious exit of William the Testy, have fabled, that
like Romulus, he was translated to the skies, and forms a very
fiery little star, somewhere on the left claw of the crab; while others,
equally fanciful, declare that he had experienced a fate similar to
that of the good King Arthur; who, we are assured by ancient
bards, was carried away to the delicious abodes of fairy land, where
he still exists in pristine worth and vigour, and will one day or
another return to restore the gallantry, the honour, and the immacu-
late probity which prevailed in the glorious days of the Round
Table.*

All these, however, are but pleasing fantasies, the cobweb
visions of those dreaming varlets, the poets, to which I would
not have my judicious reader attach any credibility. Neither am
I disposed to yield any credit to the assertion of an ancient and
rather apocryphal historian, who alleges that the ingenious Wilhelmus was annihilated by the blowing down of one of his windmills—
nor to that of a writer of later times, who affirms that he fell a
victim to a philosophical experiment, which he had for many
years been vainly striving to accomplish; having the misfortune to
break his neck from the garret-window of the stadt-house, in an
ineffectual attempt to catch swallows, by sprinkling fresh salt upon
their tails.

The most probable account, and to which I am inclined to give
my implicit faith, is contained in a very obscure tradition, which

---

* The old Welch bards believed that king Arthur was not dead, but carried awaie
    by the fairies into some pleasant place, where he shold remaine for a time, and
    then returne againe and reigne in as great authority as ever.—*Hollingshed.*
The Britons suppose that he shall come yet and conquere all Britaigne, for certes,
    this is the prophicye of Merlyn—He say'd that his deth shall be doubteous;
    and said soth, for men thereof yet have doubte and shullen for ever more—
    for men wyt not whether that he lyveth or is dede.—*De Leew Chron.*

declares, that what with the constant troubles on his frontiers—the incessant schemings and projects going on in his own pericranium—the memorials, petitions, remonstrances, and sage pieces of advice from divers respectable meetings of sovereign people—together with the refractory disposition of his council, who were sure to differ from him on every point, and uniformly to be in the wrong—all these, I say, did eternally operate to keep his mind in a kind of furnace heat, until he at length became as completely burnt out as a Dutch family pipe which has passed through three generations of hard smokers. In this manner did the choleric but magnanimous William the Testy undergo a kind of animal combustion, consuming away like a farthing rush-light—so that, when grim Death finally snuffed him out, there was scarce left enough of him to bury!

Book V
Chapter I

*In Which the Death of a Great Man Is Shown to Be
No Very Inconsolable Matter of Sorrow*

To a profound philosopher, like myself, who am apt to see clear through a subject, where the penetration of ordinary people extends but half-way, there is no fact more simple and manifest, than that the death of a great man is a matter of very little importance. Much as we may think of ourselves, and much as we may excite the empty plaudits of the million, it is certain that the greatest among us do actually fill but an exceeding small space in the world; and it is equally certain, that even that small space is quickly supplied when we leave it vacant. "Of what consequence is it," said Pliny, "that individuals appear or make their exit? the world is a theatre whose scenes and actors are continually changing." Never did philosopher speak more correctly; and I only wonder that so wise a remark could have existed so many ages, and mankind not have laid it more to heart. Sage follows on in the footsteps of sage; one hero just steps out of his triumphal car to make way for the hero who comes after him; and of the proudest monarch it is merely said, that—"he slept with his fathers, and his successor reigned in his stead."

The world, to tell the private truth, cares but little for their loss, and if left to itself would soon forget to grieve; and though a nation has often been figuratively drowned in tears on the death of a great man, yet it is ten chances to one if an individual tear has been shed on the occasion, excepting from the forlorn pen of some hungry author. It is the historian, the biographer, and the poet, who have the whole burden of grief to sustain; who—kind souls!—like undertakers in England, act the part of chief mourners—who inflate a nation with sighs it never heaved, and deluge it with tears it never dreamt of shedding. Thus, while the patriotic author is weeping and howling, in prose, in blank verse, and in rhyme, and collecting the drops of public sorrow into his volume, as into a lachrymal vase, it is more than probable his fellow-citizens are eating and drinking, fiddling and dancing, as utterly ignorant of the bitter lamentations made in their name, as are those men of straw, John Doe and Richard Roe, of the plaintiffs for whom they are generously pleased on divers occasions to become sureties.

The most glorious and praiseworthy hero that ever desolated nations, might have mouldered into oblivion among the rubbish of his own monument, did not some historian take him into favour, and benevolently transmit his name to posterity—and much as the valiant William Kieft worried, and bustled, and turmoiled, while he had the destinies of a whole colony in his hand, I question seriously whether he will not be obliged to this authentic history for all his future celebrity.

His exit occasioned no convulsion in the city of New-Amsterdam or its vicinity: the earth trembled not, neither did any stars shoot from their spheres—the heavens were not shrouded in black, as poets would fain persuade us they have been on the unfortunate death of a hero—the rocks (hard-hearted varlets!) melted not into tears, nor did the trees hang their heads in silent sorrow; and as to the sun, he laid abed the next night, just as long, and showed as jolly a face when he arose, as he ever did on the same day of the month in any year, either before or since. The good people of New-Amsterdam, one and all, declared that he had been a very busy, active, bustling little governor; that he was "the father of his country"—that he was "the noblest work of God"—that "he was a man, take him for all in all, they ne'er should look upon his like again"—together with sundry other civil and affectionate speeches, that are regularly said on the death of all great men; after which they smoked their pipes, thought no more about him, and Peter Stuyvesant succeeded to his station. . . .